CW01678081

Finding the E to Thrive

Finding the Energy to Thrive

Navigating the Maze of Life and Embracing Your Path to Wholeness

Katie Dean, PhD.

BEYOND
BELIEF
—PUBLISHING—
YOU HOLD THE FUTURE IN YOUR HANDS

Copyright © 2025 Katie Dean, PhD.

All rights reserved. No part of this book may be reproduced or transmitted in any form or by any means without written permission of the publisher, except in the case of brief quotations embodied in critical articles and reviews.

This material had been written and published solely for educational purposes. The author and the publisher shall have neither liability nor responsibility to any person or entity with respect to any loss, damage, or injury caused or alleged to be caused directly or indirectly by the information contained in this book.

The author of this book does not dispense medical advice or prescribe the use of any technique as a form of treatment for physical, emotional, or medical problems without the advice of a physician, either directly or indirectly. The intent of the author is only to offer information of a general nature to help you in your quest for wellbeing. In the event you use any of the information in this book for yourself or others, which is your constitutional right, the author and the publisher assume no responsibility for your actions.

Statements made in this book have not been evaluated by the Food and Drug Administration. This book and its contents are not intended to diagnose, treat, or cure any infection, injury, or illness, or prevent any disease. Results vary and each person's experience is unique.

ISBN: 978-1-957972-15-2

Praise for
Finding the Energy to Thrive

"Katie is a beacon of light and her story will guide you to the inner knowing that will support your search for the energy you desire."

~ John Stringer
Award-Winning International Bestselling Author
Creator and Alignment Coach

"What a wonderful book and such a creative woman! The strength of spirit and self-confidence are what I feel between the lines of this dramatic yet inspiring story. I believe *Finding the Energy to Thrive* will be valuable to many people."

~ Maryna Zhukova
Multiple Award-Winning International Designer
Owner of MaryDes Designs Ltd.

"A compassionate, empowering and truly thought-provoking guide to support you on your journey to vibrant health."

~ Lloyd Burrell
Bestselling Author of *Healing with Vibration*
Creator of the Award-Winning Docuseries *Electric YOUniverse*

"Katie Dean has a gift for sharing knowledge in a way that is caring, heartfelt and gently opens you to explore new ground. Your body already knows how to heal itself and through *Finding the Energy to Thrive*, Katie will show you how to activate and support this innate process."

~ Lisa Warner
Author of *The Simplicity of Self-Healing*
Creator of *Whole BEing Healing*

"Katie's story demonstrates what is possible when we lean in, cultivate self-trust, and follow our Divine intuition."

~JoeVitale
Author and Speaker
Featured Teacher from the Hit Movie
and NY Times Bestseller, *The Secret*

"*Finding the Energy to Thrive* invites you to question the reality you have been taught and discover that the recovery you seek is already available when you simply change your perspective."

~ Dr. John Demartini
International Bestselling Author of *The Values Factor*

"Katie writes with wisdom, gentle humour and compassion. This is a book that will change lives."

~ Keith Leon S.
Author and Book Publisher
24x Award-Winning Filmmaker

Table of Contents

Part 4
Preparing for Your Escape From the Maze

Conclusion
Drawing your Roadmap

Foreword

The first time I met Katie Dean in 2023, I knew I was in the presence of someone truly special—someone filled with wisdom, compassion, and a deep-seated determination to make a difference in the world. Over time, I've witnessed her grow, evolve, and allow her inner light to shine ever more brightly. She is living proof of what becomes possible when we trust our inner wisdom, step into our power, and commit to healing and transformation.

Now, she has written a book, *Finding the Energy to Thrive*—a heartfelt and courageous account of her journey to recovery from chronic fatigue syndrome. But this is not just any book on chronic fatigue syndrome (CFS) recovery. Despite being told she would always be trapped in illness and low energy, Katie refused to accept that as her fate. Instead, she made a powerful decision: *to seek a way back to vitality on her own terms*. In these pages, she shares how the CFS journey is like navigating a maze. This is a perfect metaphor for what I experienced in my own personal recovery from fibromyalgia and chronic fatigue syndrome, as well as those of my clients, students, and former patients.

At first, like many, Katie focused solely on supporting her body with physical interventions. But when full recovery remained elusive, she dug deeper. That's when she discovered the key: healing is not just about the physical body—it's about addressing the bioenergetic body as well. Unresolved trauma, emotional blocks, and energetic imbalances can hold the physical body in a cycle of illness. Once Katie shifted her focus to clearing those energetic disruptions, her healing unfolded in ways she never could have imagined.

Katie's story is more than just a personal triumph; it's a beacon of hope for others navigating similar struggles. With honesty, humor, and grace, she welcomes readers into her journey, offering a compassionate invitation to explore the fascinating world of metaphysical (beyond the physical) healing.

What I love most about this book is how accessible it is. So many books on healing can feel overwhelming, but Katie's writing meets you exactly where you are. It's inspiring without being preachy, inviting without being pushy. Her **Energy Saving Aid** sections are a brilliant touch—gentle reminders that honor the reality of energy depletion and brain fog, while distilling the chapter's wisdom into simple, actionable insights.

If you are holding this book in your hands, you've already answered a powerful call—the call to reclaim your energy, your health, and your life. Let Katie be your soulful guide. Whether your healing unfolds quickly or takes time, know that every step forward is leading you toward greater peace, joy, and freedom.

May you move through this journey with curiosity, compassion, and trust in the infinite wisdom within you. You deserve to feel vibrant, whole, and fully alive.

~ Dr. Karen Kan, Doctor of Light Medicine™
#1 International Bestselling Author and Visionary
Pioneer in the Fields of Healing, Consciousness, and Spirituality

Introduction

Journal: February 2023

I was running through the maze at Cliveden[1] *with my seven-year-old and four-year-old nieces, Rose and Imogen, when I suddenly realised why the metaphor of a maze is perfect for an exploration of chronic fatigue syndrome (CFS). Before I explain that, I should underline that for me to be running anywhere with two small children felt nothing short of miraculous. I had spent twenty years living with CFS and been told I was unlikely to recover.*

The three of us were thoroughly lost in the maze. My nieces were running on ahead, shrieking with glee. I was urging them to slow down so we could work out which path to try next. At certain points, we had tantalising glimpses of our destination—the centre of the maze—through the hedges framing the path down which we were running. Then we would turn a corner and find a dead end or discover our journey taking us further away from our destination. At one point, my two nieces stopped running. Rose turned to me with a serious face and confided she was very scared. She thought we were lost and might never reach the centre. And, even if we did make it to the centre, she reasoned we might not find our way out, and we would be stuck in the maze forever. I confidently reassured her we were going to be fine. We would find our way out. Even if we couldn't, somebody would come and find us before it got dark. Secretly, though, a part of me shared her fears: What if we never got out? And that's when I realised how appropriately this reflected my own twenty-year journey through the maze of CFS. A part of me had always believed I would reach my destination and

---

1 Cliveden is one of the many historic houses looked after by the National Trust—a charity set up to preserve UK sites of natural beauty or historic significance. This stately home is located close to me and was once the family home of the Astors. The house is now a five-star hotel and restaurant. It is set in acres of beautiful countryside through which the River Thames flows. This happens to have been the inspiration behind Kenneth Grahame's book, The *Wind in the Willows*.

make it safely out of the maze. Yet, I mostly felt lost, scared, and running headlong from practitioner to practitioner or treatment to treatment, with no sense of logic and no real idea why I was following those paths, except blind hope … or desperation. I regularly found myself going 'round in circles, sometimes with a faint sense of déjà vu—isn't this treatment similar to that other thing I tried, which didn't help? And I frequently ran down blind alleys, hit dead ends, had to gather myself together, retrace my steps, and try another path. Yes, the maze metaphor definitely fits! Back to the real-life maze at Cliveden: I am happy to report that my nieces and I did reach the centre of the maze and found our way out again.

Two months later, we revisited the maze. This time, before entering, Rose asked me if I had a pencil and a piece of paper.

"Why do you need those?" I asked her.

"So we can make a map," she replied, with the amazing good sense and wisdom of a seven-year-old.

Sadly, I hadn't come prepared with either pencil or paper. Inevitably, we managed to lose our way again. Yet, we somehow found the centre and found our way out again, having a lot of fun in the process. Next time, we will draw that map.

That opening journal entry shares a little taste of my writing experience. It turns out that writing a book is every bit as much of a journey as recovering from CFS. I find the process of journaling to be a powerful way of exploring my inner world and gaining the clarity to help me move forward in any area of life. I also hope that reading excerpts from my personal journal will help you get to know me a little better. So, as we proceed through these pages, I am going to be sharing a journal entry at the start of each chapter, giving you a taste of my CFS experience as I lived it at the time. Then, we are going to look back over what I learned from that experience and the research I carried out to facilitate my own recovery; it may help you understand your personal maze. At the end of each chapter, I invite you to carry out a simple practice designed to uncover the blocks that may be keeping you stuck or bring insight into how best to address your specific symptoms and challenges. I have designed these practices drawing on my personal experience of living with CFS. They have the power to open your mind and support recovery. They will also empower you to live with more self-love and compassion, which will ease your path, even if you continue living in the CFS maze.

So, taking inspiration from the wisdom of my little niece, I am here now, with pen and paper, to help you draw a map of your CFS maze and, hopefully, prevent you from getting as lost as I did on my own journey. I can't guarantee you won't hit a few dead ends or find yourself revisiting some of the same paths, but I have every faith you can create a map to take you out of your confusing, scary maze and help you find the energy you fear you may have lost forever. I will do my best to make this adventure as fun and entertaining as I can, so we all enjoy the experience.

What Will This Book Give You?

Unlike many books written by those who have recovered from CFS, this does not promise you a protocol or treatment system. It may show you the recovery path you need to take. Or it may end up providing you with greater safety and comfort as you live with CFS. Either way, my intention is to explore the maze, taking you with me and acting as your guide. I will be pointing out sights of interest—ideas that have the potential to inspire and assist you. This is about empowering you to make choices that will support you, whether that is in seeking recovery or living day-to-day with CFS.

I have split the book into four sections and a final concluding chapter that will bring everything together and provide you with your next steps, should you wish to take them. In section one, we are going to be exploring three elements. First, you will get to know me as I share my CFS story. Second, I am inviting you to explore new awareness around yourself and your approach to living with CFS. Third, we will be exploring the common understanding of what it means to receive a CFS diagnosis and an alternative understanding that seems to be commonly adopted by those who successfully recover. Together, this creates a picture of where you are right now and paves the way to exploring some new paths.

In the second section, I will be inviting you to explore a model of yourself and your world that you have probably never seen before. We will be looking at your bioenergetic field, how this is related to your physical body, and how understanding that relationship and the creative process it utilises will empower you to see CFS in a completely new way. For some of you, this may feel challenging. For others, this will be the breakthrough that leads you to find your recovery path. I invite all of you to take and use whatever resonates and politely set aside anything that isn't making sense today. My experience has led me to recognise the benefit of gaining awareness, even when I may not be ready to use it all. Many of the critical paths that supported my recovery were things I struggled to understand initially. As my experience evolved and my recovery unfolded, having the awareness of different areas allowed me to bring in those that supported me at each new point in the journey.

In section three, we will be exploring the common physical symptoms of CFS and revealing their links to your central nervous system. This system—the controller of your body—provides critical keys to understanding and unlocking the roots of your physical symptoms. We will take a look at major treatment options available and consider why some may be helpful at some points and unhelpful at other points. To be clear, though, none of the material in this book is intended to be used as a diagnostic or treatment tool. It is information that can empower you to seek help from qualified professionals in areas most effective for you. I am not a qualified medical practitioner, and I do not claim to be able to diagnose or treat you. Nor do I intend to provide you with any diagnosis or treatment recommendations. It is important to recognise that you alone have responsibility for how you choose to use the information I am sharing in these pages. It is simply information based on my lived experience, research, and personal understanding. I am not recommending any specific course of action for you to take.

In section four, I will be sharing what I learned about the experience of recovery. I believe your expectations of what the recovery journey is going to look and feel like will play a large role in how successful you are in completing that journey. I have witnessed other people getting stuck at various stages because their lived experiences didn't match up to their expectations. This can lead to creating new stories about what it means to have CFS. They may be stories like *recovery isn't possible.* Whilst I am not promising recovery for all nor suggesting that I have all the answers, I wanted to share these perspectives to increase your awareness. Everyone I know who is living with CFS has incredible courage and resilience. I wanted to write a book that empowers people to channel those qualities into discovering the best path for them with the greatest ease. I hope many more people will find the path out of the maze. I also humbly acknowledge that whatever I have learned and shared on these pages is just a small part of a larger story. We are all travelling this journey together and opening new paths as we go.

Throughout the book, I am inviting you to spend some time journaling your responses to sets of questions. That practice is going to help you become aware of your reactions to this information and empower you to use it to create your personal recovery roadmap. So, this book is partly informative and partly designed as an invitation to you to take some transformative action.

Practical Considerations

Having lived with CFS for two decades, I am well aware of the challenges it brings. When it comes to reading anything, brain fog and fatigue create huge barriers for many people. I remember when I first began reading self-help books to try to find my own path to recovery. Back then, I was experiencing a lot of brain fog. I found I could only read in relatively short bursts. Much of what I read got lost along the way, and I found myself having to repeat sentences and paragraphs to understand them. I also found it helpful to make notes about the things that struck me as being really important. So, I have tried to consider all that as I created this book.

I have split each chapter into sections so you can take regular breaks if you need to. At the start of each section, I have included something which I call an *Energy Saving Aid*. This is basically a summary box containing a few sentences about the main points covered in the next section. I don't mean for this to become a replacement for reading the entire section. There are a lot of details and nuances that will help to explain the big ideas. At the same time, I hope these summary boxes will help you to take on board the key points. You can also use them as reference points to help you find portions of the book that you would like to revisit. Lastly, please let these be visual prompts to remind you to take regular breaks. You may need to take longer periods of rest, or simply spend a few minutes relaxing and grounding before you tackle the next section. The brain and eyes, which you will be engaging as you read, are some of the biggest energy consumers of your body. We tend to associate fatigue with physical exertion. In fact, mental exertion can require far more energy than physical movement. So, if your energy is in short supply, make sure you use it wisely!

ENERGY SAVING AID

This is an example of the Energy Saving Aid. It will include a bullet-point summary of the main ideas I am covering in the next section of the chapter.

- *Please use this as a reminder to take a break.*
- *The summaries can help you follow the flow of ideas and quickly refer back to any sections that you wish to revisit in order to deepen your understanding.*

You may be feeling some trepidation at the size of this book. So, if that is the case, do you need to read it all? Obviously, I feel that everything I have included is of importance. However, each section of the book deals with a discrete angle of this illness. Within each section, the individual chapters can easily be read as stand-alone information. So, you may derive benefit from focusing on just one area at a time. For example, if you are recently diagnosed and struggling to understand what your symptoms mean, you can move directly to chapter nine, which focuses on the symptomology of the illness. If you have been living with CFS for a long time and already tried a lot of different treatments, maybe you want to begin with section four to try to understand if there is anything you are missing in your expectations around what the recovery path should look like. Perhaps you already have a clear understanding of the physical and psycho-emotional elements of CFS. In that case, section two will bring you a new layer to explore. Each of you is going to derive immediate benefit from different portions of this book. The quickest way to discover which portion is most beneficial for you today is by using the Energy Saving Aids. Read those to gain an overview of each section, and then delve deeper whenever you find information that seems helpful. Like a conventional guidebook, I intend for this book to be something that you—metaphorically—carry with you and consult regularly throughout your recovery journey. It is not necessarily something to digest fully in one go.

What Am I Inviting You to Take Away from This Book?

The answer to that question is very simple. I intend this book to empower you and offer you a new perspective on yourself and your symptoms. I am ending each chapter with an invitation to you to complete a journaling practice. If you accept my suggestion to complete those practices, they will bring you more self-awareness, self-love, and self-compassion. Those are the basic foundations to support your journey through the CFS maze. Although you can use any paper or journal for following these practices, I have also created the *Energy to Thrive Journal for Mapping Your Path to Wholeness* to accompany this book. So, I invite you to use that to support your journey of self-discovery which will ultimately create your personal roadmap out of the CFS maze. At the end of that journal, you will find an invitation to continue working with me as your guide, using the Kolorlan System I developed to support my recovery and now share to support others.

I recently found myself presenting the ideas contained in this book to a private group. At the end of the presentation, someone was kind enough to tell me they had found my story inspiring and asked me if I could share any tips for recovery. Well, this book is littered with tips, alongside the information that has helped me. But if I were to answer that question in a sentence, I would say this: I set a firm intention to recover, and I simply showed up every single day, even when it felt challenging to do that. As I will share in part four, some days are going to feel challenging, and other days will feel like you're moving forward. By developing awareness, love, and compassion, you will be empowered to meet whatever experience comes your way with grace. Let your intention be your guiding light, and just keep putting one foot in front of the other. Think of this book as if someone has presented you with a periscope. You can use it to take a bird's eye view of the maze and maybe begin to get a sense of where you are heading. I invite you to return to these pages and the practices whenever you meet a dead end or begin to feel lost. As you raise your metaphorical periscope once more, you will see new paths that perhaps you missed the first time around.

I hope that gives you a sense of where you will be travelling alongside me and how it might help you. Thank you for accepting my invitation to act as your guide. Now, I would like to encourage you to take your first recovery step and visit this webpage: https://findmyenergy.co.uk/energy-to-thrive-contract. It will take you to a contract, which I request you sign. The contract is between your conscious and subconscious mind, making a commitment with yourself to follow your own recovery path with love and compassion wherever it leads. You might be thinking this is nothing more than a silly exercise. In fact, our subconscious is fully alive to and hugely influenced by the symbolism of ceremony. Far from being a silly exercise, there is more power in this simple gesture than you might imagine.[2] Keep your contract somewhere safe, yet accessible, and draw on its power whenever you need some additional strength to complete your journey. When you have done that, it's time to move into the CFS maze.

2 This idea originates in the understanding I have gained from studying as an NLP practitioner and Life Coach. It also reflects my own experience and my extensive explorations into the mind through multiple courses offered by the National Institute for the Clinical Application of Behavioural Medicine (NICABM) and leading lights in the field of trauma, including Thomas Hübl, Dr. Richard Schwartz, and Dr. Gabor Maté.

Part 1

Preparing for your Journey

Chapter 1

Meet Your Guide

Hello, I am Katie, and I am going to be your guide through the maze of chronic fatigue syndrome (CFS). I am here to show you the points of interest and offer you some guidance as to how they might be helpful for you in your recovery journey. So, you are going to be having a lot of contact with me over the course of this book! I think it would be a good idea if I began by sharing my CFS story to help you get to know me and find out how much of your experience resonates or looks like mine.

I thought I was going to be writing a very different book to the one you are reading right now. Back in 2015, I began journaling about my experience, with the intention of turning that record into a book that told my story. Although I was writing it as if I were trying to explain myself to a trusted friend, it still turned into a stream-of-consciousness epic from which it would have been difficult for you to gain much value. However, I have been using some of those journal entries in this book to set up frameworks for each chapter as we go along. So, I want to set that precedent here. I am going to share the introduction I wrote in 2020 when I first—seriously—began the project of writing my story. So, the "journal entry" you are about to read outlined my intention back then, and it remains my intention today. I should just mention that, at the point when I was planning that first book, I had the idea of using a play on words and entitling it *All About Me*, in reference to the original name for this illness, M.E. —Myalgic Encephalomyelitis. I was also planning to write under a pseudonym to keep my real identity a secret.

> *ENERGY SAVING AID*
>
> *Throughout this book, I have included boxes like this one to summarise chapter sections and help you grasp the main points if you are struggling to read, due to low energy or brain fog. I am not going to do that for this chapter. Because this is my personal story, it is here to allow you to get to know me a bit better. So, I'm not trying to "teach" you anything. Just read as much or as little as you wish to satisfy your personal curiosity. If you do end up reading the chapter fully, please make sure to complete the practice at the end.*

Journal: The Intentions I Set in 2020

Who am I and why am I writing this? I am nobody. I am everybody. My story may be about a small portion of my experience of a chronic illness called M.E.—Myalgic Encephalomyelitis, but it is also the story of anyone who has experienced long-term illness, or prejudice, or loss in any form. The pun on words is both intentional and convenient. M.E. is the illness that I have experienced, about which I write. It needs writing about because it is so little understood. It affects millions of people around the world, yet there is no effective diagnosis, treatment, or cure for the condition. It's not a new condition: It has been officially recognised since 1969. However, many people still prefer to dismiss it. There has been, and is, relatively little research into the condition. Much of the research being carried out is funded by charitable donations.

This is also a story: My story of how this illness has impacted my life and how it makes me feel. So, it can only ever be my experience. It is all about me. That may seem self-indulgent, but unless we each tell our stories, how can we ask other people to understand how we feel and offer us support? During the years of my illness—now approaching two decades—I have come to know other sufferers. Each of us has a unique story to tell, and they all share the same basic characteristics of loss, confusion, and, yes, I'm sorry to say, prejudice. I have had to experience the narratives of others. Those who look in and judge where they know nothing. Worse still, those who observe and judge when they should know better.

So, I'm directing my story at those who may relate to these experiences and need to know they're not alone. I also want to offer those who are outside of these experiences an opportunity to observe and learn. I am aware this will make some people feel uncomfortable. They may respond to that with criticism, disbelief, or judgement. That is one of the reasons I wish to divorce these words from my physical identity. The other reason is to make a statement. Anyone who has had a diagnosis of M.E. may feel like they've disappeared from life and become invisible. This is commonly a physical disappearance: being too ill to leave the house and becoming socially distanced from friends and family. It can also be emotional distancing. The illness creates barriers that even the most caring friends and family cannot breach. This is true of any illness or traumatic experience. It's almost impossible to feel what another person feels. Whatever the cause, the result is the same: a deep isolation. Then, the stigma that has attached itself to this illness also creates another kind of invisibility. All too commonly the medical community, government institutions, or employers want to brush the patient under the carpet. They don't have answers to the problem, so it's easier to pretend the problem doesn't exist. Or they blame the patient and attach unhelpful labels that leave those patients feeling invisibility may be the best option. All these forms of dismissal or disappearance leave you feeling invisible. It's as if you don't matter. You don't deserve to be helped or heard. So, this is a single, lone voice coming from the void to say we all deserve to be heard. We all deserve compassion and help. We don't expect miracles, but a simple acknowledgement that we exist would be a great starting point. Yes, that lone voice is all about me. But it's also about millions of other people in similar situations. So, I hope, for that reason, it's a story worth telling.

Setting the Scene

My childhood was pretty ordinary. I grew up in England with parents who loved and supported me and a younger brother to whom I have always been close. My earliest dream was to write a book. That dream then took second place to becoming a ballerina. So, I grew up with a passion for ballet classes and a normal state school education. At some point during my teenage years, it became clear that the dream of becoming a ballerina was not going to materialise, although my passion for ballet remains to this day. Thankfully, my education was working out well, and I ended up leaving school, aged eighteen, with 4 A-levels, 1 S-level, and a place to read History at Cambridge University. That's not to say that my first eighteen years of life were free of challenges. I was badly bullied at school for five years. My parents' marriage experienced some rough patches. Despite the fact that I was lucky enough to have a "plan B," the loss of my dream of becoming a ballerina felt like a huge blow.

Luckily for me, the town of Cambridge also happens to have a brilliant ballet school! So, I spent the next six years dividing my life between the University library, the ballet school, and all the expected parties and frivolities that come with being a student. In short, I learned that I appeared to have boundless energy and no need to spend eight hours a night sleeping. Balanced against the many positives, I will acknowledge that life at Cambridge University is no picnic. The workload was extremely heavy, but I had learned to thrive under pressure, so I loved the intellectual challenge. Less enjoyable was the amount of sexism I met. The adjustment of leaving home and taking the first steps into adulthood felt challenging at times. Nevertheless, at the end of those six years, I left Cambridge with a bachelor's degree, a master's degree, and a PhD, but still no sense of what I was supposed to be doing with my life. Somehow, I had forgotten about the dream of being a writer. Or, perhaps, that had come to seem like a rather unreliable way of earning money.

Whatever my reasoning, I found myself in a job in London, working as a Strategy Consultant, helping businesses—of all sizes—to solve problems of all types. Need a business plan? No problem; we can help you do that. Want some funding for your next big project? OK, we'll help put you in touch with some venture capitalists. Not sure how to persuade people to buy your newest product? We can help: We'll put together a marketing plan for you. Don't know what price to charge for this shiny new product? Well, we've got you covered there too: We'll do all the analysis and help you find the perfect price for your product in your market. Hopefully, you get the picture. You may never have previously been aware that such a thing as a Strategy Consultant existed. You might be wondering why the companies themselves don't work out their marketing plans, set their prices, and whatever else they need to do. Well, many companies do carry out all those things all by themselves. Yet sometimes, for various reasons, they find it more convenient to ask someone else—us—to help them. Believe me, they pay good money for our services ... because we provide their answers much, much faster than those answers would be forthcoming if the company were to do this internally. How does that happen? Long, long working hours and very high levels of stress! For example, I found myself working on a four-week project for a very well-known UK company. Quite by accident, during that project, I met one of this company's employees and learned he had been contracted to carry out the exact same project but given six months to do it! That may have explained why my working day was typically 7:00 a.m. until 3:00 a.m. —no, that's not a typing error—and I was working seven days a week, while his working day was 9:00 a.m. to 6:00 p.m., for five days a week. So, in my experience, it's not that strategy consultants are necessarily cleverer or somehow have access to magic information; it's just that we're crazy enough to believe we have been blessed with superhuman bodies that don't require little things like food and sleep.

Now, I have to be clear here: Whilst it is true that my company were happy for me to work these hours, I was absolutely complicit in this crazy life. Nobody was standing there with a literal whip; I actually found this work interesting. OK, maybe not interesting enough to enjoy working all night once a month or surviving on twelve hours sleep a week—yes, the monthly all-nighters went on for several months and I did really have one week where I totalled just twelve hours' sleep across five nights—but certainly, I had the ambition and drive to accept this is just how it is. I believed once I had moved a little further up the career ladder, I would find myself at a place where I could get a little more sleep. Meantime, you sleep when you're dead, right? Well, after two years of this lifestyle, I learned the hard way. This kind of lifestyle is likely to bring death much sooner than you may desire! Actually, I count myself very lucky; I didn't have a heart attack or find myself diagnosed with cancer. Instead, at the tender age of twenty-six, I just collapsed one morning on my way into work. Nothing serious enough to require a hospital visit, but enough to make it clear that I wasn't going to be working that day.

I managed to get myself back home and into bed—and there I stayed. My mind couldn't quite comprehend the enormity of what had just happened to me. I remember spending at least two weeks literally sleeping around the clock. Home was back with my parents at that point. My Mum would wake me to give me food, and I would collapse back into bed as soon as I had eaten. I remember calling in to my office each Monday to say, "I'm still not very well, but I hope I'll be back in the office next week." I remember my doctor writing me weekly sick notes to confirm my continuing illness. At first, he listed the reason for my absence as "exhaustion." After six months of being poked and prodded by various specialists and having my ongoing swollen lymph nodes, sore throat, and swollen tonsils fully assessed, the reason changed. Now, I was diagnosed with chronic fatigue syndrome (CFS), and my doctor was writing sick notes to cover a month or two months at a time. Nobody seemed to think I was really going to recover from this. Nobody, that is, apart from me. I can't claim credit for much there, other than complete denial! I simply refused to accept that I was going to have to spend the rest of my life without being able to work or socialise, permanently feeling like I had the flu, and discovering that something as basic as a trip to the bathroom felt every bit as exhausting as doing ten intense ballet classes, back-to-back, without a break.

2002–2015: The Years of Struggle, Denial, and "Making Do"

My initial CFS crash occurred in 2002. I spent several weeks bed-bound, several months largely housebound, and five years off work completely. That was followed by another five years attempting to get back to work but living in a boom-and-bust cycle of gaining enough energy to try a little taste of "normal" life, followed by a crash that left me bed-bound for days, then housebound again for a few weeks before I began the cycle once again. Yes, I had made progress, but it was unsteady progress, and my energy was hugely unpredictable. I was also largely in denial about how ill I was. I continually pushed my body beyond its limits—hence the boom-and-bust cycle. I became very, very good at detaching from my body. It was stuck in pain: constant sore throat, swollen glands, and frequent bouts of nausea. My initial reaction of "this cannot be happening to me" had become one of "I will not allow this to happen to me." So, I developed the skill of simply ignoring my symptoms until they escalated enough to force me to stop briefly.

That's not to say that I did nothing. Alongside the constant fighting to "not be ill," I did what I could to try to find a treatment. Someone recommended a practitioner who worked with bio-resonance therapy. I had no idea what that was, but I was happy to give anything a try! The bio-resonance machine identified a number of food intolerances, which led me to explore my diet and make some changes that allowed me to regain some significant energy. However, after that initial step forward, my progress stalled and I decided to stop the bio-resonance therapy, although I maintained the dietary changes. Three years into my illness, my doctor heard about a treatment designed specifically for CFS: Mickel Therapy. It turned out to be a specialised talk therapy, aimed at bringing my central nervous system out of its ongoing stress response. So, I tried that, but it was not the "cure" we had been hoping for. That experience led me to reject any idea of my illness being in any way stress-related. Ironically, the refusal to examine my mindset stalled my recovery significantly. I learned about the principles of pacing, but again, these were not as effective as they might have been because I was too insistent on pushing through instead of genuinely listening to my body. Last but not least, I began a regular yoga practice.

Looking back now, I can see how all these things were inadvertently creating a more supportive environment for my physical body and even how some steps were helping my psycho-emotional body, in spite of my reluctance to really explore the mind-body connection. Mentally, I had a sense this was not "meant" to be my life, but I also had a strong dread that I might have to accept it as my reality. In 2012, I finally accepted I was not going to be returning to my old career. Alongside the onset and development of my illness, I had also been developing a new hobby: beading. For those who haven't come across this mysterious art/craft before, it is basically using tiny glass beads to create jewellery and 3-dimensional works of art. So, the loss of my career happened to open up a new door: the chance to turn my hobby into a source of income. It just so happened that this hobby was therapeutic in its own right. As these pages unfold, I'm going to be talking about creating calm and a safe place to support the central nervous system—CNS. Well, quite by accident, this is what beading gave to me. Yes, it was scary to be faced with the prospect of supporting myself financially when my energy levels and health were so unpredictable, but I felt, through my diet, through understanding the desirability of pacing my activities, and from the rather rudimentary knowledge of my nervous system, I might have created enough stability to just survive. Certainly, being in control of my own destiny and spending my time creating and building something for myself was a form of therapy in itself. So, I had four years when I was earning money, enjoying my work, and able to have a small social life, and I reached the conclusion I was managing this CFS business rather nicely, thank you!

2015–2020: The Wake-Up Call

I think it was around the summer of 2015 that I began to experience a few niggling symptoms. Things like swollen lymph glands and an almost perpetual sore throat that had never really quite gone away began to re-surface more regularly. Each time, I found a way to "manage" these symptoms, so I believed I could somehow cheat my body into supporting my desire to "live." Then, slightly more disturbing patterns started to arise. I had a few temporary crashes. Again, compared to my original experience, these were short-lived, and I believed I was "managing" my way through them. On one level, I was. On another level, my refusal to take any symptoms seriously was not well-received by my body.

So, in the middle of 2016, just as my new career was taking off, disaster struck. I crashed again. Not a small crash that I could "manage," but a full-blown collapse that took me right back to my original 2002 experience, but with the added bonus of a few new, very unpleasant symptoms. I was now also suffering from excruciating pain around my rib cage and abdominal area and a lot of nausea. What had previously been flu-like symptoms now escalated to such a level that I remember going to bed one night and seriously wondering if I would wake up the next day: I felt so terrible that I couldn't see how my body could continue in that state. I was now making choices between eating breakfast *or* taking a shower: I didn't have the energy to do both. I remember, on more than one occasion, crawling up the stairs because it was too hard to walk. You might think the complete relapse would be easier to manage second-time around. That I could lie there and think, "It's OK. I've been here before, and I got out of this. So, if I've done it before, I can do it again." Yes, that was one train of thought, but at the same time, I couldn't help noticing that my belief I had any kind of control over CFS might have been rather foolish and arrogant. Not to mention that the severity of my experience this time felt very frightening.

Anyway, overriding both of those trains of thought was the one idea that "this is not *meant* to be happening to me." This idea had been ever-present from day one, back in 2002. In some sense, I like to think of this as my Intention to heal. So, it wasn't so much a plan as it was an unshakeable belief that, no matter how much evidence you present to the contrary, I am not *supposed* to spend my entire life living with CFS. There has to be a solution. So, I began taking a new path. I soon discovered, although CFS research was limited and we didn't have a cure, we were beginning to find some possible answers. In fact, between 2002 and 2016, the CFS landscape had changed considerably. Although the conventional medical view was that this was a mystery illness with no cure, there were practitioners who had noticed patterns happening in the body and had developed ways to treat those patterns. In short, a whole body of knowledge and help existed, about which I had known nothing. I had been so busy living in the mindset that I simply had to make the best of things, ideally pretending the problem didn't exist, that I hadn't really been aware of the progress being made in functional medicine. Now it was time for me to begin waking up.

First, I read Dr. Sarah Myhill's book, *Diagnosis and Treatment of Chronic Fatigue Syndrome*, and I learned that, far from being a mystery, this illness had a very logical explanation: Mitochondrial problems. It was desperately hard to read when I had so much brain fog, but this book was providing answers and a ray of hope I was keen to pursue. I discovered Dr. Myhill's practice had become so overwhelmed with patients that she had no room to take on anyone new. I also discovered she was not the only practitioner working with this understanding of CFS, and I found my way to a lovely doctor in London. He gave me my first "hallelujah" moment: a blood test that showed something wrong in my body. He also put me on a complex protocol of natural supplements, some of which I was taking in tablet form and some through intravenous drip. He promised I would heal. After about six months, I hadn't healed, and I was beginning to question if I had made any progress at all. Any benefit I was receiving from the supplements seemed to be immediately negated by the exertion of travelling to receive treatment. I won't lie that was a very low point for me. Navigating the path between hope and despair is deeply uncomfortable. Had it not been for the constant support of my family and a few close friends, plus the beading, I might not be here to write these pages.

That was in February 2017. I decided to stop seeing this doctor—although, I remain eternally grateful to him for his kindness and support and for being the first person to give me a sense of true validation and hope in my experience. I still had a nagging belief this was not *meant* to be happening to me but had neither the physical nor emotional energy to try any other treatment at that point. I spent a few months in despair. Alongside that despair, I was also resting. Completely. By May 2017, I felt inclined to try another path. I contacted the Optimum Health Clinic in London. I explained my situation and my earlier treatment and how that hadn't been the "miracle" I was seeking. They reassured me, whilst it would have been more beneficial than I realised, in their experience, it had perhaps jumped a little too far along the road, missing some critical foundational steps that should have been put in place first. Given that they have treated literally thousands of patients from around the world and given that their attitude was hopeful but realistic—no promises of cures, but a simple promise of "we have experience, and we'll do our best"—I decided to give them a try. Even more importantly, they were able to conduct consultations remotely and order lab tests I could carry out at home and send to the lab for results. So, apart from an occasional blood test, I didn't need to travel. Unless you have experienced severe CFS, you may not appreciate the sheer relief of being able to receive treatment in your own home!

I spent the next three years working with one of their nutrition specialists, undergoing functional diagnostic tests, matching up my symptoms with patterns that they knew to be common amongst CFS patients, and taking supplements and following specific diets to bring my body's rather depleted resources back into balance. Lo and behold! After a couple of years on this regime, I had regained enough energy to be working comfortably again—still my beading business, so I was working from home and enjoyed the full support and understanding of my boss ... me!—and I was just starting to venture out on small outings. I was making steady progress and hearing more and more stories about other people who had recovered completely. Nobody could offer any guarantees, but I reasoned that if someone else could recover, then why couldn't I?

I think it was around 2019 that the online conferences began. At first, these were new things: bringing together different experts in the field, all with their own practices and their own methodologies for aiding the recovery process. Each expert would give an interview outlining what they understood about CFS and whichever area in which they specialised. Most of these experts had one thing in common: they had once been patients without hope. As most had some sort of background in medicine or science, they had used their knowledge to piece together a solution that worked for them. Now, they were busy sharing that solution with anyone willing to give it a try. Honestly, this was like being a child in a sweet shop. From a place of "there's nothing we can do," I had moved to a place of "there's so much available, where should I begin?"

Having reached a plateau on the physical side of things, I finally came to the reluctant understanding I should try looking into the psycho-emotional piece of the puzzle. In 2019, I began my first meditation practice. That quickly stalled as I found myself experiencing panic attacks. I abandoned that idea and, instead, began using Emotional Freedom Technique—EFT—or Tapping. That didn't really move me much further forward, but I had reached an "acceptable" level by this point. I was beginning to start going out and about, albeit still with difficulty. I recall some very frightening experiences when I tried to go out for a night at the theatre and suffered a near-collapse, with extreme nausea, dizziness, and difficulty standing and walking. Fortunately, I recovered quickly from this episode, but it still left me questioning my long-term future. My determination to experience a better quality of life remained as strong as ever, even if I wasn't completely sure how I could achieve that.

It was around this point that we reached March 2020. If you recall, the entire world went into panic and began taking measures nobody thought they would ever see. The COVID-19 virus had just arrived in global awareness, and groups of scientists, governments, and the media all around the world were telling us this virus presented a major threat to human life that required unprecedented measures for our salvation. The entire world went into lockdown, putting the handbrake on life. For the average person this was a major trauma. For me, it was a rather interesting turn of events that brought some mixed emotions. On the one hand, like everyone else, I felt fear of the virus and complete disbelief at what was happening. On the other hand, I remember feeling a faint sense of satisfaction as I realised I already had plenty of practice living in lockdown. Housebound was my normal territory. Who knew that CFS was preparing me to survive a reality like a global pandemic? Ironically, though, the exact timing was a little strange for me. I had been trying to open up after my four-year self-imposed lockdown, and now the rest of the world was shutting down and joining me. As I have just mentioned, my early attempts at returning to a social life were not going quite as planned. I had returned to my old pattern of pushing my body too hard. So, in many ways, the 2020 lockdown was heaven for me. It removed the pressure of trying to go out and about, and I was able to rest in ways I had never really rested before. And, boy, did that change my awareness of my beliefs! Although I didn't realise it at the time, this was setting me up for the breakthrough that was about to come.

The Breakthrough: Deep Healing at the Root Level

Fast forward to about September of 2020. Through a variety of circuitous routes, my path had now reached a place where I decided I should be investing more seriously in some form of meditation, in spite of my earlier stalled attempts. Bang on cue, up pops Niki Skye—as it happens, one of the original founders of the Optimum Health Clinic—with an online meditation group starting up every Sunday. This group appealed as it was specifically focused on healing. It was attracting people with all manner of complex, chronic illnesses. Alongside the meditations, we were learning more about the healing process. What really "sold" me was the impact the meditations were having on me. This time, I did not experience any anxiety, just deep relaxation, and I found myself releasing grief and other emotions I had been storing up in my system for years. I noticed myself feeling better after each meeting. Not a cure, just a noticeable improvement. Sometimes it was only obvious for a short while; other times, it felt like an actual movement forward.

In 2021, this ad hoc, open group became a paid membership group that was going to be focusing on a path of spiritual enlightenment with healing as one of its happy side effects. Now, although I have always had a general sense of living in a world in which something "bigger than me" exists, I have no history of religious practice—unless you count studying religious history for my PhD—and no involvement in any kind of more general or New Age type of spirituality. So, was this really a path I wanted to take? For me, decision time. Did I continue to invest in this, or did I leave this path and move on to a new avenue? I arrived at the last "open" meeting with the intention this would be my final group meditation, that Spirituality was not my path, and I would see where I went next in my quest for healing. Something really weird happened during the meditation that day. I found myself simultaneously sobbing and ecstatic. My body was telling me I *had* to continue with this group. So, I didn't hesitate. I immediately paid my membership fee, and I haven't looked back since.

Over the course of the next couple of years, I came to learn about trauma and its relationship to chronic disease. I became aware that my initial meditation experience had been my body alerting me I was carrying a lot of developmental and past-life trauma. I learned about a model of healing called the Four Levels of Creation, and I also learned these meditations were not just nice music providing relaxation. They were also providing the kind of coding I'm going to be teaching you about later in these pages: the second Level of Creation. I was literally clearing my bio-energetic field of all the—trauma—blockages that had been creating my physical symptoms and consequent misery. "What?" I hear your cries. "This poor girl has been duped into believing some weird hippy rubbish and found herself in some kind of strange cult!" I won't blame you if you are taking that perspective. There have been times I've been wondering the same thing. Yet, undeniably, my symptoms were improving. By January 2022, I had stopped taking any nutritional supplements. Bearing in mind these had been supporting me for five years at that point, this was quite miraculous in itself. In May of that year, as my health was breaking through, I found my life taking an even stranger turn. My personal experiences with the meditation and the learnings I was receiving in the group opened up the pathway for me to explore energy healing. I had come to recognise my body is so much more than its physical manifestation. Whilst I had been trying treatments that only worked on the physical level, my symptoms had become manageable, but I was still looking at spending the rest of my life on supplements. The principles engrained in the Four Levels of Creation were taking me back to the real root causes and healing at that level. This wasn't simply an ideological theory: I was *experiencing* fundamental change. My experience had been so powerful that I wanted to be able to bring this to others who were suffering.

An Unexpected Turn of Events: Training as a Bioenergetic Health Coach

I found one of my many forays into online conferences about CFS and related issues had somehow got me onto a mailing list for a company called NES Health. Funnily enough, the founder of this company, Harry Massey, was a speaker who had struck a chord with me at a couple of conferences. He had been talking about something called bioenergetics. Oddly, it sounded rather like the very first treatment I tried, back in about 2003—the bio-resonance therapy. That treatment had been using energy and frequency as a possible means of healing. If you recall, it had led to the dietary improvements that had given me my first glimpse of truly regaining some energy. But the treatment as a whole—or maybe the practitioner: she was experienced and adept with the protocol but knew nothing about CFS—had not really moved me forward enough, so I had abandoned it. Anyway, NES intrigued me, and they were inviting me to attend a free week-long online conference about bioenergetics. By the end of this conference,

I had an unquestionable "knowing" that I needed to learn more. So, without thinking too hard, I followed this instinct and signed up to train as a NES practitioner.

My suspicions about the NES protocol working in a similar way to the meditations I had been using were confirmed. As part of the training, we all had to experience the protocol ourselves. What look and sound like harmless little drops of water claimed to be carrying coded information to the biofield—many people still deride as pseudoscience—causing people to have strong physical and emotional responses. Clients regularly report improvements in symptoms, a reduction in their use of medications, and increased energy and health. The reason Harry Massey became involved in any of this was because he, too, was bedbound with CFS … for seven years. He had also trodden the path of trying everything possible. In frustration, he decided to turn his attention away from "getting rid of symptoms" and to asking instead, "What creates energy?" That question led him to meet Peter Fraser, who was developing the idea that simply by correcting distorted information in the body's energy field—biofield—healing will naturally follow. After a few years of working with Peter's developing protocol, Harry found himself fully healed and, alongside Peter, in possession of a powerful tool to support the human body, both in returning to health and maintaining a state of health. Now, as a certified practitioner, I, too, am using this amazing technology to help others.

I think one of the reasons that I have continued to feel called to share my CFS story is ongoing frustration. It frustrates me there are still so many people struggling and, whilst I am not going to sit here and over-promise, we do have a much greater understanding of what is happening in the human body, and I truly have seen and experienced miracles happening. Even if the miracles are not—yet—happening for everyone, our increasing understanding has the power to alleviate many symptoms and bring people back to a more comfortable level of existence. However, unless someone tells them about it, they are going to continue to suffer in the belief that nothing can be done. I found myself on a path I never expected to take. I have experienced that recovery is possible, and I have experienced the true power of working at the bioenergetic level. So, I simply wish to share my understanding with anyone willing to explore this path.

Through personal experience, I am also keenly aware that the rollercoaster of living with CFS creates its own challenges. I have been in the situation of hearing about something "miraculous," trying it, and feeling no benefit. I have been faced with having to decide whether an expensive treatment is worth its cost. Should I risk trying this thing, or am I going to be throwing good money after bad? I have also spent time in the position of not feeling like I can afford to pay for anything, no matter how promising it sounds. During my journey, I have also questioned whether recovery is really possible, what it would look like, and whether it is just something other people enjoy. So, when I decided to take the plunge and start sharing what I have discovered and experienced, I decided I wanted to share at multiple levels. Yes, I felt the desire to be able to offer some kind of protocol I have experienced as effective. Yet I feel an equal desire to simply help people find peace with where they are today: to help them discover a way of living with CFS and feeling acceptable to themselves and able to find some joy in their life, even though its activities and range may be narrower than that of their friends and family. So, all of this may be more of a beginning than an ending. Without fully understanding why I felt so compelled to do all this, in 2023 I set up a website that I call *Find My Energy*, and I found myself giving birth to a limited company with the same name. As I write these pages, I am still shaping what that entity becomes and even more new, exciting chapters are opening up in my life.

Perhaps the quickest way to explain my own recovery is to say that I woke up. There are things I will be sharing in the following chapters that make perfect sense from my perspective now, but which would have made no sense to me in the early years of my illness and still didn't make complete sense as I was beginning to experience them. So, as you read this book, it's fine to take what resonates and leave what doesn't. You are constantly evolving and re-creating yourself, so your understanding and beliefs are constantly evolving as well. I simply invite you to remain open and see what happens as you move forward and grow.

An Invitation to Practice

This chapter has focused very much on me and my story. Yet, I have written this book with the intention of supporting you. So, I would like to now invite you to begin a practice we will be using at the end of each chapter. This is about turning the focus back to you and encouraging you to determine what you think, feel, and need. All of that is going to become the foundation for planning your road map at the end of the book. So, please don't skip these practices.

Today, I would like you to grab a journal and answer the following questions. There are no "right" or "wrong" answers to them. This is simply about helping you to uncover more awareness within yourself. You can write as much or as little as you desire. I appreciate that your energy levels may not be great and both physical and mental fatigue can make writing difficult. So, it is also OK to make your "journal" a voice recording if you find that easier. Just make sure you have a record to which you can return at the end. So, here are those questions:

- What—if anything—do you recognise in my story that resonates with your own experience?

- Have you had any lightbulb moments where something I have shared has given you a different perspective that feels helpful?
- Is there anything in my story that you find challenging or unappealing? If so, name it and write down how/why it challenges you.
- How are you feeling about accepting me as a guide through the CFS maze right now?

Chapter 2

Meet Your Driver

In this chapter, you are going to be meeting the driver who will be taking you through this adventure: the recovery maze. Who is this person? It is you. "Hang on a minute!" I hear you say, "I already know myself. I've lived with me for xx years, and I'm pretty sure this book isn't going to show me anything I didn't already know!" You may be correct. On the other hand, which version of "you" are you mostly communicating with? Is it one of the many parts of your ego? Or is it your True Self? Were you even aware there might be different parts of "you"? Most importantly, why should any of that matter when you simply arrived here seeking a recovery for chronic fatigue syndrome—CFS? Well, that is what we are here to explore in this chapter. So, I would like to start by sharing a journal excerpt to set the scene. I didn't recognise I was heading toward my second major crash as I was writing these words, but two months after this entry I found myself back at ground zero, wondering how on earth I was going to move forwards, yet also determined that I would find the recovery path.

ENERGY SAVING AID

The following journal excerpt shares some of my personal story leading up to my second crash. It is not essential to read if you are low on energy.

Journal Excerpt from March 2016

I finally managed to drag myself out of bed because my back was hurting so much that I just had to sit up. I don't have the energy I would like, given the day that is ahead of me, but I do feel pretty lucky all the same. Specifically: I feel like my legs are made of jelly and I have a headache and can't quite think clearly. I began my day in the usual way: scrolling through my Facebook newsfeed on my Smartphone. The first item in the feed was news that a friend's shop had been set on fire yesterday evening. The second item was a link to a Huffington Post article about CFS. It was written by the friend of a CFS sufferer who is severely ill, and this friend describes how they had previously dismissed the illness as "something you just get over," but were shocked to discover the true severity of the condition. Both news items left me thinking that, whilst there are things I may like to change about my life, I'm basically pretty lucky.

This whole train of thought led to the image I frequently carry around in my head—my personal image of what it feels like to have CFS. On a day like today where I know I am going to be really, really busy with things that "have" to be done now, and where I know I have a couple more, busy days coming up, I inevitably need to assess. I would like to be starting this day with a lot of energy, but I'm not. The assessment then takes the form of "How bad are the symptoms? Will I be OK to carry on regardless, or should I be looking at cancelling something?" The answer today is, as long as I eat well, remember to deal with the "busyness" in a calm way and take some time out for rest, I'm going to be just fine, and I believe I'm going to get through this busy week and not crash at the end … as long as I'm careful.

So, much as I want to write this journal, I'm not going to use up precious energy here today. I just want to leave you with my personal image. I'm walking along a cliff top. I'm on soft, green grass, the sun is beating down on me, and it's a cloudless day with a beautiful blue sky. The cliff top stretches on as far as the eye can see and beyond. No matter how long I keep walking, I'm never going to move into new scenery. To my right, the cliff drops down and the sea extends beyond that. The cliff is very high. In some places it is steep: a sheer drop to the beach below. In other places the drop is staggered, so there are little ledges all the way down. To my left, in the distance but always visible, is a beautiful city. Sometimes it is a magical place, perhaps like the Emerald City from the Wizard of Oz. Sometimes it is just a plain normal city, or sometimes a pretty little village. It is always a little undefined, but whatever form it takes it is the place I long to be—the perpetual target to which I am heading. Just, somehow, I can't seem to make it away from the cliff edge. Sometimes I manage to ease myself farther inland and can see the city growing closer. Sometimes I find myself perilously close to the cliff edge, gazing down at it and trying to work out how I can avoid falling. Sometimes I fall. Occasionally I fall at one of the sheer points and find myself right down on the beach below, gazing back up to the cliff top and searching for an easy route back up. Sometimes I find there is a gentle path that takes me back to the top fairly quickly. Sometimes, I have to struggle, carefully trying to make it from ledge to ledge, feeling unstable and fearing that I will fall back down to the beach. Sometimes that fall happens, and sometimes I manage to cling on to the cliff edge and somehow make it to the top. On other occasions, when I fall over the cliff, I'm at a point where I land on a ledge part way down, and I can find a way back to the top quicker than when I've fallen all the way to the beach. I have been living in this place for almost fourteen years now. It has many advantages and much beauty, but really, I would like to return to the city, to the place where I grew up, where all my friends live and where the rest of the world exists. Some days I think I am getting closer. Some days I think I will never leave the cliff, and I would actually like to just close my eyes on the beach and let the sea take me away from everything.

I chose to include that particular journal excerpt because it is one of the most personal expressions of my CFS experience. I also feel like the image encapsulates my twenty-year journey with all its highs and lows, fears and hopes. As this book unfolds, I am going to be asking you to consider information that will challenge your beliefs and make you feel uncomfortable. There may even be times when I seem to be "preaching" idealistic notions so far removed from your current experience that you'll wish to throw this book away. I wanted to begin by showing you I have experienced all the anger, pain, frustration, shame, guilt, self-hatred, worthlessness, fear, and grief that come with this illness, along with occasional beacons of light in the form of gratitude, hope, self-compassion, and even the joy of those "aha" moments that provided me with breakthroughs.

At the start of each chapter, I will share an excerpt from my personal journal to remind you that behind the teacher, there is also a human who has not always been wise. To be perfectly honest, much of the time this human would not even have followed her own advice! So, I offer these pages with the greatest respect to you. They are an invitation to explore new ideas and create your own adventure. They are not a dictate to tell you what to believe or how to think and behave. I invite you to remain curious and open. Please also remember you have the free will to work with what resonates and politely put to one side all those parts you are not yet ready to embrace.

ENERGY SAVING AID

These are the essential points that are helpful for you to take away from the following section:

- *Whether or not you are aware of this, you have an internal dialogue constantly taking place inside your head. If you are aware of it, then that means you are also aware of the part of you that is listening to that dialogue. This part of you may be something you identify as your Soul, or as your True Self, or more simply as The Witness.*

- *That part has the capacity to step outside of your inner dialogue and simply observe it without engaging in the physical pains, uncomfortable emotions, or challenging thoughts you are also experiencing. The part that engages in the physical, emotional, and mental aspects is your ego mind.*
- *If you wish to drive the optimal route through your personal maze, you will need to hand the car keys over to your True Self, not your ego self. There is every chance you have been driving with your ego self in charge up until this point. Most of us do because we don't recognise there is another option. However, the ego self is not well-placed to make the best decisions on our behalf. So, it is time to start getting acquainted with your True Self.*

Getting to Know Yourself as Your Own Guide

I want you to sit with an idea for a moment:

In case you haven't noticed, you have a mental dialogue going on inside your head that never stops. It just keeps going and going. And ... And if right now you are hearing, "I don't know what you're talking about. I don't have any voice inside my head!"—that's the voice we're talking about ... There is nothing more important to true growth than realizing that you are not the voice of the mind; you are the one who hears it.[3]

Those are the words of Michael Singer from his book, *The Untethered Soul*. That book is an exploration of what it means to step outside the ego self, outside all the selves that represent the views of your friends, family members, and society, and to find the True Self or the Soul. I mention this as an invitation to explore. By all means, go and read

3 Michael Singer, *The Untethered Soul*, Chapter 1, pages 7 & 10

the book, but in the meantime, I invite you to be aware that there are many different parts of you.

Incidentally, this idea also lies behind the therapeutic model developed by Dr. Richard Schwartz: Internal Family Systems—IFS. In brief, this model acknowledges that your mind has many different parts. Rather than this being a sign that you are suffering from a disorder like schizophrenia, Dr. Schwartz argues this is the natural state of being. The problems arise when all those different parts get out of alignment with one another. The IFS model works to reintegrate them all, and it does this by accessing the Self—with a capital "S." Over his many years of research, Dr. Schwartz has now come to view this part as the Soul. You can view this part as your Higher Self, or your connection to the creative Source of the Universe, or Universal Consciousness.

Why am I telling you this? Simply, I want you to become aware that we all have a part which is our true nature and which is capable of love, compassion, and wisdom. This part of you may be drowned out by all the conflicting, argumentative, judgemental parts, but it is in there somewhere. This part of you is your true driver. If you want to make your way out of the CFS maze, you need to hand the car keys to this part of yourself. So, I want you to become aware of which parts of you are reacting, planning, and plotting as you read these pages. You don't have to give them names—although, you can if you wish!—or understand them all, but I am inviting you to try to isolate and be guided by the part that represents the Self. It is aware of all the conflicting feelings, thoughts, voices, and pains—whatever is happening in your body and mind. If you are truly tuned into this part, then you will begin to notice it has the ability to rise above all of the noise and simply observe. This part notices you have a debate running in your head yet doesn't take sides in that debate. It witnesses all the different viewpoints and simply says, "Isn't that interesting." It can observe your emotional landscape, and yet not take on those emotions: simply see they exist. This part may notice you are experiencing physical pain, yet it does not begin telling a story about that pain: It simply sees the pain is present. I am asking you to try to find and connect with that part because it will truly support your recovery process. It has the capacity to operate with discernment rather than judgement. It exists in the present moment, away from the past or future.

I invite you to pause for a moment and try to see if you can sense what I mean. Can you hear the debate in your head? Tune in to the part that is listening to that debate: your true Self. Can you feel pain in your body? Tune in to the part that is noticing that pain: your true Self. You don't need to "get it" all right away. I simply want you to become aware that this part exists. If you already have a meditation or mindfulness practice, you may already be acquainted with this part of yourself. Or, you might be meeting it for the first time right now, and it may take some time for you to recognise it and befriend it, and that's OK. As you read this book, you are going to discover many parts of you that have different opinions about what you are reading. I want you to use this Self part to tune in to all those different opinions, observe them, do not judge them, and just witness that they are there. So, now, taking that awareness forward, let's look at what we mean by judgement and discernment and why the first is less helpful than the second.

ENERGY SAVING AID

These are the essential points that are helpful for you to take away from the following section:

- *We all have a natural tendency to judge everything we experience in life. We judge it to be "good" or "bad."*
- *In truth, this is not objective. The experience can be both*

"good" and "bad," depending on your perception, expectations, and desires. It can also be neither of those things. You are the one who chooses to judge what it is. Most of us do this subconsciously—reacting from the ego mind.

- *So, how are you currently viewing your experience of CFS? Do you judge it to be "good" or "bad" or a mixture of both? Have you even thought about it in those terms?*

Judgement Versus Discernment

"There is nothing either good or bad but thinking makes it so.[4]" How many times have you heard or seen that quote? Have you ever thought about what it really means? And what on earth has it got to do with being ill? As we have just outlined, if you are going to guide yourself out of this maze, you will need to align with the part of yourself that is able to observe from a neutral perspective. Developing that skill means letting go of judgement and developing more discernment. Let's start by looking at the meaning of these two words. They serve a similar purpose: to try to understand the world around us so that we can act—or react—in ways that will help us. In both instances, we use our knowledge—or what we believe we know—to determine whether a thing is positive or negative. Will it help us or harm us? However, judgement is a decision about whether a thing is "good" or "bad" or neither. Discernment is the ability to judge *well.* So, let me try to explain that.

Let's start by going back to Shakespeare's quote. To put it back into context, it comes from a passage in which Hamlet and Rosencrantz are discussing the country Denmark. Hamlet hates the country. Rosencrantz believes it has many merits. Both are talking about the

4 William Shakespeare, Hamlet, Act 2, scene 2.

same thing, yet each sees it through a completely different lens. So, which of them is right? Both of them, and neither of them. What does "good" or "bad" mean? Taking this example, let's consider if Denmark is a "good" place to take a holiday. Well, that totally depends on what you want from your holiday. If you love surfing, then Denmark is probably not "good" for a surfing holiday. If you love the stories of Hans Christian Andersen, then Denmark might be a great place to visit because it is his birthplace. Basically, your perception of what is "good" and "bad" is going to be determined by your desires and expectations of any given situation.

So, let's bring this back to your current situation. How do you view CFS? Perhaps you feel angry and resentful at the things you have lost because of the way your body is behaving. Then you probably label this illness as "bad." Almost certainly, the illness has forced you to look at your life differently. You will have needed to adapt and change to your new experience. It is possible some of those changes have brought in something that improves your life in some way. If you see that, you might be tempted to say, *"You know what? This illness is the best thing that could have happened to me."* Then, there is a third perspective. The illness is just a thing that happened to you. The resulting losses or benefits did not arise because of the illness but because of the way you responded to it. So, if you had chosen to respond differently, the things you experienced would have been different. Then, your perception of the "good" or "bad" qualities of the illness would be different. And, of course, your perspective of this thing is going to change over time. When you are having a bad day, this illness is the worst curse in the world. When you are recovering, or recovered, you can look back and see how the experience changed your life for the better. Because, yes, I can confirm that whatever your new, healthy life looks like, it is going to feel better than the life that led to you becoming ill. So, let me turn to the practical side. Why is it helpful to set your judgement aside, and how can you do that?

ENERGY SAVING AID

These are the essential points that are helpful for you to take away from the following section:

- *Judgements do serve a useful purpose. Being able to understand that something was "bad" for us will keep us safe and prevent us from making the same mistake twice. Similarly, understanding that something is "good" for us can inspire us to bring more of that into our lives.*
- *However, when the ego-self is making the judgement, it is building upon its knowledge. This is made of the things it has been taught by others and the things it has observed from its own experience. If that knowledge is true and wise, then helpful decisions may result from the process of judgement. This would be more like "discernment." But if the knowledge is somehow faulty or applied in the wrong way, or to the wrong situation, then the judgement will be less helpful, and any action guided by that judgement will also be sub-optimal.*
- *This principle applies to the way in which you have been—and will—approach your recovery from CFS. You may believe there are no reliable treatments available at present, so you are stuck. You may find a sense of peace and acceptance with this. Or, you may feel living with CFS is so bad that you simply have to find a way out, and you will try whatever it takes. Once we remove judgement, we see both of those options are equally valid: they are simply choices to be made by each individual, depending on how they view their circumstances and the world around them.*

The Purpose of Making Judgements and How That Relates to Discernment

As I said at the start, we make judgements in order to understand the world around us, so we can navigate it better. Judgements are both necessary and useful. It is necessary to appreciate that cutting your finger off is going to hurt and also deprive you of a useful part of your body. So, that is definitely "bad," right? Yes, but only if the finger is healthy. If the tip of your finger has untreatable gangrene, which is likely to spread to the rest of your body and kill you, then cutting your finger off is still going to hurt, and it is still going to deprive you of a useful part of your body, but it is also going to save your life, which is a "good" thing. So, as you see, judging something is a useful skill, but only if you are judging it from a place of knowledge and understanding. Then, you are judging it *well*, or rather, exercising discernment.

I have just said that we make judgements based on our knowledge and interpretation of that knowledge. So, where does our knowledge and understanding come from? The answer is the things we experience for ourselves and the things others tell us, based on their experience. So, the next useful question is, how do you know that this experience is reliable? Well, that is really the big question. A lot of times that experience is not reliable. Or, perhaps it is reliable in a specific set of circumstances, but the circumstances you are judging today are not the same, so the experience does not apply in the same way. That is why you are also going to end up with different answers to the same question. My experience of CFS is not going to be the same as yours. So, the things that seemed "good" to me may not have the same positive impact on you. Which is why I am not writing a book that tells you to take a set of steps and then expect recovery. I am fully aware a particular set of steps may produce recovery in some but will not do so in others. Or maybe I am just really weird, and the steps I took to recover will not help anyone else at all. This is why we find ourselves experiencing a situation where we are presented with numerous different solutions to our problems. Each advocate of that solution can convincingly argue its merits. Those who oppose the solution can equally convincingly argue why it does not work.

So, have I now led you into a black, depressing hole? Perhaps you are fearing you will be stuck in your maze forever and wondering why you even picked up this book. Well, I can give you the glib response that even if you remain ill forever, all you have to do is focus on the positives and it won't seem so bad to live that way. That is certainly a viable option. For many years, it seemed like the only option staring me in the face. So, with that in mind, I did the best I could to build a life that accommodated the limitations imposed by my illness. Yet, at the same time, it was not an option I wanted to accept. So, that left me with a couple of other choices. To keep searching for answers, just hang in there, and hope the science would catch up. Or, to give up and end my life.

So, if I have managed to convince you that you can choose *how* you experience CFS from a mental rather than a physical standpoint, your first option is to simply accept where you are. Then, as you live with that acceptance, live from a viewpoint that judges this illness as "good." To put it another way, live your life from a *Pollyanna* perspective, in which you focus on the things you can do and ignore—as best you can—the things you have lost. For some of you, this will seem like the best way forward today. Maybe it will always seem like the best way forward, and you can view it as a "good" solution. It is certainly going to be helpful whilst you remain lost in the maze.

For others, though—and this was me—this solution was not the one I wanted to accept. At least, not on a permanent basis. You see, the "flip" side of this is that life becomes an "existence" in which you are imprisoned by a set of bars that appear to have been imposed on you against your wishes. How many of us really desire to exist? And how many of us desire to "live," but feel forced to "exist"? Then, how many are prepared to fight, come what may, to "live"? And, in case you are thinking otherwise, none of those options are objectively "good" or "bad"; they are simply choices to be made consciously or sometimes unconsciously. Come to that, how do you define "living" versus "existing"? Even that answer is going to be vastly different from one person to another. So, if you decide not to accept the current state of your body, but to seek change, let's start to explore how this idea of judgement or non-judgement can help you.

ENERGY SAVING AID

These are the essential points that are helpful for you to take away from the following section:

- *How can letting go of judgement support your recovery process? I am going to define judgement as the process of relying upon "knowledge" that may be influenced by prejudice: in other words, a belief system. The prejudice distorts our understanding of the true value of a treatment, so this may guide us to try something that is not supportive or to avoid something that could be really helpful.*
- *Ideally, we want to find a way to step outside of that. By identifying beliefs—either yours or other people's—that may be prejudiced in some way, we can step outside of them, take account of the prejudice, and try to weigh things up with discernment. Again, this is easier to achieve from the perspective of The Witness than the ego mind.*

How Can You Use Discernment to Help You Through the Recovery Process?

Whilst you are on the path of seeking recovery, you are going to be presented with a lot of different options. When we are presented with a list of possibilities, we make choices. We choose how many of those options to try. We choose the order in which we try them. We choose when to start and when to finish with each option. We make those choices by applying our knowledge to make a judgement. Is this option likely to be "good" or "bad." But how are you defining "good" and "bad"? Hopefully, your definition of "good" means *"likely to help me to recover,"* and your definition of "bad" means *"has the potential to cause me harm."* However, as I said earlier, your judgement is going to be based upon experience or knowledge. Neither of these factors is one hundred percent reliable. In practice, you are constantly open to trying treatments that do not provide the outcome for which you hoped. To take an extreme example, if some "quack" comes along and suggests jumping out of a plane with no parachute is going to cure your CFS, I think you can see fairly easily this is unlikely to help you heal. Technically, it presumably will cure your illness, but I imagine it would also cure you of "life" in the process! So, that may not be the outcome you seek.

Bringing it back to more "sensible" examples, you are going to be presented with a lot of treatment options that could sound pretty weird, depending on your prior ideas of what medical treatments "should" be. Once you begin moving into the realms of functional and energy medicine, you may be moving further away from scientific "proof." Or, actually, is that just a myth perpetuated by the media and conventional medics? So, at this point, it becomes really important to be able to exercise *discernment*. Ironically, that can mean letting go of judgement.

Let me try to explain what I mean by the idea of letting go of judgement. I define this as letting go of the "knowledge" influenced by prejudice. For example, hypnotherapy is a treatment option available for CFS. If you start looking, you can find practitioners who offer it and offer case studies of how and why it works. You can also find stories from patients who have recovered using this treatment.[5] So, it looks "good." However, you've had no experience of hypnotism in any form, so you wonder if this is really for you. Then, you remember your Aunt Mildred once went to a hypnotist about twenty years ago, and family history has it that she developed some sort of mania as a result. This looks "bad." So, which story do you believe? Well, that comes down to assessing things like the "reliability" of the information resource. In this example, you might consider whether you believe your family anecdotes about Aunt Mildred are more or less reliable than the scientific studies that support the efficacy of hypnotherapy. You might also look at the situation the evidence describes and consider how similar or dissimilar that is to your situation. Again, in this example, Aunt Mildred's experience with a stage performer falls under the category of "entertainment." The practitioner offering hypnotherapy as a treatment for illness is working in the arena on which you are focused—health. Basically, you are trying to get as far away from prejudice and opinion as you can, to reach something closer to "truth."

---

5 Just a sample result that came up when searching for supporting evidence for this point. This is not something I personally have tried, but it may be an avenue you wish to research for yourself: https://www.emilypyne.com/healingwithhypnosis/2018/12/4/how-hypnotherapy-helped-me-get-rid-of-chronic-fatigue-for-good

ENERGY SAVING AID

These are the essential points that are helpful for you to take away from the following section:

- *The steps you take along your recovery path are always going to involve an element of uncertainty. Will they benefit you or not? Nobody can say for certain until you try it for yourself. The outcome of those experiments is going to bring about opportunities for judgement. You may be judging yourself, or you may find other people judging your decisions in wanting to try certain things and judging the outcome as they perceive it.*
- *The first thing you can do is to let go of other people's judgements. Recognise they are simply someone else's story. They do not belong to you and need not harm you unless you choose to receive harm from them.*
- *The second thing you can do is become aware of your own judgement as it sits in the form of expectation. Every step you take on the recovery path is simply a step. It may bring immediate, obvious benefits or it may seem to do nothing. It is also possible it feels like a step backwards. You are going to be tempted to judge all of these things and create stories about them. That is simply a waste of your precious energy. In the next section, we will explore why and what to do instead.*

How Life Looks as You Try to Recover and How Judgement Can Improve It … or Make It Worse

As you seek recovery, your life is going to become—or may already be—something like a circus ring. Picture this: You are in the middle of the ring, standing in full view on the high wire. Below you sits the trampoline that will catch you if you fall off the wire. The audience—made of versions of you, your friends, acquaintances, colleagues, and family—sits around the arena, watching you. In emotional terms, the high wire represents hope, the trampoline represents despair, and your audience represents judgement. Each new treatment is going to be the equivalent of walking along the high wire. Sometimes, you are going to make it a really long way, balanced on that narrow line of hope. On other occasions, you will only take a couple of steps. Then, you are going to fall off and find yourself bouncing up and down on the trampoline. At first, the bounces will be low as you wallow in despair. Gradually, they will get higher as you find your next promise of hope—new treatment. The audience watching this is going to offer up their reaction. Everything from, *"Well, of course that wasn't going to work. Why would you expect that crazy idea to help?"* to, *"Never mind; it could be worse,"* to, *"Pull yourself together and just get on with life,"* to, *"Poor you. I'm so sorry you're dealing with this,"* and a whole load of other variations besides. You get the picture. That is a pretty big challenge. So, remember, you always have the option of just walking out of the ring and returning to your place of positive acceptance of your situation. However, you can also use your power of manipulating judgement to help make this challenge feel a little easier.

First, start by trying to—politely—step away from the judgements of others. You do not need to get angry, depressed, or anything else. Simply remember these are someone else's stories, based solely on *their* experience, knowledge, and beliefs. They are not your story. They do not belong to you, and they need not concern you in any way. So, now, let's move back to your story. How you judge each treatment stems from your expectations of what it is going to achieve. So, you can save yourself a lot of stress by simply re-framing the "good" you expect to come from your chosen treatment. Instead of hoping for a "complete recovery," hope for an "improvement." Yes, of course, you want and can find that ultimate recovery. But, as I am explaining in this book, it is unlikely to come from one place. More likely, it is going to be a combination of different things. So, re-frame your judgement to recognise that each thing you try is more like moving one step closer to the exit point in your maze. Eventually, one thing will turn out to be the final path. This is a process that requires multiple steps and will be a lot easier if you can accept each step for what it is: a step.

Secondly, bear in mind a step can appear to take you forwards or backwards. Again, this is just a judgement based on your perception of where you are sitting right now. The recovery process is not linear. So, sometimes, it can feel like things are getting worse—for example, a symptom flares up—but that is instead a necessary part of clearing a particular symptom from your body. So, it is really a positive thing. It is much easier to view this when you see each action you take as "a step," and do not judge the direction it is taking you. Naturally, I will caveat this. You do need to keep using discernment. If a treatment is causing you harm, stop it immediately. In part four, I will talk in more depth about how you can determine when something is harmful versus a temporary difficulty that is part of the recovery process.

ENERGY SAVING AID

These are the essential points that are helpful for you to take away from the following section:

- *Start becoming aware of the internal dialogue taking place whenever you try a new treatment or experience a new symptom. Are you internally criticising yourself? Are you using a lot of "absolutes" in your language—words like always, never, everyone, and nobody? These are simply creating a stress response in your body, which is not supportive of healing.*
- *We are going to explore the stress response and how it*

contributes to remaining stuck in CFS in part three. For now, simply start to notice your language and try to reframe it. Rather than telling yourself an elaborate story that brings in judgements and criticism, try stepping back and sticking to the facts. The more you can develop the witness state and be with your emotions, but not drown in them, the more you will create an internal environment that supports recovery.

Self-Judgement and Judgement That Causes Stress

More than likely, reading this chapter has already sent your mind down a rabbit hole. Things can be good, or bad, or neither. The criteria by which you judge this can be flawed. How do you know if you are judging or discerning? That is a lot to think about. As we are going to explore later, the type of thinking that this induces is basically activating your stress response and, ultimately, not helping you to recover. So, let's take a look at where this type of judgment comes from and why it is so stressful.

For many of us, part of the reason we ended up here is because we are too accustomed to analysing and judging everything. Perhaps this reflects a strict upbringing in which our ability to get things "right" or "wrong" had a direct impact on our physical or emotional safety. Most likely, you do not see it that way. So, what starts out as a sensible assessment of a situation can quickly escalate into a very destructive pattern of self-judgement. Perhaps you already know that. You may already see that in yourself. Or perhaps you have no idea what this means. So, let me give you an example. You try a new supplement with a great track record of easing one of the symptoms currently causing you discomfort. You have seen some studies demonstrating a cause-and-effect relationship between your symptoms and insufficient levels of the supplement, and your highly qualified nutritionist recommends this. Apparently, you should begin to feel some improvement in about two weeks. So, this sounds like a "good" treatment plan. You dutifully follow the instructions on how and when to take the supplement. You wait expectantly, carefully monitoring your symptoms and expecting an improvement. Two weeks pass, and nothing has changed for you. So, is this the conversation that then takes place in your head?

"Well, that hasn't worked! I thought this was supposed to be good for me, supposed to help me. I've done exactly what I was told, and I'm not feeling better. So, that was a waste of time and money. I'm such an idiot for believing I could get better. This treatment isn't good at all, and I've been conned again. Nobody knows how to help me. This is a disaster! I'm never going to get better!"

Can you see how many judgements are mixed up in that thought process? First, judgement of the treatment has moved from being "good" to "bad." The reality is the treatment did not provide the outcome you expected in the timeframe for which you hoped. That could be "good" or "bad" or neither, as I will explain below. But the judgement does not stop there. From judging the treatment, you move to judging yourself. Where does that come from? If the treatment did not provide the outcome you expected, how are you involved in that, in all honesty? And, why are you seeing yourself as "bad" when you followed instructions, so you behaved "well"? Then, there is the judgement of your prognosis and the ability of the people trying to help you. Is any part of that improving your illness? No. Is it worsening your illness? Yes, because it is a stress-program and, as you will learn in part three, that stress response both damages your body and prevents it from healing.

What if, instead of that very judgemental internal conversation, you held the following conversation?

"OK, so I still have the symptom at the same level as it was when I started. This isn't what I was expecting to happen, but it has. So, let me report this result to my nutritionist and see what options are available to try next."

Can you notice how this is done totally without judgement? It is a statement of the event and a willingness to see what happens next. No drama. No stress response triggered. So, is this improving your illness? Maybe not—although, maybe it is ... let me explain in a moment. Is it worsening your illness? No. The way your body responded to the supplement is simply information. When you report back to the nutritionist, their response could be, *"OK, that's fine. In some patients, this requires a little longer before you start to see the positive effect, so let's give it another week and reassess."* Or, it could be, *"OK, that tells me your body probably needs to take another step first or maybe alongside this supplement. So, we'll try that next."* Even if your nutritionist's response turns out to be, *"Sorry, I really hoped that would work for you. Unfortunately, I'm now out of options, and I don't have anything else to offer,"* that is still not the end of the road. Just take a look at the number of different treatment options I have mentioned in this book. I know there are more that I have not talked about, and there will be more becoming available.

It is true this is not the outcome for which you hoped. It is "bad" in the sense it did not bring recovery for you, but it is also "good" in the sense it gave you some more information about your body. If you use that wisely, maybe it tells you something. If the only options you have tried are physical, and you feel like you have come to the end of that road, then perhaps it is time to try a treatment that addresses the mental or spiritual body. Either way, I hope you can see that there is a difference in the paths I have outlined. Returning to where I began, it is also perfectly normal and natural to take the first path—judgement—even when you know it does not help. The entire concept of judgement may be an area that needs healing. If it is currently causing turmoil in the mind and leading to stress on the body, then healing it is going to be one of the steps that removes a weight and helps you find a way out.

Ironically, that brings me right back to my starting point. It is healthier and easier to try new ideas, new treatments from a perspective of curiosity, than to tie yourself up in knots trying to decide up front whether they are going to be "good" or "bad" or creating judgemental stories about the results when they differ from your expectations. So, if you can understand what judgement means, and how to avoid its potential harm, it will free you from a lot of angst keeping your body locked in the "stress" response, instead of allowing it to sit in "recovery" mode.

> *ENERGY SAVING AID*
>
> *Please complete the following practice. The self-awareness this brings is going to help you create your unique roadmap for recovery.*

An Invitation to Practice

This part of your journey has all been about starting to develop self-awareness. So, in the interest of doing that, I have put together a few questions to help give you a clear picture of where you are right now. Self-awareness isn't only about having all the answers: it is also perfectly fine to observe that "you don't know" or notice you are resisting this practice. That is all information, and it will all be helpful as we proceed.

With that in mind, I would like you to grab your journal and start answering the following questions:

- What symptoms are you experiencing at the moment?

- Are there any symptoms you have previously experienced, but which are not causing you problems right now?
- What treatments have you tried in the past?
- Did they help you, and in what way?
- Which of the following emotions do you feel now, or do you recognise feeling at some point in the past? Please tick all that apply.
    - Anger at yourself
    - Anger at doctors/the medical profession
    - Anger at friends/family
    - Powerlessness
    - Lack of hope
    - Fear
    - Confusion
    - Bitterness
    - Shame
    - Guilt
    - Feeling numb/empty
    - Worthlessness
    - Self-hatred
    - Joy
    - Hope

    - Compassion for yourself
    - Love for yourself
    - Empowerment
    - Write down anything else you can think of

- Make a list of all the questions you have right now concerning your illness or available treatments.
- As you have been following this journaling exercise, have you noticed any judgement coming up?
    - Have you been judging your symptoms/treatments or making up stories about what they mean?
    - Do you notice any judgement of yourself as you consider what emotions you're feeling?

You may find it strange that I am asking you to list all these things you already know, but there is value in writing it down so you become clear about your experience. This is all about developing clarity and self-awareness, which are critical if you want to take the shortest possible route to finding your energy again. I am also going to be inviting you to use your responses to plot your map out of your personal maze.

Chapter 3

Meet Your Vehicle

So far in this section, you have started becoming acquainted with your tour guide—me—and your driver—your Self. Now, it's time to take a look at the vehicle you are going to be driving—your body—and how that fits into the environment through which you will be travelling—your maze. I am going to be offering you two contrasting views of what we understand as illness, and then two contrasting views of the way we view the human body. We will then focus on the areas I found helpful in my recovery process. My invitation to you is to keep an open mind, explore all angles, and then consider some questions about how you are viewing your illness and your body. There are no "right" or "wrong" answers to these questions, simply different pathways to explore. So, let's set the scene with some rather painful memories of the time when I was still lost and seeking the paths that would support my recovery.

ENERGY SAVING AID

The following journal section sets the scene as I share my personal story. It is not essential for understanding recovery, so you can skip it if you need to conserve your energy.

Journal: Painful Memories from 2009 to 2012

In 2009, seven years into my illness, I finally found myself in a place where I was feeling the satisfaction of enjoying more sustainable energy, and I felt

I had the ability to start planning life. This satisfaction was swiftly replaced by my first bout of depression. I did the sensible thing and went to the doctor for help: He prescribed anti-depressants, and we discussed the possibility that my "recovery" had triggered this. The idea was, as the illness stopped taking over my life, I was hit by the realization of all the things I'd lost. At that point seven years of my life had been stopped in its tracks. I had moved from being 26 to being 33. I had watched all my friends get married, seen their careers blossom, and seen some of them start to have babies—all the while, I'd been battling to do basic things like get dressed.

So, when I finally began to recover some energy, I reacted by trying to leap right back into life. A friend suggested that internet dating might be a good idea as, given my energy was still quite low, it would be an easy way to meet people without leaving home. It sounded like a perfect plan. The only trouble is I quickly found the dilemma: Should I mention the CFS or not? I'm naturally open and honest, so I began by being totally honest about it. I was met by a series of judgements ranging from people just stopping emailing me once they heard to what is probably one of the most hurtful and humiliating episodes: I had been on three dates with someone, and we clicked on every level. We were emailing every day in between dates and quickly getting to know one another. . .and best of all, he hadn't cut me dead when I mentioned CFS. I'm not quite sure why, but on date number three, I had an instinct that made me ask if he was dating other people at the same time. He confessed that he was, in fact, dating four people: not great—I don't like being treated as an object to be sized up and compared against others, but that's what happens with internet dating, so I didn't raise an objection. Then a week later, he called me to tell me he'd decided to commit to a relationship with another girl because, although he thought I was lovely, he couldn't see a future with me because of the CFS. Yes, I'm afraid that was exactly the reason he gave. Whilst it says more about him than me, whilst it means I'm lucky not to have someone like that in my life, it was still a slap in the face on an epic scale. I felt devastated, but I tried not to let it show. Instead of processing this grief, I picked myself up, dusted myself down, and dated a couple more people, both disasters for different reasons. I was beginning to learn the hard way: We can't just ignore or dodge painful emotions. Finally, these rejections, on top of the loss of so much in my life, proved too much. Hence the onset of depression and my return to the doctor.

Fast forward six months, and the anti-depressants had lifted my mood back to normal, but they had reduced my overall health and energy back to a much, much lower level. Something in this drug had "annoyed" my body again and pushed it back into a bad state. I stopped taking the anti-depressants and began using every strategy I had learned to try to control the CFS and get my energy levels back. It took until 2012—another three years!—to get me back to a good place.

2012 also happened to be the year my career took a new turn. Instead of fighting to return to my old job, the one that had such horrendous hours which had triggered, if not been responsible for the illness, I was suddenly presented with an opportunity to turn my hobby into a career. I became my own boss and started doing something I love. Whilst I count my blessings every day that I can do this, it isn't without stress. I'm self-employed, so that means every penny I earn is hard-won and not guaranteed. Running a business is also hugely time-consuming, so there are moments when I'm in danger of working too hard again. There is also the constant frustration of wanting to do so much but not having the energy to manage it. In short, this is fraught with risk, and I sit with the constant realization that, unlike a "normal" person, if this all falls apart, I don't have the choice of just going out and getting a normal job. Although we have anti-discrimination laws, no employer in their right mind is going to take on a member of staff who is almost certain to have regular periods of sick leave. Also, no employer in their right mind is going to give my illness as the reason: I'm sure they would be able to point to some other area in which I'm "less qualified" than another candidate or give a more subjective reason like "not being a good fit for the company." The nature of this illness and attitudes towards it at all levels of society also means that getting financial help through the benefits system is incredibly difficult ... even if I felt comfortable taking that kind of help, which I don't.

I picked this particular journal entry because I suspect you may relate to some of the pain I have shared. We all have our own individual experience of discrimination, lack of support, and the confusion around where to seek help. Looking back on my experience, I feel that my lack of understanding about what was really happening in my body led to me taking paths I thought would help me but which ended up doing more damage. These are all themes we will be exploring throughout this book, but in this chapter I want to focus on the idea that words and names are representations of powerful images, systems, and beliefs. When we write—or speak—a word or a sentence, the reader—or listener—creates an entire image so much bigger than an individual word.

Specifically, we are going to be exploring words like "illness" or "disease." How do our beliefs about those words dictate our behaviours towards the circumstances the words are describing? We are also going to look at our beliefs about our bodies. As my story unfolds throughout this book, I want to show you how changing my understanding of the way I viewed my body and its relationship to my illness paved the way to finding the path to recovery.

What Do We Understand About Illness and Disease?

I want to begin by introducing you to two different models of illness: Germ Theory and Terrain Theory. You may or may not have heard of these names before, but each one represents a drastically different view of what we mean when we talk about "being ill" or "having an illness." So, let's unpack each of them.

ENERGY SAVING AID

These are the essential points that are helpful for you to take away from the following section:

- *Conventional Western medicine is—mostly—built upon the idea that a disease/illness is caused by a pathogen—"Germ"—attacking the body.*
- *In that model, the solution to curing disease is to simply identify and eradicate the pathogen.*
- *Research has been unable to identify a single pathogen—or even a common set of pathogens—that causes CFS, so the illness seems to be a mystery, and that may be why, in the past, it has been viewed as something that could simply be hypochondria. This is also why you are likely to be told there is no reliable treatment or cure for your condition at the moment.*

Germ Theory

Broadly speaking, this is the theory upon which Western conventional medicine is built. Its origins are often attributed to Louis Pasteur and his proof that spontaneous generation could not take place. In other words, a bacteria could not simply grow from nothing. This provided a foundation for others to argue that specific microscopic organisms create specific diseases. These can be in the form of bacteria or viruses—we have a collective name for them: pathogens. In this model, if you can locate and identify the pathogen that has caused the illness, you can seek an antidote that will remove it from the body, returning the body back to health.

As Pasteur's research evolved, he developed vaccines against anthrax and rabies. His research is said to have laid the foundations for

Alexander Fleming to discover Penicillin, the first antibiotic. Another scientist, Robert Koch, proved that specific microbes caused anthrax, cholera, and tuberculosis. Koch's Postulates proved specific germs create specific diseases and disease germs can be passed from one body to another, transmitting disease. I appreciate this is a very broad view of the model. If you are a medically trained reader, you will be able to add all sorts of information to bring more detail to this. However, for our purposes, this broad overview is sufficient.

How does this model relate to the patient? Well—simplistically—when a patient presents with a set of symptoms, the doctor will look for the pathogen that caused them. From there, treatment involves administering the appropriate antidote. Or, if no antidote currently exists, awaiting the research that will provide the antidote.

This works beautifully for many diseases, but what happens when you can't identify the pathogen? There is always the possibility we can redefine the symptoms as a "condition" rather than an "illness." So, perhaps we can identify that a system has started to malfunction, and perhaps we can identify the cause of that problem. Again, at a certain level, this model still works. For example, a heart attack might represent the failure of the system related to the heart. Perhaps we might be able to identify a blocked artery. With a clever surgeon, maybe we can open up the body and physically remove the blockage, allowing the system to work properly once again. What happens when you cannot identify a pathogen nor pinpoint a problem with a system? Where does that leave you? One option might be to accuse the patient of manufacturing symptoms to get attention. A more compassionate approach may take the view we just need more research. Science is evolving all the time. If we can just invent a more precise machine or develop a more refined drug, then we will have the answer.

Every individual who receives a diagnosis of chronic fatigue syndrome will have a different experience and perspective on this. For many years, the solution was to claim this illness existed merely in the heads of hypochondriacs. Eventually, after much campaigning, research began to emerge, pinpointing malfunctions in certain systems. However, the need to find "the one" root cause—be that pathogen or single system failure—still eludes scientists.

We have now moved forward to a place where we accept the illness is "real" and physical, not merely the result of an over-active imagination. Yet without being able to see a specific cause, we are nowhere close to finding a reliable treatment or cure. So, the message that will come with your diagnosis from your conventional medical doctor goes something like this: "Sorry, we don't have a reliable treatment right now. There may be some drugs or therapies that could relieve some of your individual symptoms, but as things stand, you're stuck with this for life."

So, how come I—and others like me—are writing books or sharing stories of recovery? You might be thinking that we were somehow just lucky, or perhaps we were misdiagnosed, and eventually found recovery through getting a different—correct—diagnosis and treatment. Or maybe we really are hypochondriacs and there has never been anything wrong with us: We simply got bored of pretending one day and decided to "snap out of it." All of those could be reasonable theories, but none were true for me and my recovery. So, what did actually happen for me? Well, having received my rather depressing diagnosis and prognosis from the conventional Western medical world, I found myself turning to something called functional medicine. This creates a useful segue into our second model of illness: Terrain Theory.

ENERGY SAVING AID

These are the essential points that are helpful for you to take away from the following section:

- *An alternative view of disease, "Terrain Theory," places more emphasis on the basic health of the body—the "Terrain."*
- *This view suggests if the body is basically healthy—functioning optimally—then it will be able to fight off a pathogen or another attack. That explains why two people can be exposed to the same pathogen, and one may become ill while the other remains unaffected.*
- *Disease occurs when the body is not functioning optimally, so it is not equipped to fight off attacks. Rather than focusing on "killing attackers," we should be focusing on increasing the basic health of the body—Terrain.*
- *This model also allows us to understand that disease doesn't always have to be rooted in a pathogen. Lifestyle has an important role to play too.*
- *In this model, recovery from CFS can be accomplished by understanding—and correcting—all the areas of basic health, including things like optimal diet, cleaning out toxins, and so on. Functional Medicine follows this approach to support and create recovery.*

Terrain Theory

Most exponents of Terrain Theory will tell you about one of Pasteur's scientific contemporaries: Claude Bernard. He maintained that the "terrain" of the human body was more critical than the pathogens that impacted it. Bernard noted that we are surrounded by microorganisms. Our bodies even provide shelter in which they can happily exist. Modern research is busy uncovering the importance of the bacteria in our digestive system. Our health depends on us having a balance of different bacteria: some carry the label "good," and others carry the label "bad." The key lies in the balance. The so-called "bad" bacteria in the digestive tract are those which might be linked to symptoms of a stomach bug, and those symptoms feel like a "problem." The "good" bacteria don't obviously create "problems" for us. Together, all these varieties create a complete environment that aids digestion.

Bernard observed that the same bacteria can create symptoms in one person, while another person exhibits nothing. He concluded that this was a reflection of the "terrain," rather than the pathogen. So, if the "terrain" is basically unhealthy or deficient in key vitamins or minerals, then when a pathogen enters, the body will have no defence system to ward it off. Unlike Germ Theory, this accounts for the observation that two people can be exposed to the same bacteria or virus and one may become very ill while the other is fine.

Legend has it that Louis Pasteur, on his deathbed, came out with these words: "Bernard was right: the pathogen is nothing, the terrain is everything." Did that really happen? Some believe it did, others believe this is a convenient legend to justify a crazy theory. Given that Pasteur is not solely responsible for Germ Theory, this is a rather moot point, in my opinion. It is worth noting that many others, including Florence Nightingale, believed in the influence of the environment on disease. The improvement in life expectancy that took place at the end of the nineteenth century is just as attributable to factors like better sanitation as it is to changes in medical procedures.

So, why the debate? Why does it matter whether Pasteur backtracked on his life's work or not? Well, if you have heard of these two theories before now, the context in which you heard them may well have been the pandemic of 2020–22. Debate raged between scientists on both sides of the fence. Terrain Theory became a tool for declaring the vaccine to be an unnecessary political tool, used as a distraction when we should have been focusing on how unhealthy our population has become. Unfortunately, some went even further, losing focus on the interesting argument around basic levels of health and moving towards what many termed as "conspiracy theories," which saw the vaccine in terms of an evil agenda, at best motivated by financial profit, at worst, some insidious form of population control. Germ Theory leant its support to the vaccine as a solution to the crisis. It pointed out other diseases that have been eradicated through the use of vaccination programs and implied the same would be true for the COVID outbreak.

The entire debate widened even further to become a question of science versus pseudoscience, with plenty of mud-slinging on both sides. However, let's not digress. That debate is not a topic for this book. What I am interested in asking is: Why does it have to be either/or? Why can it not be both/and? So, let's try to answer that question.

ENERGY SAVING AID

These are the essential points that are helpful for you to take away from the following section:

- *Instead of trying to explain CFS in one or another model, it may be more helpful to explore it as a combination of both.*
- *So, there may be a single pathogen or a set of pathogens that attacked the body at one time. Either they have not been effectively eradicated—killed/removed—or the body is still being exposed to them at the same time it is trying to get rid of them.*
- *We need to take a broader view of what we mean by Pathogen. This can include viruses, bacteria, infections, toxic chemicals, and emotions. All these things signal to the body's cells they are in danger.*
- *It is not enough to simply remove the Pathogen. The cells will also have sustained long-term damage from the attack. The body's natural healing system is equipped to deal with that, but the healing process requires energy, resources, and a supportive environment, to carry out this work. So, all of these factors need to be in place to complete the recovery process.*

A Third Option: "Both/And" Model

Let's start by returning to the specific condition of CFS. If we were to place that illness in the model of Terrain Theory, do we move any closer to finding some answers? Well, here we move into another branch of medicine: functional medicine. As its name suggests, this has more of a focus on how your body is functioning. So, when we see something like low levels of ATP—the "energy" hormone—we might ask why that is. This may bring us back to the Mitochondria,[6] and we may discover that the body is lacking the vitamins, minerals, or other raw ingredients—for example, B12, Magnesium, or D-Ribose—that support optimal Mitochondrial function. We may simply supplement with those depleted materials and see if we can improve energy levels that way.

Perhaps we still need to be looking for the pathogen that is attacking the Mitochondria. On the other hand, if we cannot find such a pathogen in existence, we might then ask what other reasons the Mitochondria could have for their sub-optimal performance. Even more intriguingly, we can explore the idea that the body is not "malfunctioning." It is making very sensible adaptations to its environment. So, that takes us a step further. We have moved beyond looking for a pathogen to looking at the "imperfections" in the environment. Now we ask, why are those "imperfections" occurring? And that may take us outside the immediate terrain of the body to consider the environment where that body is living.

This train of thought leads to a greater understanding of the processes and symptomology behind CFS. It also happens to be the model used by the Optimum Health Clinic, with which I worked between 2017 and 2021. I worked with two nutritionists who carried out multiple tests and administered protocols of supplements to help bring depleted resources back into balance in my body. And yes, my energy returned markedly. So, I can testify that this system really does work.

---

6 Mitochondria are commonly viewed as the "batteries" for our cells, responsible for producing cellular energy. Understanding the Mitochondria has been key to getting a better picture of what is happening in the biology of someone with CFS. We now know that, in addition to energy production, they also carry out other important functions, including signalling when a cell is safe or in danger. In this way, they create a communication link between the central nervous system and Immune System. So, this book contains multiple references to Mitochondria, touching upon how their various functions relate to CFS symptoms, and where it might be appropriate to use treatments designed to support Mitochondrial function.

This is also the train of thought being pursued by Dr. Robert Naviaux, one of the foremost researchers into the Mitochondria, and a scientist who has already done a huge amount to shed light upon the apparent mystery of CFS. Dr. Naviaux talks about a dual system of recovery from disease. First, it may be necessary to identify and treat a pathogen. For example, in the case of pneumonia, the patient may require antibiotics to fight the bacteria that has caused the infection. This portion of the recovery process would be termed Pathogenesis. Then, staying with that example of pneumonia, the infection will have caused some damage to the lung, which requires repair. The body will need to redirect some energy and resources to the lungs to carry out the repairs. This portion of the process is called salugenesis, and it requires the environment to be supportive and conducive to facilitating the healing process.

In the case of CFS, and other chronic diseases, the body is simply failing to complete the healing cycle. This could be because the original "injury" has never been addressed. For example, a toxin that was absorbed into the body and never fully released. Or it could be a case of "reinjury," which might manifest as continued exposure to the toxin.[7] The affected cells are constantly signalling the brain that their world is unsafe, so the brain is responding by maintaining those cells in the healing cycle, which is depleting energy and causing inflammation that may register as pain. We are going to look at this idea in much greater detail in chapter nine.

Once we address our recovery from both these perspectives—addressing all the original pathogens, and then supporting the Salugenesis healing process—will that bring about healing? Well, that depends. We need to consider that CFS rarely has a single pathogen

---

7 When I use the term "toxin" in this context, I am thinking in the broadest possible terms. So, it might literally be a toxic chemical, but it could also be a virus or bacteria. Even more importantly, we need to be considering "toxic" emotions. We will be developing that idea in part three.

at its root. More commonly, it is a build-up of different threats that end up overwhelming the body. So, the recovery process often involves following many different paths to address multiple issues. This is why it can feel like travelling through a maze. You may find a path that seems to offer an explanation of your symptoms, follow that path successfully, but still find not all of your symptoms have resolved, and you need to start following another path to unravel another layer of recovery. We also need to recognize that potential dangers—pathogens—are not only physical in nature. An emotional trauma can also create that signal of "unsafety" in our cells, and that can keep the body in the loop of incomplete healing just as much as a physical threat. That observation leads us rather neatly to my next pairing of ideas. How do we view our bodies?

ENERGY SAVING AID

These are the essential points that are helpful for you to take away from the following section:

- *In the Western world—commonly, at least—we have been taught to view ourselves as separate parts: a body, mind, emotions, and—maybe—a spirit/soul.*
- *This can lead to the view that any symptoms experienced in the physical body must have their roots and need healing in the physical body. Symptoms experienced in the mind have their roots and require healing in the mind, and so on.*
- *This immediately restricts where we look for answers when facing health issues. So, we can end up missing critical paths to recovery.*

The "Common" View of a Human

You may not have thought about it this way before, but most of us view ourselves in parts. We have a body, a mind, some emotions, and maybe a soul or spirit. I say "maybe" to that last part because I know it's possible some of you may not identify with that part of you—and that's OK. We're just here to work with where we are right now.

Having split the human into a series of parts, we see them as separate entities that are connected but function autonomously, each requiring a separate type of healing.

- Body healed by your doctor
- Mind healed by your psychiatrist
- Emotions healed by your therapist
- Spirit healed by your religious institution

Yes, of course, this simplifies things a little, but I want to make the point that we have this notion of separation.

In fact, none of these elements are truly separate. Something like depression may be considered psychiatric in nature—a problem occurring in the mind. Yet, it has physical consequences—chemicals in your brain are imbalanced. A physical issue like cancer can lead to a mental issue—depression. And then, of course, where is the divide between mind and emotions? Depression can be classified as a psychiatric—mind—disorder, but it can feel very emotional—deep sadness, for example. Cancer usually brings emotions of anger or fear. As we will be exploring in later chapters, emotions can show up as physical pain.

So, where does the *spirit* fit into all of this? Well, let's start by setting aside the link between spirit and organized religion or organized spirituality. Your spirit is the essence of who you are. It is your consciousness—not something to see, or describe, but something felt.

You may identify this as God, the Universe, Source Energy, perhaps something like Mother Nature, or even just a sense of there being something bigger than you in existence—consciousness. You can also see this element as the "True Self" identity that we were looking at in the last chapter.

You might already have noticed something about these separate parts. The body is physical. We can see, hear, feel, smell, taste, and touch our body or someone else's body. But our thoughts, emotions, and soul? Those are rather less easy to define.

For many years, one of the greatest injustices of the CFS diagnosis has been that doctors viewed it as a "psychological" illness—something happening in that rather mysterious space of the mind. This view invalidated the patient's experience of this being very much in the body. The body *felt* no energy, yet the mind longed to be actively doing things. So, as a community, CFS patients have spent a lot of time and energy fighting to have their illness classified as a physical condition. That battle is being won, but it hasn't yet led to the breakthrough treatments and cures we all desire.

Perhaps just as interesting is the question of *why* it is so important that the illness be classified as a physical condition. My observation leads me to believe that, as a society, in the Western world—at least—we attach particular qualities to the physical realm. If something is happening in your physical body, then, by definition, there must be a solution because the physical body is a machine. If a machine breaks, we can find a way to fix it. Furthermore, that problem/solution view has an external element: Someone else can fix it for you. It also tends to have a more "accidental" element: Something else did this to you and it wasn't your fault. Conversely, if something has "gone wrong" in your mind, that is somehow shameful. It has often come with a lot of blame: You chose to do this to yourself. And it comes with a terrible burden of responsibility: You are the only one who can fix this for yourself. If you don't manage to do that, then somehow you are a defective human being.

As we progress through these pages, I am going to be introducing you to some new language for exploring these differences. We will be talking about "energetic" bodies and "physical" bodies. Before we move into that, I want to introduce you to another way of thinking about yourself. What if your parts were not separate at all? I invite you to consider looking at yourself as a whole. As we move through these pages, I hope you will be able to see how this view can open up new doors to finding your recovery path.

ENERGY SAVING AID

These are the essential points that are helpful for you to take away from the following section:

- *What if we looked at those separate parts as elements of a single whole, with a complex inter-relationship?*
- *Some of those elements fall in the physical realm—things we can see, hear, touch, smell, and taste. Others fall into the "Energetic" realm—a state governed by frequency or "sense."*
- *Viewed through this lens, symptoms occurring in one part of the body may have their root cause in another part. So, simply addressing the symptom without addressing the root cause prevents the body from completing the healing cycle.*
- *This model accepts the complexities of CFS, but it also opens doors to exploring areas we might overlook that may be key to recovery.*

An "Alternative" View of Being Human

There is another way of looking at this, which sees the body and mind as two parts of a whole—the mind expresses what is felt in the body, and the body illustrates what is happening in the mind. So, the mind is an "Energetic" expression of the "Physical" entity—body. The equivalent relationship exists between the emotions and the spirit/soul. So, the emotions are the "physical" expression of the soul. They can manifest as feelings in the body or be expressed as thoughts in the mind.

Yet, as I pondered these ideas further, I came to believe that even this is a very imperfect description of what is really going on. We are still trying to create too much separation. To me, the only thing that makes sense on all levels is to see all these elements as one. Yes, each has an individual expression we can detect, but trying to separate them from one another hinders our ability to reach a true understanding of how we work. They meld together in one whole that interacts in ways too complex for us to unpick in a linear fashion.

Naturally, that is rather inconvenient. It would be much easier if we could separate everything out into a model that says, *"This does this, and it requires that to recover."* Yet, our experience of CFS—and many other chronic illnesses—suggests this simply doesn't work in practice. At best, the patient becomes something like a suitcase covered in labels. So, you may end up being diagnosed with multiple conditions, none of which has a treatment or cure. Whilst it feels helpful to be able to name your experience, unless that name comes with a solution, it has limited value.

The reason I am inviting you to consider these two ideas about who you are, or how you see yourself, is to begin looking at your CFS experience from a new perspective. If I could go back and have a chat with my 26-year-old self, I would tell her that this separation of ourselves into parts may be hindering our understanding of how we get ill and the steps we need to take to recover.

So, bringing all of this together, I want to suggest that we aren't looking at an "either/or" situation. The idea you have a physical body and a non-physical—"Energetic" —body and whatever you are experiencing is taking place in the Physical body OR the Energetic body is, I believe, unhelpful. The more helpful view is that these bodies are "both/and." So, you have a physical *and* an Energy body, but they operate together as one whole. It may be helpful to imagine them as layers, but they are not distinct. So, whatever is happening to you ends up happening in the Energy body *and* the Physical body. Similarly, if you wish to change your experience, you will need to change it at the Physical level *and* the Energy level.

To give an example, back pain may be manifesting on the physical level *and* also have an energetic root in the form of trapped anger or burdensome memories. Somewhere between the two extremes, the level of the mind will also be creating stories about this pain; for example, a story to try to identify what caused it.

It can be helpful to have this awareness that your body is multi-layered. When it comes to working out how and where to make changes, you may find that working at a particular layer is more or less effective. For example, if your appendix is about to burst, I would not recommend Energy healing as a treatment. You want an immediate, physical, surgical intervention—remove the appendix. If you have back pain for which a physical root cannot be identified—i.e., there is nothing wrong with your skeletal or muscular structure—then it might be helpful to consider working at the level of what is happening in your thoughts and emotions.

So, I invite you to hold those ideas as we move on. I have mentioned this strange idea of "Energy body" without explaining what I mean by that. Is it a "thing" or just an image? Well, it's a very big topic, and that is our next stop on this grand tour of the CFS maze. Before we dash onto that, I invite you to pause and take stock of where you are right now. I've got a practice for you to complete that will help you do this.

> *ENERGY SAVING AID*
>
> *Don't skip the following section. This part will help you map your personal recovery path. It's OK if you don't have the energy to answer all the questions in one go—you can journal entries over time. It's also OK to keep your answers short. But please don't miss this opportunity to really get in touch with how you honestly think and feel about your situation. If you skip this, the only person who you are depriving is yourself. You may have good reasons for doing that, but those reasons are the barriers to recovering the life you really desire—and deserve.*

An Invitation to Practice

I would like you to grab your journal and answer the following questions:

- What do you *think* about the models we've been exploring in this chapter?
    - Have you come across any of these ideas before?
    - How much of this makes logical sense to you?
    - Or does it all feel confusing: maybe you don't understand the point of this?
    - And if you don't know what to think right now, that's OK too—just note that down.

- How do you *feel* about the material in this chapter?
    - Is it bringing up a feeling of hope that this might be a new path you haven't previously considered?
    - Perhaps you are feeling scared that I'm about to take you down paths you don't wish to explore?
    - Or is this making you feel angry or resentful, feeling that I am spouting some kind of rubbish here?
    - Are you feeling any shame or guilt or self-blame?
    - Is this starting to make lightbulbs switch on?
    - Or something else entirely?
    - And even if you don't know how you feel, that's your answer, and it's a perfectly good answer.
- Lastly, building on the last practice: are you noticing any judgement coming up as you consider all this?
    - Are you judging yourself?
    - Are you judging me?

You can write at length if you really want to explore how you think and feel about these ideas. Or, if your energy is low, it's fine to keep your answers short. There are no "right" or "wrong" answers here. Believe it or not, just noticing you don't even know the answer is also very valuable information. I am asking you to do this so you can become more aware of what you think and feel about your experience of CFS. As with the last practice, I will be inviting you to use your answers when you come to build your roadmap out of the CFS maze.

Part 2

Understanding your Vehicle

Chapter 4

Your Bioenergetic Body

I am going to start by sharing a journal entry I wrote as I was—unknowingly—heading towards my second crash. I picked this one because it notes the link between the physical body and our emotional state. It also reflects my reluctance to explore this fully. I was determined to see my illness in purely physical terms and, therefore, seek only physical remedies. I only managed to reach a final recovery once I began to explore my emotional world and to see that this layer of "me" exists in its very own body: my bioenergetic body. So, this chapter is going to introduce you to your biofield and explain how that relates to CFS.

> *ENERGY SAVING AID*
>
> *The following journal excerpt frames the discussion themes for this chapter, but it is my personal story, so it is not essential to read if you are low on energy.*

Journal Entry: July 2015

Well, I'm properly into phase two now: "Tired but Wired." It pretty much does what it says on the tin. I feel really, really tired, but my body refuses to rest properly. It's not the kind of tiredness that has me yawning, but something a lot worse than that. My muscles don't have the strength to do much exercise. That's easy enough to manage. Worse still is the feeling that my head is at the same time filled with cotton wool, so everything is all a bit fuzzy, and it's buzzing. My brain doesn't want to shut down—it's jumping from one idea to another. I must have come up with at least a dozen possible ideas for designs or projects to promote or improve my website. I just don't have the physical or mental energy to carry them out. Interspersed with all those lovely ideas are all the trains of thought that run around with the CFS: Is this ever going to go away properly? What can I do to make it get better? What am I not doing? What am I missing? Are you sure there isn't something else wrong, something for which the medical world has a solution? It's a very familiar pattern.

Alongside this I have the feeling of being physically wired as well. Have you ever experienced a real overdose of caffeine? The sort where your heart is racing, your mind is buzzing, and you can't physically sit still. Well, if you have, you are partway to understanding how I feel. My body is incredibly jumpy, so the slightest unexpected sound makes me jump out of my skin. I can't settle to anything: I want to get up and run around, so I start to go for a walk, get a little way, and then realise the muscle fatigue is too great to continue. I make my way home again, settle down to rest, but can't. Honestly, if you're the sadistic sort looking to invent a new way of torturing another human being, then consider an adrenaline overdose—it's really awful to experience!

This seems to be another big physical area that is affected by CFS. I have seen a couple of "alternative" therapists during my illness, and one of these tested my adrenaline levels and pronounced that my body is "producing adrenaline like it's going out of fashion." It sounds lovely—I mean, what could be better than manufacturing your very own drug that gives you a permanent high, all for free? The problem is, as with any other drug, the "come down" is really horrible—it's basically back into the crash phase. Unlike street drugs, I haven't found a way to control the supply effectively.

At some point in all of this, I had returned to my GP: I was officially on sick leave from work, so I needed regular sick notes. On one of these visits, my GP told me about a "fantastic" treatment that another CFS patient had heard about. It was something called Mickel Therapy.[8] *I duly looked this up and discovered that Mickel Therapy seeks to treat problems with the hypothalamus gland in the brain. The treatment was based on the recognition that something had sent the body into "fight or flight" mode on a pretty permanent basis. Now, "fight or flight" is one of the most basic instincts. Humans share it with all other animals, and it's fantastically useful in primitive life. It is basically the mind's ability to sense that the body is in immediate danger, to shut down all "normal" function and pump the body full of adrenaline to give it the strength to either fight the danger or run from it. Then the mind is supposed to diagnose when the danger has passed, shut down the adrenaline flow, and return the body to "normal" mode. In "normal" mode, the body is focusing on the normal function and maintenance of all its systems, whereas in "fight or flight" mode this normal maintenance is put on hold. As you might expect, the body's systems can function fine for short spaces of time without maintenance, but if you stop maintaining them for a prolonged period, they all start to malfunction. Mickel Therapy was based on the premise that the body had become stuck in "fight or flight" mode for so long that it had simply stopped maintaining all its systems properly.*

Much as this idea makes great sense, it still leaves me with a little "chicken or egg" conundrum. Now, it could be that I'm just not a trained biologist, medic, or scientist of any sort and, therefore, I'm ignorant here. My conundrum is this: Whilst it's lovely to know my body produces adrenaline like it's going out of fashion and that in all likelihood my mitochondrial function is sub-optimal, why are these two phenomena occurring? I'm presuming they are related. So, are my Mitochondria malfunctioning because they are part of the system that has been shut down in this "fight or flight" mode? Or am I in "fight or flight" mode because my mitochondria are malfunctioning and my body is effectively "panicking" that it has insufficient energy to function properly, and then the constant dipping into energy reserves is stimulating

8 http://www.mickeltherapy.com is the official website which will tell you about the treatment and gives links to practitioners.

the adrenal glands to try to make up for the lack of energy? If I had an answer to that, would it help to unpick what is going on and solve this problem? Who knows, but one thing I can do is try to get a decent night's sleep. So, I'm off to try some relaxation techniques to settle me into sleep mode.

When you were back in school, you may have learned something about the human body from the perspective of biology. So, you may have learned we have organs like the heart, lungs, liver, and kidneys. We have systems like the circulatory system, immune system, and central nervous system. You may also have learned something about chemistry. Many of the interactions that take place to allow our body to operate are chemical reactions. For example, ATP—*Adenosine triphosphate*—your cell's currency of energy—is produced through a chemical reaction. Chances are, you didn't learn much about the physics of your body. Were you aware, alongside your physical body, you also have a biofield? Most likely, the answer to that question is "no." You see, biofield science is an incredibly new discipline. Like many branches of science in their infancy, it has plenty of sceptics.[9]

However, for me, learning about my biofield and how to begin working with it proved to be the final piece of the puzzle in my long recovery journey. It is also the field in which I chose to train as a practitioner, but more on that later on. For now, let me begin introducing you to your biofield.

9 This article, published in 2015, is a good introduction to the field. Rubik B, Muehsam D, Hammerschlag R, Jain S. Biofield Science and Healing: History, Terminology, and Concepts. Glob Adv Health Med. 2015 Nov; 4(Suppl):8-14. doi: 10.7453/gahmj.2015.038.suppl. Epub 2015 Nov 1. PMID: 26665037; PMCID: PMC4654789.

ENERGY SAVING AID

These are the essential points that are helpful for you to take away from the following section:

- *Your body is a complex system of communication. The basic mechanics of biology and chemistry only explain part of this story. To understand the full extent of the body's ability to communicate and thus regulate itself, we need to appreciate that it also encompasses an energy field.*
- *In 1992, the Office of Alternative Medicine in the USA agreed on a term to describe this energy field: the biofield, and researchers began to study it to appreciate how it works and how we can use energy medicine to enhance healing.*

The Human Biofield

I am going to start by quoting from the article I cited just above:

"Biofield science is an emerging field of study that aims to provide a scientific foundation for understanding the complex homeodynamic regulation of living systems. Energy medicine, the application of extremely low-level signals to the body, including energy healer interventions and bio-electromagnetic device-based therapies, is incomprehensible from the dominant biomedical paradigm of "life as chemistry." The biofield or biological field, a complex organizing energy field engaged in the generation, maintenance, and regulation of biological homeodynamics, is a useful concept that provides the rudiments of a scientific foundation for energy medicine and thereby advances the research and practice of it."

What does that mean? Basically, the way in which your body seeks to stay in balance—homeostasis, or "health"—is through regulating its many systems and organs. We can view that from a biochemical perspective. So that would mean tracking things like the mechanism through which the Hypothalamus signals to the Pituitary Gland and then the Adrenal Gland to release—or withhold—the hormones that tell your cells when your body is safe and when it is in danger. This is what the citation means by saying, "life as chemistry." However, that "life as chemistry" view struggles to explain certain phenomena we are now observing. For example, how can an intervention like Pulsed Electro Magnetic Frequency—PEMF—speed up the healing of a bone? This therapy has been around since the 1970s and has been more widely researched than many Energy medicine protocols.[10] Tracking biological and chemical changes doesn't seem to tell the whole story.

So, in 1992, the Office of Alternative Medicine—OAM—established by the National Institute of Health—NIH—in the USA, agreed on a term, the Biofield—biological field. The committee defined the biofield as:

"A massless field, not necessarily electromagnetic, that surrounds and permeates living bodies and affects the body."

In other words, both around and within your physical body, you also have an invisible field that is Energetic. Basically, in addition to your body's cells communicating via physical things like neural pathways or a circulatory system that carries blood, cells are also exchanging information through an Energy field which we cannot see or measure through direct observation. We can only see and measure the effects. So, this is not an "alternative" view of the body. It is more like an "additional" layer we haven't previously taken into account in our explorations of health and disease.

---

10 Di Bartolomeo M, Cavani F, Pellacani A, Grande A, Salvatori R, Chiarini L, Nocini R, Anesi A.; Pulsed Electro-Magnetic Field (PEMF) Effect on Bone Healing in Animal Models: A Review of Its Efficacy Related to Different Type of Damage. Biology (Basel). 2022 Mar 5; 11(3):402. doi: 10.3390/biology11030402. PMID: 35336776; PMCID: PMC8945722.

ENERGY SAVING AID

These are the essential points that are helpful for you to take away from the following section:

- *Your biofield is best understood as a wireless communication system. It communicates via frequency and resonance. The biofield contains the blueprint for perfect health, but distortions in the information in the field or blockages in communication can end up giving your cells incorrect messages. This results in disease.*
- *Traditional cultures have always understood the concept of the biofield. It may be called by different names: aura, prana, or chi, but the principle is the same. If you wish to create health, you need to ensure the energy in this field is free to flow and communicate with accuracy.*

What Does Your Biofield Look Like?

I cannot categorically answer that question. Some gifted Energy healers can sense or even see the biofield. I believe those who refer to an Aura are talking about the biofield. Traditional Chinese medicine might term it as Chi; Ayurvedic medicine might call it Prana. I have an idea it is rather like the Earth's magnetic field. We get to "see" that through the mechanism of the Northern Lights—Aurora Borealis. Solar flares from the sun release particles that hit the Earth's field and create visible light as the two entities meet. As humans, we are able to observe this light and "see" the Earth's magnetic field. So, I suspect if there were some means of mimicking the solar flare effect meeting the Earth's atmosphere but applying that to a human biofield, we would see something resembling the Aurora. This is just an idea of mine, and it may or may not be linked to "aura photography" or Kirlian photography, which claims to capture the aura around a human body. Needless to say, this idea of photographing the aura is not universally accepted. So, depending on your source of information, it could be a real "thing," or just another con trick designed to impress those who enjoy some "magical thinking."

Let me move back to theories that relate to more widely explored physics. In physics, a Field contains particles and information. Left to their own devices, the particles would dance around randomly, with no particular purpose. Once you introduce information into the Field, you can direct the particles to create matter. In this case, a human body. So, put very simply, the information in your energy field is the blueprint for your human body. We all have access to a perfect blueprint, but for various reasons, we may end up bringing distortions into the field. This can mean the information itself becomes distorted or the communication between the blueprint and the cells gets blocked. As a result, your particles are now adapting to this distorted information, and the resulting cells may start diverging from their intended purpose. When this happens, we will end up experiencing symptoms of disease. Those symptoms are really intended as a message: to nudge us into recognising there is a problem that needs addressing.

If we are suggesting your cells can communicate via some sort of wireless network—in essence, that is what your biofield is—then it is helpful to think of this as waves. Specifically, waves of light—photons—and waves of sound—phonons. Your field would also encompass the basic particles—electrons, protons, and neutrons—that form the underlying basis of your cells. Particles interact in different ways, according to the information guiding them. Those interactions change the flow of energy, and this creates waves and ripples that affect the entire field. Think of this like throwing a stone into a pond: The water will ripple out in waves around the area where the stone hits the water. The ripple/wave effect can cover just a small area, or it could reach out to the very edges of the pond—field—depending on the size of the stone you threw into the pond and the size of the pond itself. Waves have a frequency: the number of waves that pass a certain point each second, measured in hertz. If you have lots of waves squashed close together, it creates a high-frequency signal. Waves that are more spread out—fewer per second—will create a low-frequency signal.

If you want an analogy for this, your biofield would be like a mobile phone network. The biological and chemical networks of your body would be like a postal system. So, the difference in communication is like the difference between sending a text message—your biofield—and writing a letter—your physical body. The first means of communication is electrical, and the second is physical. You also have multiple fields. So, you might have fields that relate to individual cells, fields that relate to an organ, and fields that relate to a group of organs, and then a field that relates to the body as a whole. Traditional Chinese Medicine may see this as the meridians—the map of energetic pathways that link areas of the body which may not be obviously connected or even directly next to one another. In Ayurvedic medicine, the Chakras may be a way of defining fields. Interestingly, modern research is beginning to see how Chakras in Ayurvedic medicine[11] and Meridians in Chinese medicine map directly onto the anatomy of the central nervous system that we recognise in Western conventional medicine.[12]

---

11 This very accessible article outlines the correlation between the Chakras and physiology of the central nervous system: https://www.thenow.se/chakras-and-science/

12 "A neuroanatomical basis for the acupuncture meridians provides an explanation of why Traditional Chinese Medicine has no representation of the nervous system despite describing all other organs. That is, the meridians are the representation of the nervous system. The peripheral neurovascular bundles literally validate the Traditional Chinese Medicine concept that Blood and Qi (energy) flow in the meridians." Dorsher PT, Chiang P. Neuroembryology of the Acupuncture Principal Meridians: Part 3. The Head and Neck. Med Acupunct. 2018 Apr 1;30(2):80-88. doi: 10.1089/acu.2018.1271. PMID: 29682148; PMCID: PMC5908427. https://www.ncbi.nlm.nih.gov/pmc/articles/PMC5908427/

So, far from being a "new" invention, your biofield is something that traditional healing systems have always known about and worked with. More often, in Western medicine, our focus has been on biological and chemical systems—including chemical drug interventions, and we have struggled to see how a biofield could be relevnt in that context.

ENERGY SAVING AID

These are the essential points that are helpful for you to take away from the following section:

- *The biofield communicates using waveform and frequency. Disturbances in the waveforms will result in miscommunication. That, in turn, causes your physical cells and systems to begin acting in ways that result in the symptoms we label as disease.*
- *Think of this like your mobile/cell phone: if you pass through a spot with a weak signal, you may lose the call or at least find it becomes distorted. The same can happen in the biofield's communication system.*

How Does the Biofield Communicate?

The short answer is: through frequency and resonance. If your biofield is made from waves of energy, the waves that are on the same frequency will communicate with one another—we call this resonance. Waves on a different frequency will not resonate—or communicate.[13] This would be the same principle as tuning an old-fashioned radio or TV set. The information that is being sent out from the central broadcasting station—your radio or TV program—is embedded in a specific frequency wave. Remember, we said that a frequency wave can be made from particles of sound or light. So, this brings you sounds and images when you decode the frequency wave. When you tune the dial on your personal machine in your home to that frequency, you receive the waves that bring the program you wish to watch. The tuning of your individual dial matches—resonates—with the frequency of the program you wish to watch, and your TV set decodes the information carried in that frequency wave to turn it back into its original sounds and images. What happens when you move the dial slightly off frequency? Your program may become distorted or disappear altogether.

This is the same principle as a digital phone call. If you are using your cell phone—mobile phone—to make a call whilst driving, you may pass through an area where your phone's handset cannot tune into the frequency of the network's cell tower. As a result, your phone call may become difficult to hear, or it may cut out completely.

---

13 This is the classic "tuning fork experiment." If you take two tuning forks both tuned to the musical note C, for example, and strike just one of them, it will begin to make a sound. But because both tuning forks are attuned to the same note in resonance, the second tuning fork will also begin to sound in response to the frequency waves being produced by the first tuning fork. If you were to use two tuning forks attuned to different notes, say musical notes C and D, then striking one to make it sound would have no impact on the second tuning fork. That would remain silent because it doesn't resonate with the waves produced by the first tuning fork.

The same principle is at work in your biofield. When it is in balance, the waves will be coherent and able to communicate with one another. If something happens to disturb a wave pattern, it is like losing the signal in your TV show or phone call. Suddenly the organs or systems that were supposed to be communicating have lost contact. Imagine that your eyes have seen a sabre tooth tiger; your brain has processed this information and recognised you could be in danger, it has communicated that to your adrenal glands, and they have released the appropriate hormones to alert your cells. You are running away to safety. You outrun the tiger and your sensory organs—eyes, ears—detect that your environment is now safe. They communicate this to your brain, but your brain has lost the signal to your adrenal glands. As a result, the adrenal glands continue to produce stress hormones, and your cells continue to operate as if they are under threat. As we are going to explore in a later chapter, this is basically the process that is happening in a maladaptive stress response. So, hold on to that idea for a moment.

ENERGY SAVING AID

These are the essential points that are helpful for you to take away from the following section:

- *Your biofield is communicating internally and also with the environment around it. So, everything in our environment has its own unique biofield. Your body can recognise the frequency of other natural biofields and interpret their information, so it knows how to use resources like food, water, and light to support energy production.*
- *External factors like toxins, viruses, bacteria, and toxic thoughts and emotions can cause disruptions in the biofield.*

> *If your field is able to recognise and react to these, you will remain healthy and in balance. When the biofield doesn't have the capacity to respond, it will adapt to the challenge, allowing you to survive but possibly not to thrive.*

What Does This Mean for Your Health and Understanding of Illness?

So, we have introduced the idea that you and the natural environment around you have biofields that are constantly communicating information to keep your body in a balanced state. We have also looked at the idea that this information is communicated via waves and that the system can start to break down or adapt in unhelpful ways if the waves become distorted and can no longer communicate with accuracy. Now, let's develop this a little further to understand how this could apply to CFS. Your body is programmed to tend towards a state of balance—homeostasis—and this balanced state is sustained by a constant flow of energy in and out. So, what are the energetic elements that can enter the body?

- Food
- Water
- Oxygen—air
- Light
- Toxins—chemical, bacterial, fungal, viral[14]

14 Not all of these would be harmful to the body. Even those that are potentially harmful can act as a means of growth. Building resilience to a threat would allow the body to deal more effectively with that same threat in the future.

- Thoughts and emotions—through experience/education and social interactions with other people or institutions[15]

As long as all those elements are entering in a form that the body can understand and process, everything will remain in balance. For example, if the frequency of the energy waves in your food resonates with the frequency of the waves in the biofield, your body knows exactly how to process that food and extract maximum energy from it. The same principle applies in all interactions with your environment: the body automatically knows what to extract to use for benefit and what to excrete to protect itself. All of this is a system perfectly balanced not just to survive but to grow and thrive.

So, what knocks the body out of balance? When a stressor from the external environment—e.g., a virus or bacteria, or poison, or negative emotion—enters your biofield, you might think of this like causing a dent. Temporarily, the energy waves have to flow around the "attacking" object until the biofield can work out how to eradicate it. If that external threat/stressor enters fully into the system, the energy flow will be disrupted inside until the problematic object/energy waves can be removed. This would be like creating a dent or break in the natural wave pattern of your healthy biofield. The body will naturally rebalance itself, given time to do this—unless the stressor keeps recurring or the body lacks the information to process and get rid of it.

So, bringing this back to our topic of illness, or rather, disease, you can think of things like this: The initial stressor would be an acute incident—for example, a cold. It disrupts the system for a short time—temporarily blocks or distorts the frequency through which

15 Thoughts and emotions are both absorbed from external sources and generated internally in reaction to the external information. This element can be beneficial—e.g., love or wisdom, or detrimental—e.g., bullying or lies. Yet, as with toxins, even negative thoughts and emotions can have a positive growth effect when they are processed and digested.

your biofield should be communicating—but the body knows how to combat it—or works out how to combat it—and returns to a healthy balance. When the initial stressor cannot be dealt with, the body becomes stuck in a pattern of inefficient energy flow, as it has to work around the problem instead of solving it. This becomes a state of chronic ill health or disease.

> ***ENERGY SAVING AID***
>
> *These are the essential points that are helpful for you to take away from the following section:*
>
> - *Understanding the biofield and the way it works gives us a model for making sense of CFS.*
> - *It can explain the complexity of symptoms: in the field, everything is interrelated, so a change in one area will cause change across the entire field.*
> - *It can also explain the difference in the way the illness begins and the shape it takes from one individual to another.*
> - *Most importantly, this model offers a powerful way to generate recovery.*

How Does This Relate to CFS?

Hopefully, you are already ahead of me here. CFS is best viewed—in my experience—as a build-up of stressors to which the body has adapted. The problem is that each time the body makes an adaptation to work around one stressor, it automatically disrupts the balanced flow, which then creates a new stressor somewhere else. So, what may begin as a single external stress can become a series of internal miscommunications which build up into an overall system malfunction. To my mind, this model explains both the onset of CFS and the complexity of the disease.

Onset can vary from person to person. So, for some, it is a gradual process of starting to feel less energised, and then finding it difficult to fight off everyday viruses until, eventually, the system is so weakened that it collapses. For others, the onset feels more sudden. They feel as if they have been functioning fully, and then suddenly catch a virus, undergo surgery, or suffer a really traumatic experience, and they just can't seem to recover. So, it appears that the CFS was "caused" by this single event. In reality, I believe, this single event is really just *the straw that broke the camel's back*—the thing that hits a body already under so much pressure, it finally buckles. The stressors that flow into our bodies begin before we are even born. We inherit genes from our ancestors—and that gene expression will have been affected by experiences in their own lives they were unable to process. Among other things, this creates a setpoint for our central nervous system which will dictate our level of resilience to stress—in other words, our ability to process it through and out of the body.

From the moment we are born, we are exposed to a host of foreign chemicals and toxins via the air we breathe, the food we eat, and the water we drink. Yes, our bodies are naturally set to excrete harmful products. However, the state of our central nervous system—CNS—determines the time our body spends on its "housekeeping"—cleaning and maintenance—tasks. So, if we arrive here with a narrow "window of tolerance" in our CNS, the amount of time our bodies spend in maintenance mode may not be sufficient to clean out ALL the unwanted toxins, so some become stuck in our system. That gradual build-up further slows or damages the system in various ways, creating further impediments to getting rid of what we don't want. Also, from the moment we are born, we are exposed to the emotions, actions, thoughts, and beliefs of other people around us. Again, these can be helpful to our survival or feel threatening. If we are not able to process and overcome the threats, those, too, get stuck in our system—energy blockages or frequency disruptors. We will explore this in more depth later on. In addition to all of this, our environment also contains viruses and bacteria that may enter and compromise our system. Again, if the system is struggling to begin with, it may simply lack the resources to fight the invader.

This is an incredibly simplified view. For each element I have mentioned, you find hugely complex relationships occurring once you dig deeper. For example, chemical toxins may be causing damage to the epithelial tissue lining your digestive tract. That affects your body's natural ability to absorb nutrients from your food. So, as a result, any system that relied on those particular nutrients will now be trying to operate on limited resources, so it will need to scale back what it can do. It may also mean that the damaged epithelial tissue is now allowing toxic particles into your bloodstream, activating your immune system or causing damage to other organs as the blood carries those toxins around the body. This model would also explain why the illness seems so complex. If you look back over the history of research that has been carried out, you will find some people who believe this is a Mitochondrial issue. Some believe it is hormonal—adrenal or thyroid. Others believe it is immune-related—auto-immune. We are going to look into this in more depth in a later chapter.

> ***ENERGY SAVING AID***
>
> *These are the essential points that are helpful for you to take away from the following section:*
>
> - *Discovering Energy medicine and working with my biofield proved to be the final piece of the puzzle in my own recovery.*
> - *Prior to that, I had been working from the perspective of trying to understand linear systems. In a sense, the mechanics of how my body was working—or not! The deeper we delve into those mechanics, the more complex it becomes, and the more we end up hitting brick walls or circular "chicken and egg" situations.*
> - *Stepping back and understanding the biofield as a whole field of communication and governance allows us to step out of that complexity, simply focus on identifying and correcting the distorted information in the field, and allow it to flow down into the physical body and create healing.*
> - *So, our next port of call will be to discover what information is carried in the field and how we can begin to analyse and understand it.*

Coming Full Circle

As my own recovery path took me deeper into the functional side of things, I found myself once more returning to the question of cause and effect. I am not saying this is a purely *functional* view—allopathic medicine also supports this view. Once you begin to understand how different systems work, you begin to see they are deeply intertwined. So, let's take the example of ATP production. ATP is the energy currency of the body. It is produced in the Mitochondria, which are housed inside the cells. Every single cell in the body has its own set of Mitochondria and is powered by ATP. The production of ATP requires oxygen, which requires the blood to be pumping efficiently around the body to deliver the necessary oxygen to each cell. That requires the lungs and heart to be operating optimally. Yet, the lungs and heart are comprised of cells containing Mitochondria to produce the ATP to power the cell. So, we find ourselves in a circular situation. If the body cannot produce enough ATP to power its cells effectively, is that because the heart and lungs developed a problem and stopped providing enough oxygen? Or did the heart and lungs develop a problem *because* their ATP supply was compromised? We have that typical *chicken and egg* situation. So, as long as we are looking for a sequential cause and effect, I doubt we are going to find an answer to the problem.

We need to change our way of viewing the system. Instead of viewing it as a line of separate parts that relate to one another, we need to see it as a fully functioning whole whose parts operate in a way our science cannot yet fathom. The idea of a biofield with its additional layer of communication could be the puzzle piece that makes sense of all this. So, I invite you to continue with me as we explore the elements that may be found in your biofield. I have alluded to the fact that thoughts, beliefs, and emotions can disrupt and become stuck in your biofield. Basically, a thought or emotion is a waveform pattern of information. It interacts with your biofield and may either resonate or cause disruption. In the same way, a food with an energetic imprint that resonates differently to your body's resonance can cause disruption. In essence, this is really why man-made or over-processed foods are "unhealthy." Their waveform is not the same as a waveform created in nature. So, the body struggles to read this foreign waveform and cannot extract nutritional benefits from it. Science tends to explore and talk about this in terms of the mechanics: Man-made fat clogs the arteries and leads to coronary heart disease. Yes, that is the process we are witnessing on the bio-chemical level. On the biofield Energy level, this is expressed as a mismatch in frequency and resonance, which leads the body to adapt to survive. Yet, that miscommunication and consequent adaptation leads to symptoms, as the body has moved away from its natural healthy balance.

Now, if we are suggesting that physical objects—matter—and emotions—energy—both play a role in either supporting or draining the biofield system, we need a model to explain this. How is your biofield "built" and what does it contain? We need to begin looking at what we mean when we are talking about the information in the field. To understand, we are going to open things outwards and move into the realm of metaphysics, quantum science, and the process of creation. If that sounds a little scary, don't worry. We are going to be using simple analogies to explain all of this and constantly bringing things back to the main point of interest: how to recover from CFS.

ENERGY SAVING AID

Please complete the following practice. The self-awareness you gain from this will help you create your unique roadmap for recovery.

Your Invitation to Practice

I invite you to pause and grab your journal once again: It is time to explore how you think and feel about this chapter. So, please use the following questions as writing prompts. As always, you can write as much or as little as you wish. Remember to take note of the things towards which you feel judgemental. Remember that "I don't know" is always an acceptable answer.

- Are you open to the idea that you have a biofield and it has an impact on your physical body?

  - If you said "yes," then does this idea change anything about how you view your illness?
  - If you said "no," why do you feel or think this way?

- Looking back to the time before you became ill, can you identify things in your environment and lifestyle that might have caused disruption in your field or not been supportive of your physical body? Think about the following:
  - What was your diet like?
  - How much sleep did you get?
  - How much did you exercise?
  - Were you exposed to a lot of chemical toxins?
  - How was your immune system—did you often get ill?
  - How did you feel emotionally?
  - How were your stress levels?
  - What were your relationships with other people like?
  - Are you aware of any traumatic events in your past or present?
  - Can you think of any other possible contributing factors?

Chapter 5

The Four Levels of Creation

This chapter will be setting out the model we are going to explore in greater depth in this section of the book. In the last chapter, I left you with a question: What if your body is a little different than you have always thought? I alluded to the possibility that you might even have two bodies: a physical body and an energetic body. Well, this chapter is all about fleshing out that idea. I am going to offer you a new model of your body. This model comes from the understanding of the process of creation. As we build it up, it should lead you to a very different perspective on your symptoms, your illness, and, most importantly, your recovery plan. Let's not get ahead of ourselves here. First, I need to introduce the basic model. So, let me frame this with a journal entry.

> *ENERGY SAVING AID*
>
> *This journal entry is important as it sets the scene for the information I am about to share and will help you stay open to receiving new information. The basic message: This chapter contains perspectives that some people may find new, even challenging. Please just take whatever resonates and set aside anything you're not ready to work with right now. You can revisit this information as your recovery journey progresses and you evolve.*

Journal: April 2023

I have been working on my book today and found myself at a rather sticky point: the chapter in which I need to introduce the Four Levels of Creation. When I first learned about this model, it was a real lightbulb moment for me. I hope it will also be a lightbulb moment for others, but I fear that some may be more in the place I would have been, say, five years ago. At best, I might have thought it was an "interesting" idea. At worst, I would have dismissed this as nonsense. And that leads me to immediately feel a large dose of impostor syndrome. What if I actually am writing nonsense? What if everybody hates this book? Wouldn't it be better to just stop this project now? Well, after calming myself down, another interesting idea popped into my head. If I were to have a conversation with my readers, how would I help them to try to stay open to new ideas? Well, this is what I would say:

I don't know whether our human minds are built this way or whether we condition them to be like this, but I can't help noticing we are very fond of looking for simplicity. We like to put things in boxes, tie them up with a neat little bow, and add a label to warn us whether the contents are going to be "good" or "bad." Don't get me wrong. That can be very helpful in certain situations. But it can also lead us to experience unnecessary distress.

Specifically, I am thinking of a situation where a person makes ten statements. Someone comes along and listens to—or reads—those statements. The moment they recognise one of the statements is a lie, they confine the speaker—or writer—to a box labelled "insane" or "dangerous" and proceed to ignore everything that person says or writes. The opposite may also be true. The listener or reader may identify one statement that they know to be correct and which they find amazingly helpful. So, in this case, they place the speaker—or writer—into a box labelled "brilliant" or "guru," and they proceed to lap up everything this person says, without question. I get it. That system makes life really simple. We are all under a lot of pressure; we have way too much to get done in the time available to us. So, anything that can save us time and effort is welcome.

The trouble is, the more likely reality is that most—probably all—people have useful knowledge to share and useless knowledge that they also insist on sharing. If you put everything shared by that person under one umbrella, you risk either missing useful information or getting led astray by useless information. Annoying as it is, you really do need to be open to everything and then take what you find useful and leave what doesn't resonate for the moment.

Please also remember how you change. I imagine your attitude towards unicorns and fairies is a little different now than when you were five years old. Or, to take a more sensible example, are all of your political views really the same today as they were ten or twenty years ago? Do you look back on photos of you in the 1980s and really wish someone had told you that outfit or hairstyle was a really bad idea?! We evolve in relation to our experiences and our environment. As we evolve, the information that feels helpful can also change and evolve. An idea we would have rejected ten years ago may suddenly become incredibly relevant today. Or something that we passionately believed last year might feel like a bit of a mistake today.

The reason I'm saying this is, if anything you're reading in these pages feels too much to take on right now, that's OK. Just take on board what you find helpful, and work with that. Leave the rest. I don't mind whether you want to label those offerings as the ravings of a madwoman or just as something that you don't understand. But I will be sad if you deprive yourself of something that could help you just because it was shared in the same pages as something that you wish to reject or don't feel ready to hear right now. I speak from experience here: I remember being offered knowledge or opinions by practitioners early on in my CFS journey that I wasn't ready to accept at the time of offering. But as my experience evolved and my questions changed, sometimes I found myself returning to those pieces of knowledge and realising how I could use them or where they fitted on my path.

So, with all that said, let's get on to the real subject of this chapter. If I've built this up so it turns out to be something much less interesting or controversial than you're expecting, then I apologise.

ENERGY SAVING AID

These are the essential points that are helpful for you to take away from the following section:

- *We are now going to build on the idea that our "body" is one thing, including physical, mental, emotional, and spiritual elements. The physical body can be sensed with our five basic senses: it is matter and makes up the physical body element of the human. The other elements are not directly sensed with our basic senses, so they may appear invisible or intangible: they are energy and make up the energy body element of the human.*
- *Symptoms occurring at one level may have their root cause at that level as well—or the root cause and symptom may be located on different levels.*
- *If you are seeking "healing" rather than "symptom management," it is vital to understand the four levels so that you can identify where the root cause sits and address it at that level.*
- *As we move on to explore the different levels, some of the language and ideas I share may seem to belong in a spiritual context. But I am not meaning them to be viewed as "religious" or "New Age." They may share common ground with those movements, but they are also independent, and it is possible to work with the Four Levels of Creation model to effect recovery independently of your existing beliefs and without needing to reject or change those beliefs if you do not wish it.*

Introducing the Four Levels of Creation

In earlier pages, we explored the idea that, traditionally, we have tended to separate ourselves into distinct parts: body, mind, and soul. We treat all those parts as if they operate independently, so a problem occurring in one part will have no impact upon the others. I then made a suggestion: We are not separate parts. Yes, all these parts exist, but they are not separate; they are, in fact, like layers of the whole. Each layer builds upon the next in a way that could be viewed like building a house. Or, an even better analogy: like a plant.

Somewhere, buried underground, out of sight, away from our conscious awareness, is a tiny seed. It begins to develop roots and sprouts underground we still cannot see. Eventually, something breaks through to the surface, and this part grows into the plant that is visible. Now, you can alter the visible appearance of the plant by removing flowers or leaves or cutting branches, but if you want to change its state—position, you need to move the entire plant, including the roots and seeds that aren't visible above ground. You may also witness the plant begin to wither, yet see no reason why that might have happened at the level of its branches, flowers, and leaves. The problem lies at the root level. Yet it still impacted the whole plant, and no amount of trimming at the surface level is going to change what is happening at the root level. If the root level problem persists, the entire plant will die.

This is not a perfect analogy, but it may be helpful. You see, if you wish to heal a human body, it is not enough to simply mess around with what is happening at the visible—physical—level, unless the problem is *only* occurring at that level. If the problem is occurring at the root level, and you desire healing rather than just symptom management, then you need to be fixing the problem at the level where it is occurring. The trouble is if you have never previously been aware that your body had any level other than the physical, you would never think to look beyond the physical level for a root cause—or a solution.

In the last chapter, I introduced you to the emerging field of Biofield Science, and the idea we have an Energy body in addition to our physical body. Now it is time to take our viewpoint out wide and look at this from the perspective of creation. Yes, this is going to move us into territory you might feel ought to belong only in a spiritual context and should have nothing to do with your physical body or health. On the other hand, you may already be aware that "you" are not separate from your surroundings and from the wider realm of creation, Spirit, or the Universe.

I feel I also need to emphasise when I talk about "spiritual," "creation," and any linked terms, I am not referring to religion or New Age Spirituality. You may see an overlap, but if any of what I am sharing seems to conflict with ideas that you already hold, based on religious beliefs, I am not suggesting those ideas are wrong or you need to stop believing them. They can co-exist alongside the information I'm giving you here. Or, you may see ways in which the information here adds to your existing beliefs. If you are coming to this from the perspective of something like Atheism, then I am also not trying to persuade you to suddenly start following a religion or taking up a spiritual practice. You may decide you wish to do those things, but you may not. What I need to share here is a model that provides you with a framework for understanding how to recover. Whether you choose to also integrate that within some sort of religious or spiritual practice unrelated to the idea of healing is entirely up to you. Certainly, it is possible to do that, but, if that whole idea makes you feel deeply uncomfortable, it is also possible to keep this as a model for working out how to move from a place of disease to a place where you are thriving and energised.

> ***ENERGY SAVING AID***
>
> *These are the essential points that are helpful for you to take away from the following section:*
>
> - *Different models of Creation have existed for as long as humanity has existed. Ayurvedic Medicine, Traditional Chinese Medicine, Integrative Healers, and now German New Medicine all use this type of model. Yet, it is not currently taught in conventional medical schools.*
> - *We take a brief look at the five-level model used by Dr. Dietrich Klinghardt to heal chronic disease. This has helped many patients with CFS.*
> - *I work with the Four Levels model because it is the model I used on my recovery path and the model I now apply in my own practice to help others find recovery.*

Introducing Models of Creation

This idea of viewing the human as a whole, not merely a body, is not new. It is how ancient peoples and traditional Native cultures have always treated disease. It is also the model of Traditional Chinese Medicine, Ayurvedic Medicine, and, more recently, German New Medicine. Furthermore, it has been used as a model by integrative healers in Western Medicine. No, it is not taught in conventional medical school, but many conventional doctors have ended up bringing in these concepts to help heal their patients.

I want to start by mentioning the model that Dr. Dietrich Klinghardt, MD., PhD. has been developing and teaching since the 1980s. His philosophy is:

"Few people have gotten well by taking supplements alone ... Our patients need care on all levels of their existence. It works. People really can recover from their chronic illness. But patients have to shift their way of being in the world on a deep level ... For every vitamin there will be a better one tomorrow. Every deep conflict that is resolved, is resolved for good. Learning is forever. Vitamins are not ... The physical body exists within a sphere of invisible etheric bodies that each have their own anatomy and physiology. There is an alive and profound interaction between the different levels."[16]

For anyone who believes this only applies to functional medicine, you can easily substitute the word "vitamins" for the word "drugs." The same principle applies: We are always going to end up developing a "new" and "better" drug, but drugs are not "curing" disease. They are managing symptoms. I am not arguing that this is not helpful nor suggesting that we should be doing away with drugs or vitamins. Yet, as we are going to explore throughout the rest of this book, the choices you make need to be made with awareness of what you desire to achieve.

Dr. Klinghardt's model works its way through five layers, progressing from the physical body all the way up to the spiritual body. At each level, he details our experience—for example, physical would involve the five senses, what he terms the Energy Body would involve the central nervous system, then the Mental body, involving thoughts and emotions, and so on. The model also brings in the science that corresponds to each level, the appropriate diagnostic methods, and the treatment methods for each level. It is a brilliant model, and I recommend you take a look for yourself. I've linked to an article outlining it in the footnotes.

---

16 Quoted from Dr. Klinghardt's article, The Five Levels of Healing, published in Explore! Volume 14, Number 4, 2005. You can read the full article here: http://klinghardtinstitute.com/the-5-levels-of-healing/

I now want to share a modified view based on the teachings I have learned on my personal healing journey.[17] The reason I'm sharing this view, not simply using Dr. Klinghardt's model, is because this model corresponds more neatly to my own training as a practitioner and my own experience of healing from CFS, not because I wish to criticise Dr. Klinghardt's brilliant work. He has already helped thousands of people, and I trust will continue to help thousands more. You may even be one of them! But let's move on to talk about the model that I have worked with.

ENERGY SAVING AID

These are the essential points that are helpful for you to take away from the following section:

- *The creative process travels through four layers, starting with an idea—pure energy—a particle. We can think of this at the top of a pyramid: the Universe—Unity Consciousness. The creative process forms that idea into a "thing"—matter. In this case, your physical body, which is sitting at the bottom of the pyramid.*
- *The intervening two layers—Intuitive, then Psycho-Emotional—guide the creative process. You might think of this like a blueprint guiding the energy particles via information to take on wave-form, which ultimately compresses into matter, loosely following a path in which particles become atoms, then cells, then organs/systems, and then a complete human body.*

17 With deepest gratitude to my teacher and mentor, Niki Skye, for sharing this model which she developed based on her own research and experience in both the functional medicine and spiritual worlds and first shared with me in February 2023. https://nikiskye.com/the-4-levels-of-creation/

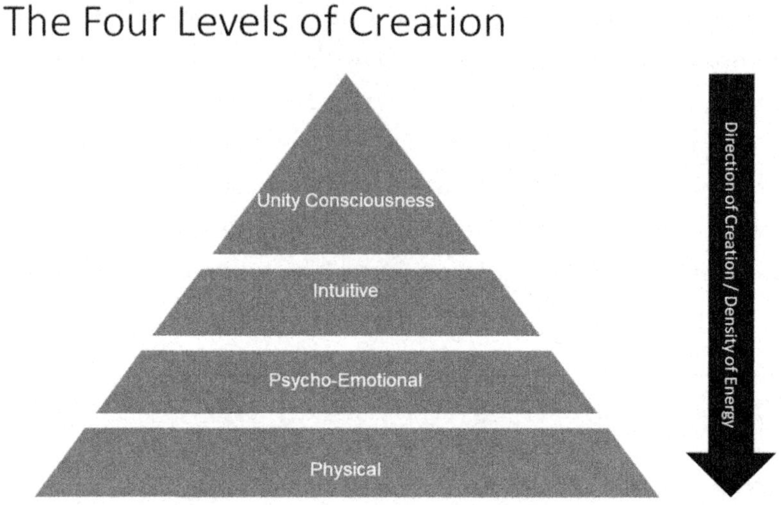

The Four Levels of Creation

In the diagram, I've given you the pyramid with the Four Levels of Creation. You can view this bidirectionally. I have laid it out as a pyramid because we're starting on the ground—our physical space—and working up towards the sky—the Universe. In terms of the creative process, you want to read this from the top downwards.

The top level begins with the idea: the inspiration or desire to create something. If we are talking about the Universe, then this might be the desire to create life. This is the level of the Creator Being—whatever you wish to name them: God, Allah, Source, etc. From your personal perspective, this is simply your idea: I want to write a book, for example.

The formation of an idea releases a seed of energy into the world. From the perspective of science, think of this seed as a particle. So, viewing this from a scientific perspective, how does a particle of energy end up becoming a human being? In the briefest of terms, it follows a blueprint for creating a human. In essence, this blueprint is your DNA. Following the information contained in that DNA, the particle will combine with other particles to form atoms. These combine to form cells. Your cells combine to create a body. Eventually, we end up with a human being. The same process applies if we are creating an animal, a plant, or an entire planet. This process also applies to the idea you came up with. Writing a book has a blueprint. No, it's not DNA, but it is a set of information that guides the process of creation.

Now, there is a lot happening at each level of this creative process. So, over the next three chapters, we are going to explore each layer one by one. If you're really concentrating here, you may notice I said *three* chapters, but I've told you there are four layers. Well, let's spend a few paragraphs exploring the top layer, *Unity Consciousness*, in this chapter. Whilst this topic deserves a whole book of its own—and many have been written already—I am devoting less space to it because I want to focus on how we can apply this model to your recovery. For that purpose, there is more depth and complexity in the lower three levels.

ENERGY SAVING AID

These are the essential points that are helpful for you to take away from the following section:

- *In metaphysical terms, Unity Consciousness is the basic idea that we are all one: a single creative force with multiple individual expressions.*
- *Our physical awareness has become rooted in individual experience; most of us have forgotten that we are all one. Those who "awaken" may suddenly remember this idea of being one with the Universe and begin to seek Enlightenment. They are seeking to access this experience of Oneness—we call it*

Samadhi.

- *The work of scientist Dr. Robert Lanza supports this idea. His model, Biocentrism, demonstrates that we are not dropped into a pre-existing, independent Universe. We are active creators, creating our lived experience all the time. So, we are the Universe, and we are also experiencing the Universe. We are not separate from the creative Source.*
- *In individual human experience, the creative step that takes place at this level is the idea: an idea pops into your head out of nowhere.*
- *In scientific terms, the creative step at this level concerns the particle(s) appearing in a vacuum, ready to combine with other particles and begin to form atoms.*

Unity Consciousness

We begin at the top of the pyramid with Unity Consciousness. This is the pure "nothing" from which everything emerges. If you wish to give it a name like God, Allah, Brahmin, Source, Creator Being, The Universe—or anything else—you can.[18] However, you can also view this in more general terms if you don't feel comfortable bringing religion or spirituality into this discussion. Unity Consciousness is the place from which everything comes. It is a perfect no-thing. You could describe it as some sort of vacuum or as a light which perceives only light. It is Consciousness—all that is. Many, many greater minds than mine have wrestled with the problem of trying to understand and

---

18 I wish to acknowledge and apologise: I am aware I have not included every religion's main deity within that list. This in no way reflects the importance or value of any particular religion, and I do not intend any offence or diminution of anyone I have left out.

describe this idea. So, I am not going to offer you definitive answers here. Just perceive this as whatever works for you.

At the level of Unity Consciousness, everything is one. We all exist as individuals, but we are an individuated expression of One: both Individual and All. Throughout history, people have described having this kind of experience, of suddenly knowing and feeling they are themselves and everything, all at once, with no division. This is the experience religions like Buddhism are seeking through meditation. If you were to go to India, say, to follow the teachings of a Guru and experience life in an Ashram, this is essentially the experience you are seeking. We call it a Samadhi Experience. This is a Sanskrit word that means being in a higher consciousness and feeling at one with the universe. The astronaut Edgar Mitchell experienced this as he was on his way back from the moon landing on the 1971 Apollo 14 mission.[19] This experience had a formative effect on Mitchell, leading him to set up the Institute of Noetic Sciences—IONS—in 1973. To this day, IONS continues to research consciousness from a scientific rather than spiritual perspective.

In 2010 scientist Robert Lanza and Astronomer Bob Berman published the book *Biocentrism*, which turned conventional thinking on its head, suggesting it isn't the Universe that creates life, but life which creates the Universe. In other words, we are not simply individuals dropped into a world some external force has created. We are the ones creating this world in every moment, collectively, AND also experiencing it individually. We are simultaneously the creators of our experience AND the experiencers of our creation. That does not take God/Creator Being out of the equation. It supports the idea we are an individuated expression of God/Creator Being, which gives us the power to create. At the same time, as individuals, we have free will

---

19 You can read a brief overview of Edgar Mitchell's life in this blog post: https://noetic.org/blog/getting-to-know-edgar-mitchell/

to determine what we create and experience. Through that process, God/Creator Being can experience the infinite possibilities of what it is and is not in order to know itself. In a sense, each of us is a seed, an idea, or a particle that goes on to create its own story, which is then simultaneously experienced by us and the Creator.

If you want to bring this down to examine the creation process at the human level, you might think of this as the space into which an idea pops. You're lazing around, thinking of nothing, and suddenly an idea pops into your mind. It has no obvious origin: It just suddenly appeared. Continuing the analogy, as you develop that idea, it will take on a life of its own. A book, a piece of art, or a project at work is shaped by you, shaped by the forces of others, and also shapes you in that process.

If we're at the level of the Universe, viewing from the perspective of physics, this is like a particle suddenly appearing in a vacuum: or, more precisely, particles—plural—of whatever number and type required to be able to attract and begin forming atoms. Again, that particle will then be shaped by information to fuse with other particles, to react to the information around it, and to transform into matter. It still exists as an individual particle within that matter, retaining its ability to change form, change direction, and influence a change in matter, and at the same time, shares the experience of—and is further shaped by—the matter of which it is a part.

ENERGY SAVING AID

These are the essential points that are helpful for you to take away from the following section:

- *In order to begin to think about how this level affects your recovery, you need to understand the principles of how it operates. In scientific terms, this is a Field. A field contains individual particles and information. There is a two-way interaction between the individual and the field, governed by the information. So, the information shapes how the particles interact, and the interactions of the particles feed back to reshape the information, which then reshapes the particle interactions further.*
- *In terms of humanity, this interaction between the individual and the collective can take place at the physical level—physical interaction with a group—and at the energetic level—mental/emotional interaction with others.*
- *From a religious perspective, we would reframe this idea to talk in terms of prayer and outcomes as the channel of communication between the individual and the Creator Being—Divinity. Yet, that can often involve a perception of separation: the human is separate from the Divine.*
- *Bringing this away from religion and into a more metaphysical realm, we see the human as an individuated part of the Unity Consciousness—the particle as an individuated part of the Field—and, in that model, when we offer up a "prayer" we aren't talking to "other"; we are connecting to the part of ourselves that sits at the level of Unity Consciousness.*

- *In this model, "prayer" is a very specific term for a more general concept. Every desire, idea, and thought can be a "prayer." So, the question becomes, are we creating consciously or unconsciously? The answer: both. Therefore, your experience will reflect both aspects. Which means that changing your experience can be a matter of uncovering where you are creating unconsciously—unaware of—thought and behaviour patterns and changing that. This is what we will explore in full in part three, as we unravel what Trauma is and how it impacts the conscious mind, subconscious mind, and physical body.*

What Is the Relevance of the Level of Unity Consciousness?

I have just thrown several huge models into that last section. So, let's look at the relevance of this to your recovery path. The big idea here is that we remain part of a collective Consciousness whilst having an individual experience. In other words, we can be affected by and create an effect on that larger collective Consciousness. What does that mean?

Science would explain this in terms of a Field.[20] Each individual human exists in their own right AND within the larger field of humanity. So, the actions of the individual human impact the lives of humans around them—for example, a person having a conversation with a group of friends. The actions of the field as a whole impact the life of the individual human. An—imperfect—analogy might be a war: This will impact individuals who did not start the war and may have no direct interest in its outcome. Both those examples look at the physical level, but this interaction between individual and collective also occurs at

20 The work of Lynn McTaggart is a good starting point for exploring this idea of fields of information and how they relate to the human experience. You may also want to read Michael Talbot's book, *The Holographic Universe*.

the energetic level. Think about phenomena like mass hysteria, mass formation psychosis, or group think. All of these are related to a group of people forming a common set of beliefs or opinions that end up creating a physical reality.[21] What has been less closely studied is how much of that reflects direct physical actions—e.g., reading an article, listening to the news, or talking to a friend—and how much is about sensing a general feeling of fear widespread within a group or across the general population, and then absorbing that sensed fear in a way that creates physical outcomes.

Religion explains this same idea of Unity Consciousness more in the context of a creative force—God or Source—and the individuals within humanity. So, in this context, we would be looking at communication through prayer and outcomes. We might interpret our illness as a message from God that we have done something wrong and are being punished. We might then use the power of penance and prayer to seek forgiveness and health. However, in this model, there may be a degree of separation at play. God can be viewed as a separate all-powerful, all-loving entity who has created humans in much the same way a human might write a book or create a piece of art. The thing created is *of* the creator, but not the *same as* that creator.

On the other hand—and this is my personal belief—you can marry both these views into one by recognising that the Creator Being is not separate from the individuated creation. We, as humans, are an individuated part of our Creative Source. That means we retain a part of the Creator within us at all times. So, when we offer up a prayer, we are simultaneously offering it inwards to the creative part within

---

21 Some scientists suggested that some of the adverse consequences of the COVID-19 epidemic may have been caused by mass hysteria, Bagus P, Peña-Ramos JA, Sánchez-Bayón A. COVID-19 and the political economy of mass hysteria. *Int J Environ Res Public Health*. 2021; 18(4):1376. doi:10.3390/ijerph18041376 The Salem Witch trials of the seventeenth century would be another example of mass hysteria.

us. Since each of us is an individuated part of the whole, that creative part within us also connects us to every other human—and beyond; we can also be connected to plants, trees, animals, the planet, etc. So, within that model, our actions, prayers, and reactions affect everything around us. As Robert Lanza's thesis seeks to prove, we are all creating our reality all the time.

I use the term "prayer" in its broadest possible context. We may tend to think of a prayer as something consciously offered to God within a religious context. In fact, in its broadest term, it can mean every thought or desire, whether consciously offered to God or not. In this sense, the phrase "the power of prayer" takes on a whole new meaning. Imagine each thought you have is heard by your inner Creative Part and is a part of the all-powerful Creative Consciousness. By implication, every thought creates a new reality. So, are you creating consciously or unconsciously? Take a look at your life: Is it the life you truly wish to be living? For the moment, just hold onto that idea and do not start judging yourself. We will explore it more deeply as this book unfolds, and you will come to learn how it is we all create things we do not consciously desire.

Next, I want to take a look at how you might wish to use this Level of Creation in your search for health. I am inviting you to consider that you can use all four levels to seek recovery if you wish. So, what would that look like at this level?

ENERGY SAVING AID

These are the essential points that are helpful for you to take away from the following section:

- *This model implies, for healing to take place at the Unity Consciousness level, you need to consciously partner with the Creative Source. Religion offers us a way to do this through the power of prayer or faith healing. Anecdotally, this may work.*

- *Scientific study and analysis of healing through prayer has proven inconclusive. Why is that? Possibly the design of the studies has been poor. Possibly we are seeking to use a tool—science—to study a subject that is inherently based on faith and cannot be proved or disproved.*

- *The model I work with sees individuals as remaining connected to the Creative Source. Individuals exist because the Creative Source wished to know itself and chose to do this by individuating so it could experience infinite possibilities. To know anything, you need to know what that thing IS and what it IS NOT. This means the individuated part must have the freedom to create "good" and "bad"—the polarities. For that to work effectively, the individuated part must have free will so it is not being orchestrated by its Creative Source—it is free to explore and create whatever it dreams up, and the Creative Source will experience that and gain greater awareness of itself.*

- *If the individual is free to create consciously and subconsciously, for its desired outcome to be realized, both conscious and subconscious minds must be seeking the same goal. If they are not, the Creative Source cannot override the free will of either part. The individual must recognise the conflict and request assistance in making a change. Until then, there may be a disparity between the individual's conscious desire and the physical reality. It may appear this is a case of a prayer not being answered. In reality, it reflects an unresolved conflict between the individual's conscious and subconscious desires.*

- *This will become more pertinent and apparent in section three when we explore Trauma and its relationship to CFS.*

How Does Recovery Take Place at the Level of Unity Consciousness?

If you wish to make the most profound changes of all, then finding a way to work at the Unity Consciousness level will be the fastest route. So those people who report healing through prayer or celebrated faith healers who affect "miracles" through the simple laying on of hands are not necessarily the charlatans you may think. These people may have succeeded in finding a way to partner at the Unity Consciousness level and change the creative process from that place rather than from a lower level of creation. So, is this just speculation, perhaps "bunkum," or could it be real? Many religious faiths include elements of healing through prayer or Divine intervention. So, from a religious perspective, this is a real possibility. How about from a scientific perspective?

Well, interestingly, we do have several scientific studies that have attempted to determine the effectiveness of prayer on healing. Unfortunately, the results are varied and support anything from "yes this works" to "actually, this makes people worse, not better," to "we didn't really see anything happening at all."[22] So, how could we

22 This study, a meta-analysis of several previously conducted scientific studies, will give you an overview of where science currently stands in answer to this question. Andrade C, Radhakrishnan R. Prayer and Healing: A medical and scientific

have such a vast spectrum of results? Some of the answer may lie in the design of the experiments. Regardless of the area of study, any scientific experiment can provide altered results if you alter the way in which it is carried out. However, of more concern is the question of whether we can use science to study religion. Science is about providing "proof" and "certainty," about working out a definable system that can be repeated and always provide the same results. Religion is about faith. So, trying to use science to "prove" the existence of God is rather like trying to use a hammer to paint your wall. It's not an effective tool for the job.

I wish to add another detail that may help to explain why prayer shows such a vast range of effectiveness. This Universe we are all collectively creating through our connection to the Universal Creator contains a Law of Free Will. My personal belief and understanding is that Creator Being decided to individuate to know Themselves. By creating a—potentially—infinite number of expressions, this paved the way for experiencing an infinite number of unique experiences. Since we can only know something through polarity—you cannot know what something is until you also know what it isn't—it means some of those experiences will be "good" and some will be "bad." It also means, to truly experience everything, the Universal Creator needed to make the Law of Free Will. Without that, it would be possible for the Universal Creator to dictate and confine Their experience. Each individuated Soul needs to have the Free Will to request *anything*, no matter how evil or how outrageous. This is why we need to remove the concept of judgement, as I suggested in chapter two. The desire of a Creator Being is to experience everything, so no one thing can be "better" or "worse" than any other thing. It simply *is*.

---

perspective on randomized controlled trials. Indian J Psychiatry. 2009 Oct-Dec; 51(4):247-53. doi: 10.4103/0019-5545.58288. PMID: 20048448; PMCID: PMC2802370.

If you are willing to work with that idea, and we now overlay it onto the question of prayer, then something interesting happens. For your prayer to be answered, it needs to be in full alignment with your individuated Free Will desire. That desire is apparent at both a conscious and subconscious level. So, let's imagine you pray for health. That is your conscious, heartfelt desire. But, at a subconscious level, you may also hold the belief you are a bad person, you deserve punishment, and your ill health is that punishment. So, this Free Will—subconscious—belief conflicts with your conscious request. The all-loving, all-powerful Creator Being may desire to answer your prayer and bestow health upon you, but doesn't that override your free will to believe you don't deserve to be healthy? So, how do we cope with that? The answer is to seek to become aware of all that you are, both consciously and subconsciously. Once you can uncover your belief in your inherent unworthiness, you can ask for assistance in first healing that.

Which brings us to the next layer of creation, but before we get there, I want to explain some additional nuances of the model as a whole.

ENERGY SAVING AID

These are the essential points that are helpful for you to take away from the following section:

- *It is important to understand the Creative process is not a one-off, linear process. It is cyclical and continuous. In other words, the process may feed down from idea to physical reality, but it doesn't stop there. The physical reality then feeds back up to the Creative Source, allowing that source to make alterations that feed down to allow the physical expression to expand and evolve. For example, your physical body is constantly regenerating itself as older cells die off and are replaced by newer cells.*

- *Second, we are examining this in a linear fashion to help make the model easier to grasp. In fact, all the levels operate together, all at once, not one at a time, one after the other.*
- *The levels are not equal in terms of the impact they have on our experience. Only 1% of our physical experience has its origins at the physical level. About 19% of our physical experience originates from the psycho-emotional level, while 80% of that physical experience originates from the Intuitive level. So, if you are seeking to create lasting change, focusing only on the physical level is going to bring about limited results. Focusing on the Intuitive level will have a much greater impact, and changes made at that level will automatically feed down to express at the physical level. However, complete healing needs to address the issues at ALL levels.*

Some Important Nuances

Firstly, as we progress through the next chapters, I will be laying the model out as separate levels or layers and describing a linear process. However, this is just to try to make things easier to understand. So, I need you to be aware that this process is not happening as a progression and each level is not discrete. All of it is happening all at once and over and over all the time.

Secondly, this is not a one-way street. In the original image, I showed the pyramid in discrete layers, with a downward arrow indicating a one-way direction of travel. This makes it easier to try to grasp the concept. However, aside from understanding your levels are simultaneous, rather than one after the other, you also need to understand the direction of communication is a flow like a circle. So, the creative process doesn't stop when it reaches your physical body. Instead, your physical body communicates back up to the Unity Consciousness level. So, if the physical body notices something is amiss, it is communicating that back up to the top to request that your creative level alters the plan to improve the physical situation. We will explore that idea more fully later on. So, really, your pyramid of creation should look more like this:

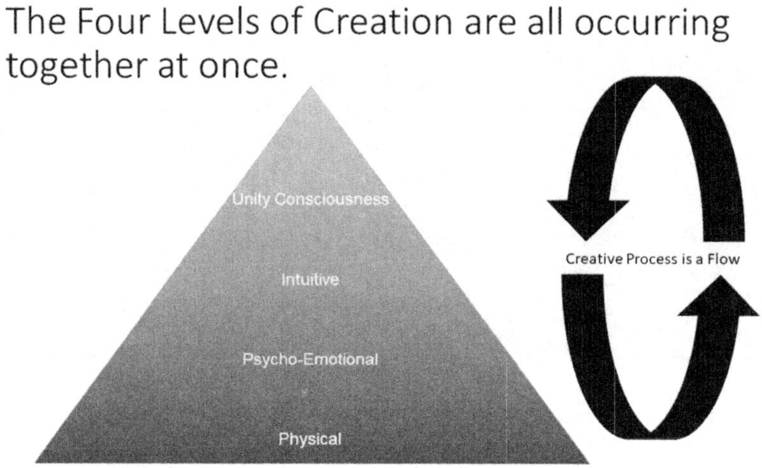

Also, this process of creation is not a "one-and-done" event. Unlike building a house, which is a single event, building a human body is a permanent evolution. Your body is simultaneously mass AND energy all at the same time. Energy never stands still. At the Intuitive level, your particles are darting around waiting to be directed by information. At the Psycho-Emotional level, your waves are constantly flowing and have the potential to change frequency in response to new information. At the physical level, every single cell in your body is alive and regenerating all the time. Your entire body is constantly regenerating. You get a brand-new liver every few weeks. You get a brand-new skeleton every ten years.

In recent years, we have also reached the exciting understanding that your genes are not set in stone in the way we previously thought. The study of epigenetics has opened our eyes to the idea genes can be switched on or off in response to their environment. Guess what? The most influential part of your environment is not what is happening in your physical space but what is happening at the level of the mind, both conscious and subconscious. According to Dr. Bruce Lipton, "Getting back to health, it comes down to a simple fact: Less than 1% of disease is associated with genetics. Over 90% of disease is a total reflection of environment, and especially our programming: the disempowering, self-sabotaging behaviours we acquired in the first seven years of life. Since those disempowering programs are based on our environment and our perception, and since we can change the environment and our perception, we have the power to free ourselves from disease and to start living that happily-ever-after honeymoon of life experiences we all believe we can have."[23] So, this process of continual regeneration gives us the potential to create lasting change or to create lasting damage.

The speed of change is different at each level. At the higher levels of creation, change can take effect in milliseconds, but this has to feed down through all the levels; the denser the energy—the higher the mass, the slower the speed of change.

---

23 Quotation from the following article: Gustafson C. Bruce Lipton, PhD: The Jump from Cell Culture to Consciousness. Integr. Med. (Encinitas). 2017 Dec; 16(6):44-50. PMID: 30936816; PMCID: PMC6438088. I also recommend you visit Dr. Lipton's website to explore these ideas in greater depth: https://brucelipton.com

The Four Bodies Within the Levels of Creation

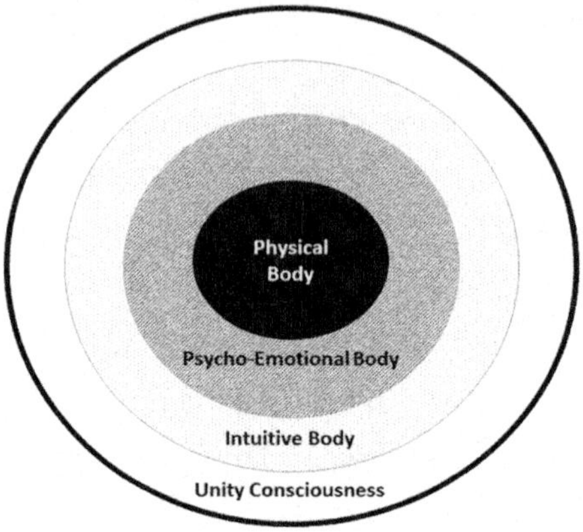

I feel it is also helpful to re-shape the model a little. Instead of looking at it as a pyramid shape, it's really a circle—in fact, more of a sphere, but as I'm drawing on 2D paper, I have to draw a 2D circle!

How the Four Levels Relate to Lived Experience

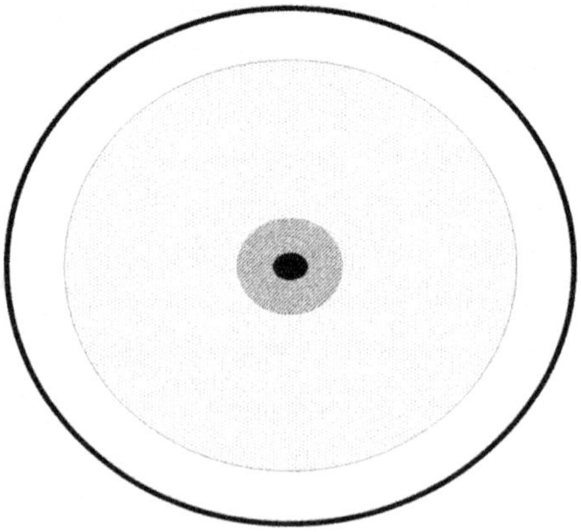

The final nuance I want to bring to your attention is the relative impact the creative process, at each level, has on your physical experience. I warn you this is not something that comes from "science." This is leaning on metaphysics. If you wish to disregard this idea, you can. It needn't mean the rest of the model is inaccurate. Think back to my cautionary tale at the start of this chapter!

So, distortions, or errors in the information at the Intuitive Level, account for 80% of your physical experience. Distortions or errors in the wave patterns at the Psycho-Emotional Level account for around 19% of your physical experience. This leaves us with just 1% of your physical experience directly influenced by distortions and errors occurring at the physical level.[24] Again, we will be using the next three chapters to explore what each of these levels mean, so don't worry if you're not understanding the significance of these figures at the moment.

If you are feeling triggered by me telling you that your physical body only occurs for 1% of your physical experience, I am not saying the errors and distortions occurring at the physical level are "small" or "unimportant" or "irrelevant." This proportion of effect relates to the relative impact of distortions at each level and the effectiveness of healing at that level of creation. This links back to Dr. Klinghardt's work and his assertion that deep, long-lasting healing needs to take place at a level deeper than the purely physical.

To put this in slightly different terms, 80% of the discomfort you experience at a physical level has its original root cause in distortions at the Intuitive Level and 19% of your discomfort has its origins at the Psycho-Emotional Level. Remember, those distortions do not simply sit at that level: They influence the levels below and end up manifesting as your physical symptom. Your physical symptoms may be huge and life-changing, or they may be small and annoying, but when those symptoms come together into a pattern we call chronic illness, it is not enough to try to attain healing by working *only* at the

---

24 Source of these figures is Niki Skye's work on healing: https://nikiskye.com/the-4-levels-of-creation/

physical level. As with any problem in life, unless you address its root cause, you will not fully solve the problem. You may be able to take some action to provide temporary respite, but the problem will recur, perhaps in the same form, or perhaps in a slightly different form.

From a physical perspective, we tend to view health issues as problems—which, of course, they are—but they are also challenges inviting a solution. So, from a perspective of creation, when a problem surfaces, it is an invitation to examine the creative process and look for ways it can be improved. Changing the process at the root level will feed into a change at the physical level because the creative process is constantly moving and evolving.

> *ENERGY SAVING AID*
>
> *Please make sure to complete this exercise, as you will be using the results to help create your recovery roadmap.*

An Invitation to Practice

I invite you to grab your journal again and start noticing—and writing about—your reactions to this chapter.

- How do you *feel* about it?
    - Confused?
    - Hopeful?
    - Angry?
    - Unsure how to answer that?
    - Something else?

- What do you *think* about the information in this chapter?
    - Does it sound similar to information you have heard before, or is it completely new to you?
    - Are you open to working with this model, or do you still feel that your body is a physical entity and nothing more?

Remember, there are no "wrong" answers here. Just note down whatever you feel, think, and notice. If you are judging yourself—or me—make a note of that as well. We are just information-gathering at this stage.

Chapter 6

Sacred Geometry – The Intuitive Level

In this chapter, we are going to explore the Intuitive Level in our Four Levels of Creation model. From a scientific perspective, this is the level ruled by geometry. Geometric coding provides the basic information that guides our random particles of energy to begin forming whatever it is that we wish to create. From a spiritual perspective, this level is where the Akashic Records reside. These record every event throughout the Universe across all time. These events create our Karma. We will be exploring how your past, whether that's the collective past of your family, race, or community or the personal past of your previous incarnations, impacts the information creating your present experience. If all of that sounds a bit intellectual or a bit woo-woo, you can also think of this level from the perspective of a personal project. Imagine you had the idea of building a house. At this point, you would be calculating things like the size of your rooms and the load-bearing properties of your building materials. Again, we are focusing on mathematics, calculations, and geometry. Of course, I will also bring this back to the perspective of your health. What has any of this got to do with your recovery from CFS? Well, read on to find out!

ENERGY SAVING AID

The following section introduces a couple of ideas that we will explore in the chapter, but it is my personal story, so not essential to read if you are low on energy.

Setting the Scene: Two Short, Pivotal Stories

I am the first to admit that, whilst I might have found talk of past lives, Karma, and the Akash interesting, these ideas were never part of my formal education, my upbringing, or the basic fabric of my life. At least, not until about 2021. I began to experience what many would recognise as a Spiritual Awakening. I'm not talking thunderbolts and miracles here. This was really more of a gradual process. So, the first story is one moment in time where that process solidified for me.

Throughout my years living with CFS, I was repeatedly told that meditation would be "good for me." I tried it on more than one occasion. Sometimes I just experienced nothing but boredom, distraction, and "monkey mind." A couple of times I found myself hyper-ventilating and going into panic. This did not feel good, and it didn't seem to be what meditation was "supposed" to be doing for me. I began to wonder if this meditation "thing" was nothing more than spiritual mumbo-jumbo. Or whether I was deeply flawed and somehow lacked a critical skill. So, I put my attempts to one side and continued to focus on taking supplements to support my physical body.

Then, in 2020, I was listening to an online conference about trauma. One of the organisers, Niki Skye (formerly Gratrix), had included a free bonus—a meditation. So, I decided to give this one a try. Wow! This twenty-minute experience found me relaxing, releasing emotions, and afterwards feeling transformed—temporarily. Finally, I began to see why so many people swear by meditation. I continued to use that meditation daily, and I eventually began working with Niki, using more and more of her meditations until I had a regular practice.

Well, by 2021, not only was I releasing more emotions and feeling more benefits, I was also having some pretty weird experiences. Not all the time; just every now and then.

I particularly remember one meditation. I fell quickly into a deep state of peace—not always what happened for me! I began to see faces around me, then heard a voice telling me that I was still gripped by a trauma from a past life and that was blocking my healing. The voice ceased, and I then began to smell burning and feel my feet and lower legs first getting hot, then beginning to burn. This felt terrifying, and I immediately came out of the meditative state wondering what had happened. I continued to sit and listen to the rest of the meditation music but didn't go back into a deep state. The meditation finished, and I continued with the rest of my day. But a few hours later, I began to remember more. I remembered being burned at the stake, and I remembered why I had been given this punishment.

I also felt like I might be going mad, so decided to dismiss those ideas. I have no "rational" explanation for this incident. Interestingly, I have always been terrified of fire. As a small child, I had recurring nightmares about being trapped in a fire. Apart from managing to set my hair on fire by getting too close to a candle when I was at university—all was well; I didn't suffer any burns, just some singed hair!—I have never had any experience of fire or burning in this current lifetime. Doubtless, a psychologist could offer some theory to explain this if I was minded to ask them.

I mention that story as a way of introducing a thread we are going to explore in this chapter. The following story, completely unrelated, will help to introduce a second thread of exploration.

During my GCSE years—aged 15–16—at school, I studied World War II in history class. I must have been about fifteen when my class was taken on a school trip to the Imperial War Museum in London. The purpose of the trip was to learn more about the War. More than thirty years later, I don't remember many of the details, but one part of this trip did stick in my mind. One of the exhibits in the museum was a reconstruction of a bomb shelter like the type that many would have used in London during the Blitz. In fact, my own grandparents lived in London and regularly used these air-raid shelters throughout the war. This exhibit wasn't simply something to look at; it was an entire experience. So, in small groups, we were ushered into the mock shelter, the doors were closed, and we were immersed in that world. The museum had recreated the smell. We were sat in dim light, on uncomfortable benches, immersed in a soundtrack that included the noise of air raid sirens and bombs falling, as if outside the shelter, and the conversation of the people inside. It was incredibly real. For me, this wasn't simply a curious experience of another time. I felt real fear and panic, as if I really was sitting in that shelter, in the 1940s, in fear of my life, in danger of losing my home and with bombs falling around me. It felt quite strange to walk back out of the room and discover I was still in the 1990s and we were not facing a war. As I say, I don't remember much else about the day, but that visceral experience has stuck with me for over thirty years.

So, there we have two unrelated stories that may leave you questioning my sanity. Or perhaps just feeling I have a powerful imagination and you're not sure why I'm telling you this. For me, yes, I have asked myself both those questions. I have also used these experiences as a starting point for exploring more facets of who we could be as humans. So, I invite you to remain open and curious as we explore together.

ENERGY SAVING AID

These are the essential points that are helpful for you to take away from the following section:

- *This introduces the idea, at this level, the building blocks are mathematics—specifically geometry. Think of this as coded information that determines the eventual shape of your physical creation.*
- *This is important because, if you wish to make a change at any level, you need to use the tools that relate to its building blocks. So, in this case, we would need to change the information—or coding—creating an outcome we find undesirable.*

Intuitive Level

If you remember from the last chapter, the second level of creation is called the Intuitive Level. At this point—from the perspective of Universal Creation—Geometry starts to come into play. Geometry is the science—correctly, branch of mathematics—from which everything is formed. How do we know this, or why would we believe it?

Well, I am not a physicist, and I am not about to attempt to deliver a treatise on the Big Bang Theory or the origins of the Universe. However, if you are interested in those topics, I want to draw your attention to a couple of scientific discoveries. In 2013, a group of theoretical physicists discovered something called the Amplituhedron. This is basically a geometric shape, resembling a jewel. Its discovery in 2013 allowed theoretical physicists to calculate "scattering amplitudes." This is the way in which particles interact to form other particles, in other words, to begin building things—creating life. Prior to its discovery, theoretical physicists performed these calculations using mathematical models developed by Nobel Prize-Winning physicist Richard Feynman.[25] The second discovery that piqued my interest is the study of fractals. In 1980, Benoit Mandelbrot created computer coding to illustrate a fractal. Interestingly, fractal geometry can be used to explain the creation process in nature. The 1980 code is named the Mandelbrot Set. It uses mathematical calculations to create a Fractal: a shape that will retain the same properties as you enlarge it and reduce it. You can view this as a computer image, and it is absolutely mesmerising.[26] Once again, we are talking about geometry and talking about this as a basis for building life.

---

25 If you want a relatively accessible article about this topic, this could be a good place to begin: https://www.quantamagazine.org/physicists-discover-geometry-underlying-particle-physics-20130917/

26 Mandelbrot developed the fractal whilst working in the IBM labs, so this article from IBM is a nice overview of his work: https://www.ibm.com/ibm/history/fractal-geometry

I also wish to introduce an interesting thread from the metaphysical perspective. The work of Egyptian scientist Dr. Ibrahim Karim has used geometric shapes to manifest incredible results in a diverse range of areas. This intriguing new area of exploration is called Biogeometry®, and it focuses on using geometric shapes to increase the Divine Energy—centre point—in buildings, humans, and animals. This practice harmonises the entire field and supports improvements in health and well-being.[27]

So, why am I telling you any of this? Basically, at this level of creation, the "tool" that creates and changes things is mathematics—specifically, geometry. We can also refer to this as coding. Think of this maybe like a computer program. This is significant because we need to understand the tools that operate at each level if we wish to understand how to—theoretically, at least—make changes at any level. I will come back to that idea at the end of this chapter.

27 To learn more about this, you can begin by reading Dr. Karim's book, Back to a Future for Mankind: Biogeometry®: Solutions to the Global Environment Crisis. New Energy Secrets of Ancient Egypt and the Great Pyramid Revealed. Some of his work has been subjected to scientific study, including a study in which Biogeometry was used to provide incredible results in treating Hepatitis C. In another study, applying geometric shapes to the buildings in which chickens were raised resulted in larger, healthier chickens without the use of antibiotics or genetically modified food.

ENERGY SAVING AID

These are the essential points that it is helpful for you to take away from the following section:

- *If we examine this level from a spiritual or metaphysical perspective, then it is the level that contains the Akashic records. This is the record of all events coded into the fabric of the Universe. Note: this is mathematical/geometric coding that creates the record.*
- *We have a Universal Akash, and we also each have our own personal Akash—the record of everything our individuated soul has experienced during its existence across multiple lifetimes. That personal record is our Karma.*
- *This is not just a theoretical idea or metaphysical concept: brilliant scientists are putting forth theories and carrying out experiments that support the possibility of a coded information store that creates the world we experience.*

The Akasha

Let's now look at what is happening at this level from the Universal spiritual perspective. This is the level at which all creation is recorded—the Akashic Record.[28] The term Akash originates from the Indian Sanskrit word Akasha—Ākāśa. This concept made its way into Western thought through the work of the Theosophical Society. In the early twentieth century, Edgar Cayce popularised the concept through his

28 This article by Alexander Nash is an easily comprehensible, scholarly look at the Akashic Records, tracing their origins back to Indian wisdom, looking at how they entered Western spirituality and how this concept has shown up in the Twentieth-Century: https://www.researchgate.net/publication/346481905_The_Akashic_Records_Origins_and_Relation_to_Western_Concepts

work. Cayce was an American-born psychic who discovered he could enter a trance-like state and channel these "secrets" of the Universe.[29] He used his skills to facilitate healing, accessing these Akashic records to discover where his patients had acquired "blocks" in their field.

That may all sound rather "out there." Perhaps you believe these concepts are somehow "made up," or symptoms of insanity, or merely con tricks used to part naïve people from their money. But were you aware we have several academic explorations of the Akashic Records?[30]

It's OK if you are feeling some doubts here. Let's just keep exploring. The link here is that these records are "coded" into the biofield of the Universe. This is a record of every single event that has taken place throughout all time. If it helps, maybe think of this a bit like the cloud storage for your computer. Yes, the entire record is stored at the Intuitive level of the universe, but your personal data is also stored in your personal Intuitive level—your little patch of the "cloud storage"! And what is your personal data? Well, that would be the events—ideas, thoughts, actions—in which you, as an individual Soul, have participated in each of your lives, along with the Karma that accrues from those events.

Is it possible to prove—or disprove—this idea using scientific principles? Some scientists believe it is. Michael Talbot's fascinating

---

29 You can read more on the official website of Edgar Cayce, here: https://www.edgarcayce.org/edgar-cayce/his-life/

30 A very quick search brought up numerous articles about the Akash published in various academic journals. They range from explorations of the religious, historic, and scientific origins of this idea to speculation about its use to us in the future. For example, this paper looking at its potential for use by the military in surveillance: Levin J., Hacking the Akashic Records: The Next Domain for Military Intelligence Operations?, World Futures, published online 8th January 2020: https://www.tandfonline.com/doi/abs/10.1080/02604027.2019.1703159?journalCode=gwof20 I am not speculating about the truth of any of these claims: they could be complete bunkum, but you may be interested to learn that the Akash is more than simply folklore.

book, *The Holographic Universe*, presents us with a remarkable theory of reality that makes sense of the latest frontiers in Quantum Physics, purports to explain paranormal phenomena, and explains many apparent riddles about the human mind-body connection. It builds upon the work of Karl Pribram, David Bohm, and many others. As Talbot explains, we have evidence our brains are holographic in nature. We do not store memories as "objects" in a specific part of the brain. Instead, they seem to be stored as information that can be recalled at will, and this information is located in the energy field around us. The same is true of our emotions—they are not stored in the brain. Some people talk about emotions being stored in the "body." Again, though, this is not the physical body: We cannot pinpoint an organ or muscle or bone and see a memory or emotion sitting in there. We are talking about the biofield: the field of energy creating and re-creating us all the time. Interestingly, our eyes also seem to work in a holographic manner. What does this mean? The image—or thing—we see is really a piece of coded information that only becomes an image—thing—when it is observed and processed through the consciousness. This links back to Robert Lanza's thesis that the world does not exist until consciousness—individual or collective—creates it through observation. So, yes, it is possible that the entire catalogue of the events of the Universe, through all time, exists as information in a field, waiting for us to observe it and bring it into our perceived reality—which is mind-blowing. Just hold onto that thought as we explore further ideas, and I will explain the relevance to health at the end of this chapter.

> *ENERGY SAVING AID*
>
> *These are the essential points that are helpful for you to take away from the following section:*
>
> - *In many cultures, past lives are an accepted fact. In the West, we may be a little more sceptical. Yet many people report having past life memories, and there is a fascinating body of psychiatric research into this area.*
> - *This is an invitation to keep an open mind because some clues to your current life experience may be coming from past lives.*

Might We Really Have Past Lives?

In case you wondered what I was talking about, the first story at the opening of this chapter talked about a past life memory. Are you someone who believes in reincarnation, or do you think this current life is all there is? Well, I am not here to tell you what you should be believing or thinking, but if we are to thoroughly understand our maze, then I need to point out all the different features, and past lives happen to be one of those features.

Having grown up in Western culture where reincarnation is not much discussed and certainly doesn't form part of our accepted belief system, I have to confess that I was somewhat of a sceptic when it comes to talk about past lives. So, imagine my surprise upon discovering there is a significant body of academic research on this topic.[31] Many Eastern religions include reincarnation as part of their belief system. It turns out this understanding of the Universe also appears in the Old Testament of the Bible. The New Testament also referenced reincarnation until A.D. 325 when the Roman emperor, Constantine

31 The Division of Perceptual studies at University of Virginia has spent the past fifty years studying reincarnation and past lives.

the Great, and his mother, Helena, deleted those references. The Second Council of Constantinople, meeting in A.D. 553, confirmed the deletions, declaring reincarnation a heresy.[32]

So, what we are looking at is a belief system. Science can neither prove nor disprove reincarnation. Many people have reported past-life memories. Brian L. Weiss, M.D. authored the book *Many Lives, Many Masters*. It catalogues his personal journey from sceptic to believer. He was working as a traditional psychotherapist and found himself treating a fascinating yet tricky case. Having exhausted a number of conventional avenues for healing, Dr. Weiss turned to hypnotherapy in one session. To his complete astonishment, his patient began recalling detailed memories of previous lives. As he worked through those memories, she began to experience healing that hadn't taken place through the earlier practice focused on her present life. Dr. Weiss, fascinated by these discoveries, turned his whole practice over to studying past life memories. His work is not unique, as he himself discovered. Edgar Mitchell had written on the topic—you may remember, we encountered him in the last chapter; he founded the Institute of Noetic Science: IONS). Dr. Ian Stevenson, M.D. had catalogued over two thousand cases of children experiencing reincarnation-type memories, and he had many papers published in the psychiatric literature. These ideas are not simply the "woo-woo" that you may have been led to believe.

Perhaps those feelings of déjà vu, or that instinct that you already know somebody, could be reflections of this phenomenon. If you happen to be one of those people who has had these experiences, then you may be inclined to believe in reincarnation. On the other hand, if you have never experienced anything like this and you have grown up in a belief system that states reincarnation is a myth, you will be

---

32 Many Lives, Many Masters: The True Story of a Prominent Psychiatrist, His Young Patient, and the Past-Life Therapy That Changed Both Their Lives, Brian L. Weiss, M.D.

less inclined to believe in the concept. Depending upon your beliefs, you are going to be inclined to either love this chapter and embrace its ideas or hate it and wish to reject everything I am sharing. I invite you to notice your reaction and simply try to remain open and curious as you continue reading.

ENERGY SAVING AID

These are the essential points that are helpful for you to take away from the following section:

- *On slightly less controversial ground, we are also gathering evidence that the traumatic experiences of one generation can be inherited by later generations. So, if your grandparents lived through a traumatic event like World War II, that can have caused alterations in their gene expression passed down to you, these will have a direct impact on your own central nervous system.*

Ancestral and Collective Trauma

The second of my opening stories touches upon the area of ancestral and collective trauma. The work of great minds like Thomas Hübl has opened our eyes to the possibility we may inherit trauma. Unlike reincarnation, science can prove this thesis. In fact, it has already attempted to do so. Studies on mice have demonstrated that the genetic changes experienced by a mouse during a traumatic situation are then inherited by its offspring up to six generations later, causing maladaptive behaviour responses in these later generations, even when they are not exposed to the trauma.[33] You might be wondering whether

33 This paper outlines one set of research findings in this area: https://www.researchgate. net/profile/Isabelle-Mansuy/publication/325707115_Transgenerational_Epigenetics_of_Traumatic_Stress/links/5b29634ca6fdcc72dbeebc0b/Transgenerational-Epigenetics-of-Traumatic-Stress.pdf

this same process applies to the human population. Well, Rachel Yehuda argues that it does.[34] Since the 1960s, psychiatrists have been speculating as to the possibility of the children and grandchildren of Holocaust survivors inheriting trauma patterns through altered gene expression. Yehuda's research suggests this speculation may be visible in the genes. We still have more questions to answer, but it seems increasingly likely the emotional imprint of trauma is carried into the physical body, affecting future generations. This is supported by the discoveries made in the field of epigenetics. Yes, our DNA does contain a blueprint of information. However, within that, we have over 90% control over which of those genes are switched on or off and, therefore, what health outcomes we experience. Our environment and our subconscious mind control that. So, yes, genetic alterations can take place as a result of traumatic experiences. Once we become aware of that change, we can reprogram the subconscious mind to alter the gene expression back to its healthy form. My experience in the mock air-raid shelter all those years ago in the museum may not have been the effects of an over-active imagination. I may have been tapping into inherited trauma memories. In the light of this section, once I became aware of that trauma, I gained the power to see it and heal it rather than continuing to live under its subtle influence.

Karl Jung's work talked about the Collective Unconscious, a consciousness shared by the entire society and which the individual can access and be influenced by. Again, this relates to the idea your personal experiences and expressions of behaviour may be influenced by the wider world around you. Could this Collective Consciousness be an expression of the Akashic record? If you choose to believe that the Akashic record exists, then what is its significance for you personally? This Intuitive Level is the level on which your Karma is

34 Yehuda R, Lehrner A. Intergenerational transmission of trauma effects: putative role of epigenetic mechanisms. World Psychiatry. 2018 Oct; 17(3):243-257. doi: 10.1002/wps.20568. PMID: 30192087; PMCID: PMC6127768.

created and stored. So, whilst the events themselves remain embedded in the Akashic Field for all eternity, the Karma is like an accounting balance sheet. Actions that benefited others accrue "credit" for you, and actions that harmed others accrue "debt" that must be repaid. So, as your current life is manifesting, it is at this level your Karmic debt and credit are held in your individual biofield. That Karma is going to have an impact on what plays out in your physical experience.[35] Yet, with the understanding you can change your environment, the challenges your Karma may attract can become invitations to experience healing.

If all of this is feeling too "out there" for you right now because you thought Karma was just a figure of speech or something that New Age Hippies believed in, but which doesn't "actually" exist, then I have been where you are right now. So, you don't have to 100% believe me here and now today. If it helps, it's perfectly OK to think you've just fallen into a new and crazier version of *Alice in Wonderland*, so all you need to do is keep reading and enjoy the story, and I promise we will return to more familiar territory soon!

---

35 As with the idea of an Akashic Record, the idea of Karma spans a whole range. At one end, we have flippant use in everyday language, "Oh, that's going to get you bad Karma," or "I must have done something really bad in a past life!" Most of us, if we think or say things like that, don't really expect it to be literally true. Moving towards the other end of the spectrum, this idea also touches upon Determinism. That is the belief events do not occur randomly but are determined by past events and, in turn, give rise to future events. Or, similarly but subtly differently, we have the idea of Predestination, which has been hotly debated between Christian denominations for centuries. This is the idea God has predetermined our fate. So, although we retain free will to act as we wish, we all have a predetermined destiny playing out for us.

ENERGY SAVING AID

These are the essential points that are helpful for you to take away from the following section:

- *We tend to think of Karma as being about a system of punishment and reward. This implies a judgement by some external "other."*
- *In fact, Karma is really about a system of consequences. There is no judgement involved. The system of Karma allows the Universal Consciousness to experience its full potential through individuating. A choice made by the individuated Soul in one lifetime will impact the experiences of that Soul in the next lifetime so the Universal Consciousness, through the individuated Soul, can fully experience a concept from both the perspective of what it is and what it is not.*
- *Infinite individuated Souls, all creating infinite experiences, allow the Universal Consciousness to fully know itself—know all that is possible.*

Karma

If you are willing to explore a little further, I want to introduce a few brief ideas about Karma. First, we tend to think of this from a perspective of punishment and reward. In other words, if I do something good to or for someone else, then something good will happen to me and vice versa. So, this can bring comfort when we see someone do something bad and escape punishment. We may find refuge in the idea Karma will catch up with them and something bad is going to happen to them in the future. For some, that can literally mean in this lifetime; others are prepared to take a longer-term view and see this as playing out in another lifetime. Perhaps you have heard someone commenting on a friend who seems particularly lucky, "Well, they must have been a Saint in their previous life!" Or, perhaps something unexpectedly bad happens to you, and you jokingly comment, "I must have been a really bad person in my last life!" However, there is a slight nuance to this perspective. Karma is about consequences, which are not necessarily the same as punishments and rewards.

Understanding Karma in terms of consequences builds on a set of beliefs about why we exist. In this belief model, we exist as a discrete part of the Universe—the creative whole. We exist so the Universe can understand what it is by experiencing everything. The original Source—creative force—chose to fulfil this desire by individuating into an infinite number of expressions. Each of us is one of those expressions, and, as we explored in the last chapter, we are having a unique individual experience AND experiencing the Universal Whole at the same time. Once created, each individuated part can explore and experience an infinite number of things in this quest to understand who it is, and all of those experiences feed back into the Universal Whole. However, you cannot understand what something *is* unless you also understand what it *is not*. So, in this model, Karma is about exploring that concept.

Let me explain that through an imaginary example. In one lifetime, I may have the experience of being powerful and abusing my power and using it to kill and harm others. I may, in fact, have multiple lifetimes when I fully experience this from different angles. So, in one, I am a mass murderer; in another, I defraud millions of people of all their savings. Throughout these lifetimes, I have come to fully experience the dynamics of power and evil from the perspective of the *doer*. As a result, I have a one-sided view of what power is and what evil is. So, I now need to experience those same things from the opposite perspective. I will now have a series of lives in which I am victimised and abused in all the ways that I previously tormented others. So, yes, there is a level on which I am living a cursed life because I previously did very bad things, but this is not because some *other* has decreed this for me and I am an unwilling participant. In fact, my Higher Self—the part of me that is in Unity Consciousness—is fully aware of why this is happening and wishes to experience it to evolve and understand the Universe to its fullest extent. We talk about the Law of Karma to indicate this idea of consequences. Think of the Law of Gravity: If I step off the top of a tall building, it is inevitable I will fall to the ground. This is not because I am being punished or rewarded for my decision to step off the building: I am simply following the natural consequences of the Law. The same is true for the Law of Karma.

ENERGY SAVING AID

These are the essential points that are helpful for you to take away from the following section:

- *We explore more nuances of Karma. In between lives, the individuated soul chooses what it wishes to experience to complete Karmic lessons. These choices may be made with other souls who agree to help by creating circumstances that allow the desired experience to take place, but we have no memory of this between-life—or indeed, past-life—experience. So, we view our current physical existence as positive or negative.*
- *We also retain free will. So, if we chose to experience something that would allow us to complete a Karmic debt and grow, we have the free will to decide how we respond to that event. Do we view it as an opportunity for growth and healing? Or do we see it as an unjust challenge and perhaps even accrue more Karmic debt from responding unwisely to the challenge?*

- *You might want to view this as a "nice little idea" or as completely crazy, or you might want to consider that this model of existence could have huge implications for the story you are telling yourself about your health challenges.*

Understanding the Soul's Purpose

In between my lives, when I return to the awareness of Unity Consciousness, I will evaluate my experience and actively participate in the decision about what I wish to experience in my next life. This process is taken in conjunction with other souls. So, I may say I wish to experience the worst possible health and ask other souls to volunteer to help me by helping to set up circumstances in which this "worst possible health" experience can manifest into physical reality.[36] The problem is, right here, right now, in the physical plane, I have absolutely no memory of doing this. So, I feel as though I am being punished and cursed by some malevolent force I don't understand.

In yet another nuance, we need to understand Karma is created for both parties at the time the "bad" act takes place. So, if I murder someone, yes, I create Karma for myself—the need to repent and understand why my actions caused pain. However, my victim also experiences Karma. This would appear more like trauma—the trauma of having been murdered in whatever manner. Both parties have a Karmic debt that needs to be paid off in their next lifetime. At the same time, we also retain free will. So, as the—previously—murdered victim, in my next lifetime, I may feel fearful and powerless. I have

---

36 This is essentially what Dr. Sue Morter terms "the bus-stop conversation." You can read about this in more detail in her book, *The Energy Codes*. Interestingly, Brian Weiss also reports this idea in his record of his patient's hypnotherapy sessions. In some sessions, she would report what takes place in between our lives, and this idea that we evaluate what we wish to learn and choose when we are going to learn those lessons was something that she revealed.

the choice of overcoming those fears and healing the powerlessness—post-traumatic growth—or acting out my trauma and trying to protect myself by, in turn, abusing others. If I choose the first path, I will erase my Karmic debt. If I choose the second path, I will accrue even more debt, requiring more clearance in future lives.[37]

The reason I am mentioning any of this is that it can be used as an explanation for why some people cannot seem to recover their health, no matter what they do. If, at the level of Karma, they have decided or agreed to experience this, it cannot be changed at the physical level without also making a change at the Akashic level. My understanding is that rebalancing can only take place between lives when the soul reviews its progress and determines whether or not it has learned all that is required to understand the desired lesson. Now, that idea may be the craziest thing you ever heard. It may make you really, really angry because I seem, like so many doctors, to be saying that your experience is your fault. That may be triggering all sorts of patterns of blame and shame you don't want to confront or explore. I sympathise with you for taking that view. You may also see this as a convenient excuse: a lazy way of justifying why we have no answers to many diseases. You may prefer to stick to the view that this "crazy talk" is simply letting people off the hook when, in reality, we need to be carrying out more research and improving our treatments until one day we have cures for everything. However, let me propose a radical compromise here. Imagine there is some mileage to this "crazy talk" and, rather than seeing this as an either/or situation—either metaphysics has the answers *or* science has them—we see this as a need for more research, taking a wider perspective. I would argue we need to understand more about how the physical body interacts with the wider universe, with consciousness, from perspectives that aren't always going to be

---

37 Again, in his book, Brian Weiss records his patient, Catherine, reporting that people don't always learn their lessons and may need to reincarnate multiple times to clear one Karmic debt.

explicable in a conventional scientific or laboratory setting. I am going to leave that exploration of Karma for you to ponder or set aside as you wish. Let's bring this level back into the context of the creative process.

ENERGY SAVING AID

These are the essential points that are helpful for you to take away from the following section:

- *In more practical terms, we can view this level of creation as a step in a project to build a house. This step involves the mathematical calculations of room size, load bearing, etc., which will determine how successfully you build your house.*
- *Viewed through the lens of physics, at the previous level, we introduced particles into a vacuum. They are currently moving around chaotically, without structure until, at this level, we introduce the information—the blueprint that tells them what physical form to take.*
- *From an epigenetic perspective, the blueprint encoded in your DNA can change its expression by altering the information it receives from its environment. So, your health may not be set in stone.*

Exploring the Intuitive Level from a Practical Perspective

So, as a more practical analogy, I like to think of this Intuitive level as the first stage of a plan. Your idea popped out of nowhere in the previous level. Now it exists as a thought, and you are starting to plan how to turn that thought into a reality. Let's say your idea was to build a house. At this point, you are calculating the length of the walls, the height of each storey of your house, the angles of your structure, the load-bearing potential of your building materials, and so on.

We can also view this from the perspective of physics and the laws of energy creation. Specifically, this would relate to the second law of thermodynamics, which—put simplistically—states that energy particles naturally tend to entropy—randomly moving around at high speed, with no order or design—until we introduce information. What is information? This would consist of mathematical codes. So, hypothetically, in the creation process, they would be the things like the Mandelbrot Fractal and the Amplituhedron at the root of creating nature or the Universe. In the metaphysical sense, this information could be your Akashic record, Karmic debts and credits that guide how your life will take shape. On the level of the human body, this information is encoded in your DNA. Importantly, though, as we considered above, the genetic information encoded in your DNA can change its expression. You can reprogram the information in your blueprint to bring in a more desirable physical expression.

Photons and phonons are some of the particles that form the basic building blocks of all life. As they come together and bind into denser forms to create atoms, then cells, and eventually a human body, we move from a place of invisible energy to a place of visible mass. How do they know what form to begin taking? They are directed by the information—the mathematical coding. So, if that information is directing things to take a—seemingly—"less than perfect" shape, this will manifest on the physical plane.

One word of caution here: I invite you to remember back to chapter two where we talked about the idea of judgement. We explored how our perception of "right" and "wrong," "good" and "bad" are simply reflections of our judgement. So, from a physical perspective, where you have no idea about Karma, no thought of Universal Laws, no sense of Spirituality, living in a body that experiences pain and refuses to allow you to follow your desires may seem like "a mistake." On the other hand, if you view those same physical issues from a spiritual perspective, they can become a "perfect Divine plan" that opens up opportunities for your soul to remember its mission and experience growth. Our very perception that our symptoms are a "problem" pushes us to seek answers and potentially discover the life lessons we forgot we were seeking.

ENERGY SAVING AID

These are the essential points that are helpful for you to take away from the following section:

- *The purpose of exploring this level is to understand how it impacts your physical experience and what you can do to make alterations if you need to.*
- *If you felt your symptoms were rooted at this level, the swiftest, most effective way to change those root causes is by changing the information coded into your biofield. Imprinted meditations and NES Infoceuticals or MiHealth device are all designed to do this.*

Relating This to CFS

Whether or not you have found this discussion interesting, you are probably wondering how it can possibly relate to CFS. I have made references to trauma and epigenetics, and we will be exploring those areas in much more depth later in the book. I am asking you to consider these ideas to help you see what might sit at this level of Creation or this level in your Energy body. Possibly none of this will affect you. Certainly, I never considered any of these angles until I had thoroughly explored my physical and psycho-emotional bodies—the areas we will cover in the next two chapters. I would not have been led to contemplate them at all except for two strong personal beliefs. The first was that I could find complete recovery. The second was since I had explored other areas and was still experiencing symptoms, I must be missing something.

So, if you believe there could be a problem at this level, how would you go about fixing it? By using the tools that operate at this level: geometry, coding, and information. In essence, if your physical body is experiencing a symptom that originates at this level, you are looking for the "faulty" coding or "faulty" information leading to that symptom. I use the term "faulty" with a pinch of salt. In truth, if we accept we incarnated here with the intention of growing in wisdom, then those so-called "faults" are simply the clues to the areas on which we need to focus our attention in order to grow.

I am going to come back to explore treatments towards the end of the book after we have explored our vehicle and environment fully. So, I simply want to note, the treatments I used that work with coding or information are the meditations from Niki Skye, which I mentioned at the start of this chapter, and the NES Infoceuticals, in which I ended up training as a practitioner.

ENERGY SAVING AID

Please complete the following practice. The self-awareness you gain from this will help you create your unique roadmap for recovery.

An Invitation to Practice

This chapter has covered a lot of ground and is likely to elicit a lot of different responses in you. So, I want you to grab your journal and answer the following questions:

- Which parts of this chapter felt good or brought up positive emotions in you?
- Which parts of this chapter felt challenging or brought up negative emotions in you?
- What do you *think* about the material in this chapter?
- Have you ever had any experiences you feel might be related to reincarnation or past lives? If yes, name them.
- Do you have any fears that seem a little irrational, and you can't track back to events of which you are aware in this lifetime? If yes, name them.
- Think about the experiences of your ancestors and the community in which you grew up and now live. Which of those experiences might have been traumatic? This could be examples like mine—grandparents living through a war. It could be cultural or historic—racism or sexism. It could be current in the community in which you were raised or live now—poverty, racism, sexism, etc. Make a few notes about these experiences.

Chapter 7

The Psycho-Emotional Level

In this chapter, we are going to explore what happens at the Psycho-emotional Level of Creation. I am going to start by inviting you to explore this level from the perspective of physics. Don't worry, though: We are keeping it simple! Then, we will move on to take a look from the metaphysical angle. What happens at this level also has an important relationship with the ideas of Karma we explored in the last chapter. Finally, we will take a look at how this relates to CFS. Just as this level develops from Karma at the previous level, it also feeds into what is happening at the next level—the Physical Level.

Before we get into all of that, let me prepare the way for you. The following journal entry comes from a point in my journey when I had no idea about the Four Levels of Creation. To me, CFS was a mysterious inconvenience causing me a lot of trouble, and I saw no alternative but to try to make the best of things. I found myself constantly coming up against people who were less than supportive, and I began to notice the impact my own emotions were having on my physical symptoms. I still had no real thought of being able to take back control and change this situation unless someone could find the *thing* that was wrong with my body and fix it. This might be where you are right now, although the fact that you are reading this book suggests to me you are also aware of the possibility there "should" be answers to your dilemma.

> ***ENERGY SAVING AID***
>
> *The following journal excerpt frames the discussion themes for this chapter, but it is my personal story, so it is not essential to read if you are low on energy.*

Journal: August 2016

A couple of things have happened that I do want to talk about. CFS is not a psychological illness in the sense that my brain did not invent these symptoms. The various discomforts I experience on a daily basis are actual problems in my physical body, problems that I now find we can measure and define, maybe even correct. That's why I'm waiting for this physician's appointment in four days' time. Yes, one part of me is counting the days because one part of me cannot wait to feel that I am taking some constructive action to fight this illness. The other part of me is trying not to think about any of this because there are no guarantees that this "constructive action" will have any constructive results. It is hard to both keep a blind faith in an eventual good outcome and remain realistic about what that good outcome looks like. I'm not asking to live a wild life: I would just like to be able to do a Jewellery Maker TV show. Not too much to ask.

Why is this relevant? Well, because even though CFS is not a psychological illness, there is no denying it has a psychological impact, and the way in which I react to that impacts my ability to heal. How so? you may ask. Well, two things are going on at the moment: one is a longer-term niggle, the idea that maybe I could have done something to cure this sooner. The other is an unfortunate occurrence that took place last week.

First to the unfortunate incident last week. Yesterday I should have been teaching a one-day workshop at a local summer school for adults. I've taught at this venue for three years now and always had a great time. So, it was a really tough decision to have to pick up the phone, call the organisers, and explain that I'm just not capable of teaching at the moment. I haven't even been able to teach my normal two-hour workshops from my own home to a group of ladies who are really good and need comparatively little help from me. Yet, still a part of my head was thinking I could maybe somehow drag myself through a six-hour workshop for a group of twelve, fairly inexperienced people who would need a lot of help. After much agonising, "sensible me" prevailed and made that phone call. It's not the first such phone call or email I've had to make recently; in fact, it is just another in a long line of "life-cancelling" actions I've been taking since May. I know I'm disappointing and letting down a lot of people, but up to now those people have been incredibly kind and understanding and simply wished me well in my recovery. The guilt I've felt at knowing I'm leaving someone else to scrabble around and find a Plan B for their event has come entirely from my own head, and I mostly manage to put it into perspective. I make no secret that I have CFS, so there is an inherent risk in booking me. I have been managing that risk very successfully since 2012, either by planning my energy to ensure I have some when I need it or simply by pushing through when those plans go awry. Suddenly, just as unexpectedly to me as to everyone around me, I cannot do that at the moment.

Anyway, to get back to this latest conversation, I was not met with an expression of sympathy and good wishes, but by the assertion "You can't cancel the course. You have eleven students, and we can't lose all that money." My initial response was to ignore the fact that I cannot even manage one hour's conversation with a friend at the moment without ending up glassy-eyed, unable to focus or think, feeling faint, and having to lie down. What the lady on the other end of the phone was saying echoed a large part of my own mind: I don't want to give up; I'm sure I can find a way to fight through this. Nobody has told me that fighting through is damaging my body, so it feels rather pathetic not to fight on. I feel like I'm giving in, and that has never been in my nature. I found myself hanging up the phone having agreed to either look for another tutor to stand in my place or to teach the class for half the day. Panic began to set in: deep down, I knew I didn't have the energy to teach even half the day. I desperately just wanted to be taken seriously and allowed to take the sick leave I need. I resigned myself to starting to pack up beads ready for the course: I had several hours of preparation work ahead of me whether I taught or not. That bit, it seemed, was non-negotiable, so the best way of dealing with it would be to start now, so I could do it little by little and still rest in between sessions of work. My Mum phoned. When I told her what had happened, she exploded verbally: the anger she felt at that woman's attitude poured into my ear. The upshot: I found myself in floods of tears. My own anger was a little slower to follow.

I began by calling a couple of local beaders to ask if they were by any chance free. No joy. I called the summer school back and said I was only prepared to bring in the instructions and beading kits, spend only one hour getting people started, and then the ladies would have to be left to their own devices for the remainder of the day. In addition, I wanted to contact all the students to find out which project they would be doing and what colour beads they wanted—they had a choice of three projects, many colours—so that I could provide specific kits to save time on the day. That hour needed to be spent teaching, not messing around choosing beads. The lady said she would put this to the rest of the summer school committee and let me know in the morning.

Morning came and went with no news. Meantime my own anger was starting to surface. Why should I be treated like this? What if I had been phoning to say I had just had a heart attack—would the reaction have been the same? What if I got run over by a bus the day before the course— would they have reacted in this way? What if I woke up on the day of the course with gastric 'flu—would they have asked me to come in and vomit my way through the day? Surely not. So, why does CFS not count—why am I "not allowed" to actually be ill?

To cut a long story short, I called the summer school again in the afternoon of the second day. They had apparently been trying to find a new tutor with no success either. So, they had decided I was going to come in and teach from

10 a.m. to 12 p.m., and then a committee member who had some beading experience would supervise the group in the afternoon. I knew that even this arrangement would set me back physically, and why should I jeopardise my recovery in this way? In desperation, I put out an appeal on Facebook, and a fellow beader who lives 300 miles away came to my rescue. This time I emailed the organiser and told her exactly what I thought of her attitude. I was polite, but I made it clear just how angry I felt and how disappointed at her attitude that CFS should not be taken seriously. Her response: She was "upset," and, as it happened, she had a friend with CFS, so she did take it seriously and, moreover, she had just been trying to act in everyone's best interests. That was like a lit match to paper. Nothing in her reaction had been in my best interests: I wrote back and pointed out to her that it was not in my best interests to have been phoning and emailing to try to find another tutor. Now that I had done so, I was still looking at several hours' work in class preparation, none of which was in my best interests and for which I was not being paid, as the teaching fee would now go to the lady who had stepped into the breach. Neither was it in my best interests to have been given a guilt trip about how I was letting everyone down—did she think I didn't already know that? The only thing in my best interests was to be resting.

This did something to work through my anger, but some damage had already been done: The anger had led to an adrenaline kick that threw off my sleeping and resting pattern, and I was beginning to feel the effects. This is not a peculiar effect of CFS, nor is it a strange weakness in me, nor a reflection of my inability to deal with life. The fact is, when any of us feels under threat and this manifests as anger, it triggers a chain reaction of hormones that have physical impacts. It requires energy to be angry. This type of energy also takes away from the body's normal "maintenance" function. If your body is producing energy at 100%, and let's say it takes 2% of that energy to be angry, you are in effect losing two percentage points, so you're still functioning at 98% which is fine—you will hardly notice the difference. If your body is just producing 30% energy and you lose two percentage points, that leaves you at 28%. This is, relatively speaking, a much bigger impact. So, yes, this whole debacle had an impact. You might be sitting there thinking I'm stupid for getting angry about it—just ignore the silly woman and her ignorant reaction. Yes, fair point, but her ignorant reaction did increase my workload at a time when I should be focusing on rest. That ignorant reaction is also something I have to fight frequently. Why should I sit back and take it when someone tells me, albeit implicitly, that I'm not ill? I know the anger doesn't help me, but I'm not a saint, and I feel that anger was entirely justified, so the only path left is to work through it as fast as possible and then pick up the pieces.

I said there were two things that had been preying on my mind. The second is a question of time, more particularly a philosophical look at the strange relationship we have with time. As I have mentioned before, in my head I feel as though the last fourteen years of my life haven't happened. This is nothing other than a bad dream from which I will awaken as my twenty-six-year-old self and continue into that alternate reality where I get married and have kids or have the career on which I had embarked when I left university, or manage to do both. Yet, those past fourteen years have seen huge changes in my life: I've had a different career, but I've barely been able to notice it happening because of the constant battle to find the energy to allow it to happen. This year, reality hit, and I realised my body is not going to return to twenty-six with the prospect of having a family still ahead of me: That particular road is closed now. As I sit here, the last relapse has pushed me into researching more into the illness, and a part of me is asking why I did not do this before. Why did I not find a specialist before now? Why did I not get my thyroid tested? Why have I not pushed to have other vitamin and mineral levels tested? Reality check time: It is fourteen years since I was diagnosed with this illness and, although there isn't a lot of research going on relative to the amount being carried out for cancer, say, there has been some. In fact, some of the explanations I'm now reading did not exist fourteen years ago. Fourteen years is a really long time, given the pace at which human understanding grows and changes in the current age. Fourteen years is also a really long time in my life, but because I've been trying to blank that out, it's hard to see how much has changed in the world around me. This appointment may be another blind alley that leads nowhere, but it could be there is now knowledge that can help me which did not even exist when I first became ill. Sobering thought and time for me to stop, as I can feel the tiredness creeping back, so I'm off to rest.

Why pick out that entry from my journal? Well, at some point, I came to recognise my energy levels and physical symptoms were not only being affected by my physical activities. Emotional challenges and mental stress also played a part in my experience. Perhaps less obviously, from your perspective, this entry also indicates how much I resisted the illness and how hard I fought to ignore it and carry on with life as best I could. Denial was certainly a very large part of my coping strategy for many, many years. Now, I am not berating myself for this—although I did condemn myself for a while when I realised what I had been doing. At the time, given my level of knowledge and understanding, this combination of denial, attempting to cope, and attempting to carve out the best life I could was a brilliant adaptation.

I believed I had no choice but to live with CFS for the rest of my life. I was determined to live that life as fully as possible. It was several more years before I gained a new perspective: the idea that the illness might be inviting me to address some fundamental issues. By addressing those, not only did I end up overcoming the terrible physical pain I was experiencing, but I ended up living from a place of enrichment I had never imagined possible. So, with that background in place, let's move on to explore what is happening when we reach the psycho-emotional level of creation.

ENERGY SAVING AID

These are the essential points that are helpful for you to take away from the following section:

- *The psycho-emotional level creates 19% of your physical experience. That doesn't mean that your physical symptoms aren't real; simply that their root cause is in thoughts, emotions, and beliefs. So, if you want to experience improvement in your physical symptoms, you need to heal the disruptive emotions/thoughts/beliefs.*
- *These thoughts/emotions/beliefs reside in the biofield in the form of waves with a frequency. Waves of a particular frequency will attract waves of a similar frequency.*
- *If you detect problems being caused by low-frequency waves, you can raise their frequency by exposing them to higher-frequency waves and allowing the two sets to synchronise at the higher level.*
- *These principles of—Quantum—Physics underline how we can create change at this level and experience consequent improvements in energy and health.*

Psycho-Emotional Level

You may remember, I suggested, in the Four Levels of Creation model, the Psycho-Emotional level is responsible for 19% of what you attract and experience at the physical level. In other words, 19% of your physical symptoms are occurring because of issues rooted in the psycho-emotional arena. As my journal excerpt illustrated, my anger—emotion—had a direct impact on my hormones—physical—which created sleep issues and further depleted my energy. So, let me explain what is happening at this level. And, yes, you may start to feel like you're on firmer ground as we explore this layer. As you may have imagined from its name, this level is where you will find thoughts, beliefs, and emotions—what we might label as the "mind."

From the perspective of physics and the scientific creation process, this is where we get into Quantum physics and your little particles start doing really crazy stuff! They now take on a dual potential. They can be particles AND they are ALSO waves. If you want some evidence for this idea, then we can turn to another mind-bending physics experiment: the Double Slit Experiment.[38] In essence, it is the idea that a particle is BOTH a particle AND a wave until it is "observed," at which point it takes on the form of one or the other, depending on the perspective of the observer.[39] Yes, this is far crazier than the Mad Hatter's Tea Party. So, it's fine to follow Alice's lead here and simply enjoy the cupcakes and not worry if you don't fully understand the conversation right now! The reason I wanted to mention this is because it might help to give you a sense of why we were just talking about particles being guided into form by geometry in the previous layer, and now we're moving on to waves that begin working according to another set of rules: the rules of Quantum Physics.

---

38 This Wikipedia entry about the experiment will give you an overview and various links to explore if you wish to delve deeper: https://en.wikipedia.org/wiki/Double-slit_experiment

39 Specifically, that idea is the Relational Interpretation of what the experiment is telling us. You will also find other interpretations, not to mention plenty of discussion and disagreement amongst different scientists!

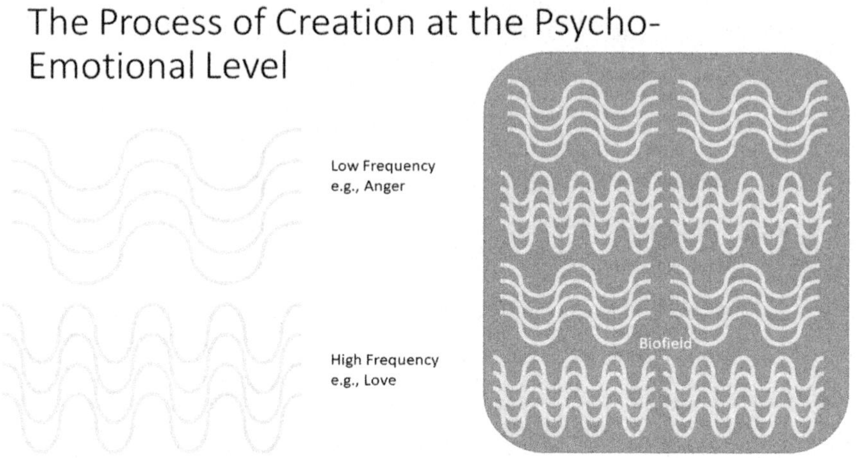

We also touched on this when we were exploring the biofield—your Energy body. This waveform creates a means of communication in the energy field, through resonance—waves on the same frequency talk to one another. So, in the image above, you can see two different wave patterns. The top pattern has fewer waves per second—or fewer waves across the same left-right distance—so is lower frequency. In emotional terms, this could be something like anger. In thought terms, this could be plotting to harm someone. The bottom pattern has more waves per second, so it is a higher frequency. Again, in emotional terms, this could be a positive emotion like love. In thought terms, this could be planning a kind gesture for someone.

On the right-hand side, we have a representation of the biofield, but this could be any of your body's fields. So, since I've just given an example using thoughts and emotions, let's see this particular field as the central nervous system. Within that field, you see wave patterns. When the thought or emotion with a matching wave pattern comes into the field, it will resonate with—"trigger"—the corresponding wave pattern(s) already in the field. The wave patterns can correspond to processes or cells, or whatever is required for the body to respond to its environment.

Sound is created through vibration. So, when one object vibrates at a certain frequency, it creates something known as a resonance. If it is near another object that holds the same resonance, then those two objects can communicate. To demonstrate this, you can use tuning forks. Take a tuning fork tuned to the note C and hit it to make it vibrate and produce a sound. If you sit it near another tuning fork also tuned to the note C, that tuning fork will automatically begin to vibrate and produce a sound, even though you haven't touched it. It simply responds to the vibrations of the first tuning fork. If you put the first tuning fork next to a tuning fork tuned to the note D, that D-fork would do nothing because it isn't resonant with the first fork. Here we are in a field of sound and light governed by frequency and resonance. So, if things are a little "off" in this field, we need to use tools of frequency and resonance to make changes.

What would those tools look like? Well, let me introduce you to another idea from the realm of physics. Noise spontaneously synchronises over time. Think of an audience clapping—given enough time, the random pattern of clapping will come together to form a unified pattern. UCLA Department of Physics and Astronomy created a beautiful short video demonstrating this phenomenon in action using metronomes. In the video, five metronomes are placed next to one another. The metronomes are set off one at a time. So, initially, they are all moving at different intervals. Over the course of a couple of minutes, they spontaneously synchronise, until they are all moving in the same direction at the same rate.[40] So, using this physics, it is possible to detect fields whose wave patterns have been distorted—second chart above—they will be sitting at a lower frequency.[41] Then,

---

40 You can watch the video here: https://youtu.be/T58lGKREubo

41 I am not saying this is the precise mechanism of the scan—I am simply trying to relate this to principles that may help you understand the idea of what is happening here.

if you expose them to a correct wave pattern—a higher frequency—over time, the lower frequency wave pattern will adjust to synchronise with the higher frequency wave pattern like the metronomes in the video I linked above. So, that element of the psycho-emotional level is now back in balance.

At this point in the creation process, we are starting to take all our calculations and turning them into a blueprint. Continuing with the analogy of the house, this would be like the architectural blueprint. Interestingly, to link this entire chain of events so far, we can turn to the science of Cymatics.[42] In simple terms, when you place a layer of fine powder—e.g., flour—onto something like a glass plate, and then expose that glass plate to a sound frequency, the powder will form into geometric patterns. This suggests that we have geometry—information—as the basis of frequency—sound.

This scientific explanation sets up an idea we will explore in parts three and four. In part three, we will be looking directly at the central nervous system and exploring how traumatic events lead to physiological adaptations. In effect, a traumatic event leads to a lowering of frequency in an area of the biofield, which translates into physical symptoms or issues in the physical body. Because the root cause of the physical symptom is at the level of the emotional frequency, just focusing on addressing the physical symptom is not going to change the distorted or lowered frequency. So, the problem will not fully resolve. You might experience some level of respite, and you may also discover the symptoms change and shift. Full resolution will only come about when you address the emotional issue at the level of frequency. We do have tools, treatments, and protocols that work at that level. So, that is what we will explore in part four.

---

42 Experiments of this nature have been attributed to Galileo in the 1630s, Robert Hook in 1680, and Chladni in 1787. Modern study by Hans Jenny—1967 and 1972 books Kymatic—has continued to fascinate. You probably won't be surprised to hear that modern analysis has also termed this study a pseudoscience.

ENERGY SAVING AID

These are the essential points that are helpful for you to take away from the following section:

- *This level also has metaphysical implications. In the last chapter, we looked at Karma. That is stored as coding in the Intuitive level, but it also has an emotional charge stored at this level—Psycho-Emotional.*
- *If you have incarnated with a lot of Karma to clear, you may be carrying a lot of low-frequency vibrational energy in your biofield. This will attract low-frequency events—challenges. They are not designed to be a punishment, but rather an invitation to see the low-frequency patterns and take steps to raise their frequency.*

The Law of Attraction

Before we move on to the more comfortable physical level, I will just link this level back to the exploration of Karma we began in the last chapter. Your experiences are recorded as data in the Akashic record using geometric coding. However, as we know on the physical plane, an event is often accompanied by a set of emotions in response to that event. The same is true on the Karmic level. Those emotions are also stored here in the Psycho-Emotional Level, in the form of *charge*—the common currency at the electro-magnetic level. So, for example, you might find you have a deep, deep fear of something, but you can't recall an event that took place in this lifetime which could explain your fear. Perhaps you have a fear of sharks, yet you live in England and have never been near shark-infested water in your life. Maybe you watched the film *Jaws* when you were quite young, and the movie really, really scared you. So, yes, that could have caused your fear of sharks. What if your fear had begun before you ever watched *Jaws?* Well, you might say, "Everyone knows sharks are dangerous. I've just heard stories about people being killed by sharks." What if you were killed by a shark in a previous life? The event would create a record in the Akash—a piece of data. At the same time, it creates an emotional charge: a fear you never resolved because you died before you had the chance to process the trauma. So, in your next life, unprocessed trauma is creating a little disruption in your bio-field at this level of creation.

If you do have any interest in spirituality, then you may have come across the idea of the *Law of Attraction*. In the last chapter, I talked about how Karma can be viewed as a tool for gaining experience and spiritual growth. Well, the *Law of Attraction* is the mechanism that enables it to happen. So, that disruption in your biofield caused by the shark attack, is basically like a wave at a very particular frequency. That frequency is going to attract events, people, and opportunities vibrating at the same frequency. Those would be the souls who agreed to help you in your mission or the people from past lives with whom you have unresolved Karma. The opportunities are an invitation for you to process your traumatic experience fully and move on to experience something different. Of course, you have the free will to choose whether or not to do this.

Let me try to illustrate this idea with a fictional example. Imagine your best friend wins a holiday in a tropical location and invites you to join them. You jump at the chance. As part of this amazing prize, you both get to go on a boat trip in waters where sharks could, possibly, be present. You know about the possibility of sharks, but you really want to do this boat trip, and nobody is going to make you go swimming, so you feel OK about this. However, by some random accident, you somehow manage to fall overboard; but it's OK, you're wearing a lifejacket and can swim, and the boat has stopped and is just working out how to get you back on board. So, you are safe—except for your fear of sharks and for your awareness there could, just possibly, be a shark waiting to come to attack you. Now, it is possible this event could lead to a trauma response in you. Remember, we are going to be exploring your central nervous system and trauma in part three of the book. So, if this scenario happens, and your beautiful boat trip leaves you with PTSD, it opens up two possible pathways. It might prompt you to seek help, end up being successfully treated for the PTSD, and in the process also overcome your fear of sharks. Or, you could simply end up traumatised—or perhaps, more accurately, retraumatised—by the event and, instead of seeking help, just decide you can never safely go near the sea again. You have the free will to choose your outcome: post-traumatic growth or permanent loss.

Of course, you may also take a more conscious decision to overcome your fear of sharks. Perhaps you find yourself with a desire—and opportunity—to go swim on the Great Barrier Reef, but you know there are sharks off the coast of Australia. You may not be certain they are waiting for you at the Reef, but the general possibility is enough to put you off the idea. However, swimming in the Reef is on your bucket list, so you decide to stop being held back by your fear and to find a way to overcome the fear and enjoy a wonderful experience. Whatever resonates—or not!—with you, I simply wish to illustrate how understanding this model of creation can help you to identify the root cause of a problem and to treat it at the root, so it resolves permanently. We are going to delve deeper into that idea in a later chapter.

ENERGY SAVING AID

These are the essential points that are helpful for you to take away from the following section:

- *Thoughts, emotions, and beliefs are held as Energy vibrating at a particular frequency in your biofield. These end up manifesting as behavioural patterns and physical symptoms that feel challenging.*
- *If you wish to adjust—improve—symptoms resulting from low-frequency thoughts/emotions/beliefs, you need to use treatments that work on the level of frequency.*
- *You may not have considered this before, but your illness might be here as an invitation to experience growth. How do you achieve this? By becoming curious and examining your symptoms, learning lessons, and stopping your resistance to them. You have greater healing power than you may realise.*

How Does This Level Relate to CFS?

There are three ideas I would like you to take away from this chapter. The first is the idea your emotions, thoughts, and beliefs are held as Energy in this field. If you could look at them, they would appear like waves, each wave vibrating at a specific frequency. That frequency will resonate—communicate—with other waves of the same frequency. Eventually, those Energy waves will compress to the degree they manifest into something physical, but we have not yet reached that point in our exploration. However, when they do take on that physical form, they will manifest as patterns of behaviour. We engage in those patterns in order to try to protect ourselves, based on our current understanding of what is threatening us and how we can best deal with those threats. In reality, if that understanding is based upon low-frequency emotions—for example fear—and beliefs—for example, I am powerless—then the resulting behaviours will attract more situations to reinforce our perspective. If we can become aware of our patterns and recognise different choices are available to us, we can begin to enjoy different experiences. This is a very brief outline of the concept of trauma we will be exploring in depth in part three. So, don't worry if this is not yet making sense to you.

The second idea is this: If you want to make adjustments to the frequency of your waves, then you need to do this by using other waves. In other words, working with frequency and resonance. That means the type of treatments capable of making adjustments at this level are treatments operating using frequency and resonance. Sound Therapy is a very obvious example. Emotional Freedom Technique—EFT or Tapping—is another common example. NLP—Neuro Linguistic Programming—will also work at this level. Again, we are going to talk more about specific treatments in part four, so I just want to introduce those ideas for now.

The third idea is the possibility your illness is here to invite growth. It manifested in response to a challenge. The illness is forcing you to slow down and step out of life, and it is keeping you safe from being exposed to that challenge. So, it is a sensible adaptation to a challenging environment. You are welcome to accept that adaptation and make adjustments to live with your symptoms. Or, you can address the challenge, not by suppressing, ignoring, or by-passing your symptoms; they need to be explored to unpack the messages they are trying to deliver. Understanding and addressing those messages opens the doorway to growth.

I appreciate these may not be messages you wish to hear. I hope my opening journal entry helped to illustrate I was not willing to explore this viewpoint at first. In my own journey, I have tried all three variations: ignoring the messages, adapting to them, and then, finally, listening and learning. So, wherever you are right now and wherever you choose to travel in the future is OK. I am simply bringing your attention to another point of interest in your maze. I also need to emphasise that whatever challenges or discomfort you are feeling in relation to these ideas may be greatly alleviated in part three of the book. We will be moving away from the spiritual or metaphysical discussion and into a much more practical level. So, I invite you to remain curious, open, and patient as we follow the paths to reach that point.

ENERGY SAVING AID

Please complete the following practice. The information this uncovers is going to help you create your unique roadmap for recovery.

Your Invitation to Practice

Please grab your journal and write down your responses and reflections in answer to the following questions:

- Has this chapter brought up any uncomfortable emotions for you? If so, which emotions, and which parts of the chapter brought them up?
- What do you think about the ideas in this chapter?
- Make a list of all the things you wish to be able to do in life, but which you can't do because of your CFS.
- Make a list of all the ways having CFS has improved your life. For example, maybe you feel happier spending time on your own or happier because you don't have to do a job you dislike, or maybe someone looks after you. To be clear, this is NOT me suggesting you are deliberately making up your illness or

even that you are enjoying the experience: I am sure neither of those things is true. Yet every experience in life brings us challenges and benefits, and I am inviting you to view your CFS experience from two perspectives. Believe it or not, this understanding is going to help you see where you can focus most effectively on your recovery path. So, even though this request is going to challenge you, don't skip it!

Chapter 8

The Physical Level

This level is where we finally experience a physical object: something that we can see, hear, feel, touch, smell, and taste. At this level, we are working with classical physics, chemistry, and biology. So, if you are anything like me, this will be the level on which you have primarily focused your search for answers to CFS. Since this is the level with which you are probably already most familiar, and since we are going to be exploring elements of this level in more depth in part three, the focus of this chapter is going to be on bringing things together. We will look briefly at this level and the tools you can use to make changes here. Before moving into that, let me set you up with a journal extract from my own CFS experience.

> *ENERGY SAVING AID*
>
> *The following journal excerpt frames the discussion themes for this chapter, but it is my personal story, so not essential to read if you are low on energy.*

Journal: November 2016

I had the second set of blood test results on Tuesday. It turns out there are three things showing up as blockages on my Translocator protein. Before I come back to them, a little aside on the Translocator protein. In "science speak," Translocator is simply about chemicals moving from one side of the Mitochondrial membrane to the other. A protein helps them to move, and it is the movement of this protein that has been partially blocked in my case. The movement is important, as this is essentially the recycling of ADP—Adenosine Di-Phosphate—back into ATP—Adenosine Tri-Phosphate—ready for the Mitochondria to use to fire off more energy for the cell.

Right. Back to the blockages. One substance is thought to be a residue from antibiotics. Interestingly, the last time I had any antibiotics was just a few weeks before I collapsed in November 2002. I leave you to draw your own conclusions. Moving forward, I apparently need to find out what the antibiotic was, and I'm going to need to take care if I'm prescribed antibiotics in future. Although, as we all know, we should all be avoiding antibiotics except under the direst of life and death situations.

The second substance is a chemical called Polyoxymethylene. This is commonly used in detergents. My first act was to take out all my bottles of household cleaners and cosmetics and check their ingredients. To my disappointment, most of them do not list the ingredients. Tracking down whether or not this chemical is used in any particular product is harder than one might think, I have just discovered. So, I have taken the decision to "go eco." Even then, I've had to search a lot to be sure that I have a "truly" eco brand. It may or may not surprise you to know some brands are jumping on the eco bandwagon when in fact their ingredients are perhaps not as "natural" as they might be. Having said this, it will be impossible for me to completely eradicate my exposure to this chemical, as it will also be in my water supply. I don't have to drink tap water, but I do have to wash in it and use it in my household appliances, not to mention everywhere I come into contact with it outside my home. All those chemicals in the household cleaning products we use don't simply disappear: They are washed into our water system, and the purification through which it goes to make it "safe" to drink doesn't remove all the many chemicals we have added to it. It is probably worth my while to say I have never thought of myself as a particularly "green" person. I may make the odd nod towards looking after the environment, not being too wasteful, and so on, but I am neither fully informed, nor much of a participant in a truly "green" lifestyle. That may change, to some degree at least. If you do see me popping up in future as a green activist, then you will know this transformation came about as a result of physically experiencing the negative effects of modern life, not as a theoretical argument about the way we choose to live.

The final blocker is a substance my own body manufactures. I won't bore you with the scientific name—I'm not sure I can even pronounce it!—but the substance is designed to help the cell to oxygenate. When the cell is inhibited, this natural substance is turned into a compound that attaches itself to the genes of either the cell or the Mitochondrion—or presumably both; I'm not sure. In some very rare cases, i.e., mine, it attaches to the Translocator. I gather I may have caused some small excitement in the lab, as every good scientist likes to see evidence of a rare phenomenon, so I'm happy to have obliged.

The positive news from all of this is that, with the right support from supplements—levels of several key minerals in my Mitochondria have also been tested and reveal deficiencies—there is a very good chance of healing, my specialist tells me. With any luck, if I give them the materials they need, my little Mitochondria will recognise the foreign agents and get rid of them. So, there is a lot more science coming in here, with which I am not yet totally—at all?!—familiar, but it involves Lysosomes and a process called Super Oxide Dismutase. So, I'm off to do some research.

I now feel as though I am standing here holding a jigsaw puzzle in its box. It is a very large, very complicated jigsaw puzzle, but I want to try to put it all together. I'm not sure if I have all the pieces. Perhaps it will turn out some are missing. Perhaps some pieces from a completely different puzzle have got mixed up in the box. Maybe I will find more pieces hiding down the back of the sofa before I'm done. Before I can answer that, I need to patiently sit here and see what the supplements do. I have taken one day's worth of the detox—please do not confuse that with "detox" diets that polarise people as they argue whether these are potentially harmful fads or genuine science: my "detox" is not one of those; I simply don't have another term to use—part of the package and eight days' worth of the energy building package number two. I have hope, but no guarantees. I also have a promise this is not the end of the road and there is a Plan B to try to tackle these blockages if Plan A doesn't come up trumps.

I decided to share that particular journal entry as it marked a huge turning point for me. It was only after my second crash, in 2016, I finally found a specialist able to carry out some blood tests. He requested testing of my Mitochondrial function. For anyone who is not familiar—I certainly wasn't before all this started—your Mitochondria are like the batteries for the cells in your body. They produce the energy—ATP—that powers each cell. When you are considering an illness largely defined by lack of energy, it surely makes sense to look at the body's source of energy, doesn't it?

By this point in time, I had been living with CFS for fourteen years, so why had nobody done this sooner? In fairness to the original specialist to whom I was referred in 2003, I don't think the blood test for checking Mitochondrial function was available at that time. All that to say, it took fourteen years before I was given any physical evidence of a problem in my body. I had always been convinced my body had something physically wrong: these symptoms weren't simply coming from my mind, and were most certainly NOT any form of hypochondria. So, to find myself finally holding a piece of paper with lab test results confirming my beliefs, felt miraculous.

Was this the solution for me? Unfortunately, not. It was the start of a long, winding road that has brought me to writing this book. That road also ended up taking me back to review my beliefs about the connections between mind, emotions, and physical symptoms. In other words, my journey started at this level of creation and worked its way back up towards the top level. I will be sharing more of that as we continue, but that rather more hopeful journal entry does seem like a good introduction to our exploration of the physical level of creation.

ENERGY SAVING AID

These are the essential points that are helpful for you to take away from the following section:

- *The Physical level is where you are probably most familiar. This is where your physical body resides, along with everything else that you can see, hear, touch, taste, and smell. At this level, classical physics, biology, and chemistry govern things. In terms of disease and healing, the focus is primarily on biology and chemistry.*
- *Bringing all the levels together, you can use the analogy of building a house. At this level, the physical house appears. Whether it is complete and built as planned will be determined by how well the architect carried out the calculations, how accurately the draftsman drew the plans, and whether or not the builder followed the blueprint. If something is "wrong" with the house, you need to identify at which level of creation the original error occurred, and to make the correction at that level. This makes perfect sense within the analogy of building a house, but have you ever considered what that means if you are building a body? The Four Levels of Creation model is about considering that we may need to take a wider view of our physical symptoms and their origin if we wish to truly resolve them and heal.*

The Physical Level

So, now, after exploring metaphysics and psychology—geometry and physics—we arrive at the physical level. This is the point at which the creative flow manifests as a physical object. On this level, the action is governed by the laws of classical physics, biology, and chemistry. This is the point your physical body comes into being. So, your particles have become atoms, then cells, and are now building the human body. Or, to continue with the other analogy I have been using, the architectural blueprint for your house is now being turned into reality as builders lay bricks, plumbers add the piping, electricians wire it up, and roofers seal the structure. If that process has flowed without incident, then you have a perfect physical manifestation of the idea you originally created.

What if the physical manifestation isn't perfect? Or what if it develops some faults? Could it be the builder cut a few corners and didn't read the architectural plan properly or didn't use the materials recommended? Potentially. Could it be that the draftsman made a mistake whilst creating the blueprint and accidentally forgot to mark in a door, or wrote down the wrong number on the measurements of the room? Again, potentially. Or, could it be that the architect made a mistake in the mathematical calculations? Yes, that could also have happened. The error also could have occurred at just one of those levels or multiple levels. If there were multiple errors, perhaps they each occurred independently, or perhaps the error on one level caused the error on the next level. The point is, unless you are aware that all these levels exist, and unless you manage to identify at which level the error took place, and also manage to correct it at that level, you are not going to end up with a perfect house. My personal recovery journey led me to understand the same thing is true of the physical body. Even though we may be experiencing physical symptoms that are very real and can be documented through lab tests, the reason *why* these symptoms are occurring may lie at a different level of the creative process.

So, returning to our house-building analogy for a moment, let's consider what happens when there is a problem at the physical level. Let's imagine you receive a call to say your house is complete and ready for you to enjoy. Excitedly, you rush along to admire the beautiful structure. When you arrive, you feel a little confused: Something doesn't look quite right. You stare at the structure for a moment, wondering what is "off," and then realise it's missing the front door. Frankly, that's a bit of a disaster. So, how are you going to fix it? You could start by going and shouting at the builder. After all, he was the one who didn't put the door in place. "Well," he turns around and says, "The blueprint never mentioned anything about a door!" Sure enough, when you check the blueprint, the door is missing. You may go back to your draftsman and demand to know why he didn't put the door on the plans. Perhaps he acknowledges that he got distracted and simply forgot. Or perhaps he says it wasn't in the calculations. Maybe the issue goes even higher and it turns out the original idea was missing the door for some reason. Was this an oversight, or was it a deliberate experiment to see what a house would look like if it had no front door?

Now, to develop this analogy one step further. If you had gone to the builder and complained about the lack of a door, he might have said, "Well, it wasn't on the plans, but I'll just put one in now. Leave it to me." If he didn't have enough understanding of the mathematical calculations underpinning the structure, he might just knock a door through where he thought best—but guess what? In the process, he weakened the structure and the entire house came tumbling down.

You may be sitting there thinking, "Yes, but this is just a silly story. The house doesn't even exist. I thought we were supposed to be talking about my health and my body here." Have you considered that if we—

collectively; I am not assigning any judgement or blame here—have only been looking at one level of creation, we may have been missing critical information and insights? You may feel that isn't the case. Perhaps you believe we are looking at the correct level; we just haven't done enough research or gained enough knowledge yet. I have no proof you would be wrong. All I have here is my personal experience and the research carried out by others. The more levels I explored, the more fully and sustainably my body healed. The more I sought to understand what was working—and not working—for me, the more I discovered research that supported this idea of flow between the layers. So, let's move on to look first at the flow between levels and then at the tools that fit into the physical level.

ENERGY SAVING AID

These are the essential points that are helpful for you to take away from the following section:

- *In each of the previous Levels of Creation, we have seen how each layer bleeds into the next: the issues at one layer have an impact on what happens in the next layer. The same is true with the physical level.*
- *We look at three discrete areas in which scientific research has shown a clear correlation between thoughts and feelings and the physical symptoms that result. In other words, the psycho-emotional level has a direct impact on the physical level. These three examples are: the science of Psychoneuroimmunology, our understanding of genetics, and the curious case of the symptomology of Multiple Personality Disorder.*

A Beautiful Flow

If you remember, in the last chapter, we looked at how the Intuitive level flows into and overlaps with the Psycho-Emotional level. In that case, we identified that Karma sitting at the Intuitive level could bring in trauma patterns, which reside as a frequency wave pattern at the Psycho-Emotional level. Well, the same type of flow occurs between the Psycho-Emotional and Physical levels. In other words, we have scientific studies—and whole branches of science—that have documented how Psycho-Emotional issues create Physiological symptoms. Covering all that would be an entire book—maybe even an encyclopaedic set—in its own right! However, I would like to share some fascinating examples that grabbed my attention as I was learning more about this idea.

First, let me mention an entire system of research: psychoneuroimmunology. Robert Ader and Nicholas Cohen coined this term in 1975 as a way of framing the study of the interrelationship between the nervous, endocrine, and immune systems. In some sense, as I mentioned earlier in this book, the idea of this inter-relationship is as old as time. In ancient tribes, a Shamanic healer would look for emotional or spiritual issues, as well as physiology when treating a patient. Indigenous populations throughout the world have, traditionally, had an awareness that we are a whole person. So, this "new" science could be seen as Western ideology catching on to ancient truths.

Science has been mapping the close link between the nervous system, the endocrine system, and the immune system. In essence, what that means is your nervous system may perceive a danger. This threat could be physical, mental, or emotional. The nervous system signals to the endocrine system the body is under threat. The endocrine system responds by sending out "stress hormones"—danger signals—to the body's cells. The cells pick up this signal, and the immune system launches an attack. This is brilliant if the danger happens to be a virus or bacteria. However, if the threat is emotional in nature—for example, an argument with a loved one—the physiological immune system is less well-placed to do anything. In an ideal world, the threat is addressed, and the nervous system picks up that the danger has passed. It sends the "all-clear" signal to the endocrine system, which, in turn, releases the "safe" hormones to let the immune system know it can stand down. Studying this is bringing to light how this system, if not understood, can end up creating physical symptomology. For example, if the original danger is emotional and it is not resolved, the immune system is left in fight mode and may be attacking the physical body. The result: an illness with the label of some kind of auto-immune disease. A common example could be thyroid disease. Focusing on treating this at the physiological level, solutions might be thyroid hormones, perhaps even the removal of the thyroid gland. As anyone with a thyroid condition will tell you, this solution often feels like walking a tightrope of trying to control the symptoms via medication rather than a "cure." So, from a psychoneuroimmunological perspective, what happens if we begin looking at the whole person and addressing underlying emotional issues as well? That does not mean focusing solely on the emotions; it is about creating a comprehensive model of treatment. This may include using nutritional and supplemental interventions, getting the biorhythm back on track, looking at exercise and movement, and then bringing in meditation and mindfulness. Physiotherapy, psychotherapy, and pharmacological drugs may also be needed. So, this is taking a multi-layered, multi-disciplinary approach to an illness.

That is just one example. This science is still delving deeper and has not yet become fully mainstream, but it certainly turns traditional thinking about auto-immune disease on its head. In part three, we are going to be looking at how that idea applies to our understanding of CFS. Again, when viewed from a purely symptomatic perspective,

CFS is confusing. Yet if you start to bring in the nervous system and understand its role as a master controller of the body, an entirely new perspective opens up.

So, is this the only science making concrete links between thoughts, beliefs, and emotions and physiological symptoms? No. In the last chapter, I mentioned the science of epigenetics. If you recall, this is the study of how our genes interact with the environment. Dr. Bruce Lipton's research indicates that only 5% of our genes are "set." The remaining 95% can be switched on or off. He speaks about the environment being the factor that determines this switching process. In other words, if you wish to change your genes, change your environment. What do we mean by the environment? Is this physical? In part, yes, but it also includes your emotional environment and the landscape of your thoughts, beliefs, and behaviours.

I particularly love a study that Dr. Lipton details involving Telomeres. These are the specific DNA-Protein structures found at both ends of your chromosome. They play a vital role in preserving the information in our genome. In the normal cell division process, a part of the Telomere is—deliberately—cut off. This doesn't contain any critical genomic information, so its loss doesn't affect your genetic blueprint. However, it is finite in length. Or, at least, it was thought so until 2009. If it is understood to be finite, then, at some point in your life, your genome would have lost its Telomere and, as the process of cell division continued, you would begin losing your DNA sequencing. That would lead to ageing and death. In fact, this will happen eventually. However, it turns out that Telomeres can grow. If we live wisely, we can consistently maintain our Telomeres and, hence, prolong a healthy cell division, allowing us to enjoy better overall health for longer. Your Telomeres require an enzyme called Telomerase to facilitate this growth. In 2009, Dr. Elizabeth H. Blackburn, Carol W. Greider, and Jack W. Szostak were jointly awarded the Nobel

Prize in Medicine or Physiology for making this discovery. Having discovered Telomerase, further research looked at how the enzyme is created and what ingredients we require to maintain—or increase—its supply in the body. Yes, there are physiological factors, but Dr. Lipton and others have discovered that emotions like love and gratitude also contribute to creating a healthy supply of Telomerase. Literally, a gratitude practice can help to lengthen your life. As Dr. Lipton puts it, gratitude is the elixir of youth!

The final intriguing piece of research I would like to leave you to consider relates to the psychiatric condition called Multiple Personality Disorder. The name says clearly what this diagnosis means: a single person who exhibits multiple personalities. Each personality is fully formed and very different. One might be a seven-year-old boy and another a forty-five-year-old woman, for example. They exist in the same physical body at the same time. At any given time, one personality will manifest, whilst the others remain dormant. This manifestation may exist for a few minutes, a few hours, or even days or weeks. The person experiencing this will experience themselves *fully* in the dominant personality at that time, perhaps with no awareness of the other personalities. If you want to see this from a non-medical context, the film *Split*, directed by M. Knight Shyamalan, is built around a character with this diagnosis.

However, the reason I mention this here is to bring to light the fascinating observation that these different personalities can also have a completely different physiology. So, for example, one may be asthmatic and another not. Fascinatingly, when tested, the body will exhibit the physiological traits of the condition. So, this is not simply the mind "thinking" it has asthma and mimicking asthmatic symptoms: the entire physiology changes. When the personality switches to the non-asthmatic version, the physiology changes again, so asthma symptoms are no longer present, and neither are the biomarkers of the condition. This switch can take place in a second, which throws into question everything that we believe about our physiology being formed separate and unchangeable.

I invite you to explore further along these avenues if you wish. I hope those examples have created a new perspective for you to consider. In Western society, we have tended to take the view something in the mind can be changed and something in the body cannot. Also, we are somehow more responsible—more to blame—for what we create in the mind, and more of a hapless victim of our physiology. Rather than appreciating if we can create our experience, it is very empowering, we have tended to take the view that those who create a less-than-desirable experience are somehow inferior. I would like to invite you to consider that all of us are creating our experience; once we fully acknowledge that, we become empowered to create what we truly desire, rather than suffering the illusion of victimhood if our experience feels unpleasant. For now, though, let's turn back to the physical level. If you wish to create change purely focusing on that level, how would you do this?

ENERGY SAVING AID

These are the essential points that are helpful for you to take away from the next two sections:

- *If you wish to focus purely on physiological symptoms and physical tools, then you may be looking at things like pharmaceutical drugs, surgery, nutritional supplements, and yoga. Basically, a diverse range of protocols work on the physiology, biology, or chemistry of the body in some way.*
- *If you are looking at some newer modalities like PEMF therapy, EFT, and Vagus Nerve Stimulators, consider how they work. Are they focusing on biology and chemistry or are they using the principles of physics?*
- *At the end of the day, the important point is to recognise we operate as a whole person, and we need to be considering both the origin of problems and the tools to solve them from the perspective of all levels of our being.*

What Tools Should We Be Using at the Physical Level?

Typically, when we are talking about healing or recovery, we will be looking at treatments. So, let's think of those as "tools." This will probably come as no surprise to you: The tools that work best for the purely physical level are going to be physical tools. So, I am thinking of things like pharmaceutical drugs, nutritional supplements, and supportive tools like a plaster cast or bandage. Also consider actions applied to the physical state: for example, medical surgery or changing lifestyle habits, such as trying a different diet. If you have been researching treatment protocols, then you might be aware of some newer machines and modalities. I am thinking about things like the

Vagus Nerve Stimulator, Heart Rate Variability monitors, Pulsed Electro-Magnetic Frequency machines, or protocols like Emotional Freedom Technique. As we are about to explore, the idea all of these new tools and modalities operate at the purely physical level is open for debate. How do you know what is operating physically and what is operating at one of the higher levels of creation? You need to ask *what* the machine is doing or *how* it operates. A machine that operates via electrical or magnetic pulses could be operating on the psycho-emotional level because it is attempting to change the frequency of a part of the body.

Talk therapies are another area where the delineation may seem unclear. Again, in my understanding of this model, the answer lies in how the therapy is designed to work. If it is designed to talk about your reactions to events and guide you to change the way you respond in future, then I would classify this as operating at the physical level. If talk therapy also combines some element working with the Energy body, then it is designed to be effective at creating change at the Psycho-Emotional level. Before this opens up arguments as to which healing modalities sit at which level, I invite you to consider the purpose of this model is to bring you to a new awareness. I am not trying to get into a strict definition of what sits where. A general idea you may need to consider different levels and mix together different healing modalities is all that you require right now. Let me return to bringing the entire Four Levels of Creation model into perspective.

Is Any of This Relevant to Health and Healing?

I acknowledge that the entire Part Two of this book may have felt like a complete digression away from the subject of CFS or even from the more general discussion of illness and healing. You may not have signed up for an exploration of ideas that seem to belong to the realm of metaphysics or Spirituality. So, why did I include this? Well, I have noted a few times that the main reason for my attempting to explain any of this was to introduce you to the idea that your body is greater than the physical elements you can detect with your five senses. This is not a new idea. In fact, my entire CFS journey has been peppered with references to this idea. I have very clear memories of reading Louise Hay's book, *You Can Heal Yourself*, back in 2012. I loved the book, but I was not open to the idea of considering my physical symptoms as messages from my emotional or spiritual body at that time. My bookshelf now also contains Inna Segal's book, *The Secret Language of Your Body*. That also describes a system whereby physical symptoms can be read as messages from trapped emotions or current experiences. John Sarno is another great doctor whose work led him to explore the idea of pain being a symptom of a mental or emotional block. Another of my personal favourites is the book, *Letting Go: The Pathway of Surrender*, by Dr. David R. Hawkins.

Now, I am not insisting you immediately switch to the belief nothing occurs at the physical level and everything is about emotions and beliefs. There is certainly more and more evidence to support that view, but it is important to recognise it is a belief system just as the idea every ailment needs to be healed by a conventionally trained medical physician is a belief system. My personal belief system has undergone some pretty major shifts. Let's look at those two potential belief systems as polarity points: the opposite ends of a spectrum. Transitioning from one end to the other is not—necessarily—going to happen in one great leap. I now sit at the "midway" point where I liked to reference Louise Hay, or John Sarno, or Jacques Martel, or David Hawkins to provide me with balance. Not because I suddenly came to the belief *everything* is about my emotions but because I like to see if I am covering all potential areas. Yes, my physical symptoms may need a visit to the doctor, a pharmaceutical painkiller, or a modification to my diet. At the same time, they may also be alerting me to an emotional or psychological area I would benefit from exploring. I could elect to follow *either* the physical route *or* the emotional route, but I feel I derive more benefit from considering *both*.

If you are open to recognising "you" may be made from more than just your physical body, it opens up the possibility the issues you experience in your physical body could have root causes somewhere else and there could be ways in which you can try to address those root causes at a non-physical level. Think of yourself like an iceberg. There is a tiny part at the top everyone else can see above the water line, but the majority of you is not visible unless someone happens to look beneath the water line. If only the watchmen on the Titanic had eyes below the water that April night in 1912! The relevance of this idea is that as long as we focus all of our awareness on the physical level, we risk missing something important below the water. We also risk missing a possible understanding, by correcting something sitting below the water line, it will end up changing things above the surface. This is how complex systems operate. Even if you are aware of all the levels, it is still very difficult to determine precisely how one change below the surface is going to end up manifesting in another area.[43] The beauty of making this realisation is that a symptom which previously seemed to be impossible to resolve may suddenly become very treatable. Simply by considering a different level of creation and working with tools designed to heal at that level, you may experience miracles. I have felt it myself and seen it in others.

We are going to develop this idea in much more detail over the next few chapters. So, hold on to the ideas for now, and I hope this model is beginning to open up a possible framework for understanding your experience of CFS. Once again, it is important to emphasise we are working with a complex system. So, we are not looking for *the one* cause or *the one* treatment. We are seeking to create balance within

---

43 If you wish to explore those ideas, then we would need to turn to the mathematical model of Chaos Theory or look at something like the Butterfly Effect.

the whole, and that may involve working with layers of treatments. Each layer flows into the next. Cumulatively, they form one beautiful, complete whole. To conceptualise this, we have needed to break things down: in effect, to draw a map. In parts three and four, we will be exploring how you begin to determine which paths are going to be helpful for your personal journey.

ENERGY SAVING AID

These are the essential points that are helpful for you to take away from the following section:

- *I briefly put the Four Levels of Creation model into my own recovery journey and explain why I feel my personal experience is testimony to the effectiveness of using this model for recovery.*
- *This sets up the next section of the book, where we will move back to looking at the physical experience of living with CFS and how that could map onto the model.*

What Is the Point of This Theory?

You may have found this a fascinating, thought-provoking journey so far. Or maybe you didn't understand any of it. Perhaps you even feel I have been leading you a merry dance through paths of fantasy there to bamboozle you and make you vulnerable to some kind of insidious manipulation. So, why have I taken you along this path? Because it has been my personal experience the human body is responsive to and reactive to its entire environment. That means the parts we can see, hear, smell, taste, and touch and the parts about which we can only theorise and argue. I freely confess if you had told me twenty years ago I would be writing something like this, much less hoping anyone would take it seriously, I would not have believed you. To be honest, I am still a little sceptical as to how many people will take it seriously, but I'm happy to welcome you on whatever level you feel comfortable today and invite you to explore further as and when you feel ready.

I started in 2002 from the firm belief my CFS was purely physical and needed a purely physical treatment. I explored many avenues on that level. Yes, I received benefits, but I still had CFS. This left me with a choice:

- Accept CFS is for life.
- Try a different path.

I chose to try a different path. Without realising I was doing this, I moved to the next level of Creation: The Psycho-Emotional layer. Again, I explored a lot of avenues, using psycho-emotional tools like Mickel Therapy and Emotional Freedom Technique. Again, I found myself improved but still not recovered. So, once again, I found myself contemplating a choice between accepting my situation and trying something different—and, yet again, I chose to explore a new path.

I didn't realise it when I started down this new path, but I stumbled upon the next layer of Creation: The Intuitive level. And, yes, this has been mind-blowing and nonsensical and brought me to explore ideas and concepts I never thought I would be open to. However, right now, my life is opening up into a world I could not have imagined to be possible. My aim was to get back to where I started before getting ill. I found I have discovered a level of existence I have not previously experienced. I wanted to share my discovery to open up a path for others to follow. Whether or not you choose to take your version of this journey is entirely up to you. Let's remember, we are still only partway through the story. So, having explored your vehicle—body—from a new perspective, it is time to move on and take another look at your environment—the CFS maze. In the next section, we are going to begin that exploration at the physical level by taking a look at some common symptoms of a CFS diagnosis. Then, we will work our way back up through the levels, specifically exploring the role played by trauma.

> *ENERGY SAVING AID*
>
> *Please complete the following practice. This will help you become aware of the information you need to create your unique roadmap for recovery.*

An Invitation to Practice

Once more, I invite you to take your journal and use the following prompts to continue adding to your self-awareness:

- How does this chapter make you *feel*?
    - Note down any emotions you are feeling in response to this information. If it doesn't make you feel anything, that's OK, too—just make a note of that.
- What do you *think* about the information in this chapter?
    - Note which ideas are new to you and which are familiar.
- Has any of the information in this chapter changed the way you think and feel about the other levels of creation?
- Bringing your focus back to your own experience, list the symptoms you are currently experiencing. Considering each of your individual symptoms or the set as a whole, answer the following questions:
    - Have you sought treatment for this symptom/symptom set?

  - Have you experienced any improvements as a result of any treatments?
  - Have any symptoms improved naturally? If so, what was happening at that time in your life?

- Has any of the information in this section prompted you to think differently about where you are looking for answers about CFS?

Part 3

Understanding the Terrain of the Maze

Chapter 9

Exploring the Physical Symptoms of CFS

I am going to invite you back to slightly more familiar territory: your actual physical symptoms. One of the most confusing things about CFS is the range of different symptoms and different experiences each individual has. It can appear the CFS label is simply an umbrella term for so many different things, none of which we understand. What if that were not the case? What if these seemingly different symptoms track back to a single root? What if that single root could be explored through the model we set up in the last part? These are all questions that I am going to be introducing and starting to unpack in this chapter. Let me first set the scene by sharing a journal entry describing my own experience as I was seeking treatment after my second total crash.

> ***ENERGY SAVING AID***
>
> *The following journal excerpt frames the discussion themes for this chapter, but it is my personal story, so, not essential to read if you are low on energy.*

Journal: January 2017

Rereading my journal entries for last year, I can say with certainty that nothing in them even comes close to expressing just how terribly ill I was feeling. I have named certain symptoms, but I begin to see the complete inadequacy of words for conveying how those symptoms feel. I have detailed a lot of the emotions, thought processes, and tough decisions it engenders, but I cannot find a way to convey the level of pain and discomfort that has become part of my everyday life. Maybe that shouldn't surprise me—or you. After all, if you get a cold and tell all your friends you have a sore throat and painful sinuses, even if you say on a scale of one to ten of pain, you're at level 9, it still doesn't convey to them how it feels to you. They may be able to think back to their own experience of a cold and their own pain level as they try to understand, but, most likely, their scale and yours will be different. All I can say is that reaching the point I reached originally in 2002, and again last summer, is a point where the pain, discomfort, and general feeling of illness is so great and so distressing I was literally thinking, "How is it possible to feel like this and not be dead or dying?" I daresay this makes me sound like a very melodramatic character; all I can do is assure you I don't believe that is how others perceive me, and I certainly do not believe myself to be so.

The second huge trend is noticing how much of this has been focusing on psychology and stress. Reading this, it makes it sound as though I am at once saying, "this isn't a psychological illness," but every treatment I describe and every "tool" I talk about using to try to cheat my body into giving me a little more energy is based on psychology of one sort or another. I see I have written pages of musings about how I perceive the illness and whether those positive or negative thoughts are having an impact on my symptoms. I have suggested I can clear or improve symptoms by "dealing better" with personal relationships, with my workload, and with any other "stress" that I could seek out to label. I had, in fact, "bought into" the myth that this is psychological and can be fixed through psychology, in spite of feeling very deeply within my body that the pains, discomfort, and general malaise were all physical.

I have just spent three and a half months undoing that notion. Only in re-reading this do I now realise how much of a hold it had on me and how ridiculous it now seems. The beginning was, of course, the piece of paper that stated my Translocator Protein was 26% blocked and which identified the three chemicals responsible for that blockage. That magical piece of paper with those validating test results brought me feelings of wonder and excitement as I stood amongst the—metaphorical—jigsaw puzzle, determined to try to put it back together in a better way.

As I sit here writing this today, those feelings of elation seem a long way off. I have become accustomed to the notion I finally have evidence of a physical problem with my Mitochondria. The more I have gotten to grips with what that evidence means, the more it makes sense that I should have been feeling so truly awful. Think about it—and how about this for an analogy?—do you have an electric toothbrush? One that is battery-powered? As the battery begins to run down, the speed at which the bristles revolve is reduced. This happens gradually, so you may not even notice at first that the revolutions are a little less. Then it becomes noticeable. Before long, the length of time the battery will work is severely reduced, so instead of the usual two-minute clean, you find it stopping of its own accord after thirty seconds. You know this means the toothbrush is no longer doing its job effectively. Even though one day or two days used in this way will make little difference, if you spend a whole year cleaning your teeth badly, you are likely to develop dental problems.

Well, those batteries are my mitochondria. The three substances that have gathered—I don't know whether it was gradual or sudden, but I do have reason to believe that a lot of this blockage occurred whilst I was at university—are all preventing that highly efficient ADP-ATP recycling process from taking place in full. I have been told that a 26% blockage is pretty severe: I'm not sure what level of blockage would equal death, but if you're thinking that 26% isn't too bad as a level, well, in some measures, that may be the case, but where the Translocator Protein is concerned, it's bad. So, without their full battery power, my poor little cells have been rather like that toothbrush with its slow revolution. They have still been doing their job, but at a slower rate. I imagine them like little people: think of sitting in an office and your boss popping in and adding a pile of paperwork to your desk. You groan but have no choice other than to get on with it. Then the boss pops back and drops a bit more paperwork in, but you haven't even got through the first lot yet. Maybe you scan through and surreptitiously label a few bits of paper as irrelevant, so throw them away to reduce your workload. Can you believe it? The boss is back with another load of paper, and he's not giving you any extra manpower to deal with this. Again, you throw some away, but before long as this continues, you find yourself drowning in paper and just give up. These are my cells: It's not so much that their workload has increased, at least not at first, as their "manpower" for doing it has been reduced. In my research, I learned that the energy production cycle does, in itself, require energy. So, eventually, with so little energy to expend, not only do the main tasks of the cell fall by the wayside but so, too, does the energy production. This is a downward spiral with potentially catastrophic results. Now, Dr. Myhill has been very clear in describing CFS as a symptom, so whether it manifests as tiredness, nausea, vomiting, disturbed sleep, or whatever, it is still a manifestation of the body's emergency call. It is designed to stop human beings in their tracks so their bodies can take time out and focus all their attention on energy-building so they have the power to do their jobs.

The second point is, with every single cell struggling to do what it should, that means every single organ in my body is functioning suboptimally. Since a lot of organs need to work in conjunction with one another, this fact also results in a "double whammy" where the organ itself is affected, but so, too, is its inter-relationship. For example, all organs require oxygen to function properly. They receive that oxygen from the blood supply. The heart pumps blood around the body. So, with the Mitochondria in the heart going slowly, the heart rate is lowered, the blood pressure is reduced, and, consequently, the rate at which oxygen is delivered to other organs is reduced. Move round to say, the liver, and it's already going slowly because it has reduced energy. Once it also has reduced oxygen, its ability to work is further impaired. Toxins then begin building up, which slows the body down, and so the downward spiral progresses.

All of these facts have been demonstrated in my body for years: I have had very low blood pressure for years, frequently to the point where I am on the border of fainting. I had the opportunity, back in 2005, to see my blood under the microscope and be shown it is poorly oxygenated. It feels to me that these, and other definable physical symptoms, have been ignored by my doctors for years because they weren't going to kill me, and they didn't know what to do about them. Neither, it seems to me, did they appreciate the significance of any of this. I could go on writing pages detailing how different organs are unable to function "normally" and how I am experiencing various pains and highly unpleasant symptoms as a result. The fatigue is just the icing on the cake. In and of itself, it is undesirable and inconvenient, but having a constant feeling of being "unrested" and having a frequent desire to lie down is nothing as bad as the extreme nausea or severe headaches, for example. The sore throats, painful eyes, and swollen glands aren't great, but this is pain that I can block out. By virtue of the name given to the illness, the frequent dismissal by the medical profession, and the lack of research, your average person may not even have heard of the condition. If they have, they just pick up on the "fatigue" and usually wonder what all the fuss is about. After all, we're all tired most of the time in this busy modern life. Trying to convey to someone how different this is, how life-changing, how—I don't even have words—seems an impossibility.

That was my experience of my symptoms. Now, let me take you through some of the discoveries I learned when I began researching in earnest. It turns out scientists have been very curious about the body's energy production mechanisms and a whole host of other mechanisms that can relate to some individual CFS symptoms. Each specialist, investigating their particular area of interest, holds little puzzle pieces. The more of these I researched, the more I began to see a common thread to which that system—or symptom—can be traced; then we stop.

> ***ENERGY SAVING AID***
>
> *These are the essential points that are helpful for you to take away from the following section:*
>
> - *The range of different symptoms that can be experienced by people living with CFS is huge. When listed, they appear to affect so many different systems within the body, it is hard to make sense of it all.*
> - *Additionally, everyone's experience is subtly different: some people experience all the symptoms, others just a few. The severity also varies drastically from person to person, all of which adds to the confusion.*
> - *We have just explored the idea your body is greater than its physiology. It also has a biofield which contains information about your mental and emotional state. I would like to suggest if we turn our focus to that idea and start looking at a root cause of stored trauma, everything about CFS begins to make much more sense.*

The Confusing Landscape of CFS Symptoms

One of the most confusing things about Chronic Fatigue is the long and varied list of symptoms that can come with it. This includes the obvious fatigue—better described as exhaustion in many cases. However, other common symptoms can be—in no particular order:

- Digestive issues like Irritable Bowel Syndrome (IBS)
- Nausea
- Headaches
- Sore throat
- Flu-like symptoms
- Difficulty sleeping
- Night sweats
- Allergies and sensitivities to food or chemicals or other environmental factors
- Irregular heartbeat
- Shortness of breath
- Muscle weakness

This is not a comprehensive list. You will find other common symptoms listed on many medical websites, and you yourself may be experiencing other symptoms not listed here.

The point I want to make is, looking at that list, the symptoms don't appear to make sense. They affect so many different areas of the body. When you look at individual patients, the range and severity also vary a lot. It is possible to have all of these symptoms, but it is also possible to have just one or two. The number of symptoms doesn't necessarily correspond to the severity of the patient's experience. In other words, you might find yourself bed-bound but only be able to list exhaustion, sore throat, and headache as your symptoms. It is no wonder researchers and doctors have been stumped by the illness. Yes, there is room to argue we simply haven't put enough funds into researching, which is why we have few helpful answers. I wish to suggest another idea.

In the last section, we explored the idea your body is much bigger than its physical expression. Thoughts, emotions, past lives, and more can all impact that physical expression. So, let's begin to explore an aspect where the physical and emotional elements of you are closely bound together: Trauma. When I mention that word, what do you think about? Does your focus immediately go towards emotions like fear, anxiety, and panic attacks? Perhaps you think of the impact of Trauma being largely psychological; for example, PTSD. Or, are you aware that Trauma can also be physical in nature? To have your limb amputated would be physically traumatic, as well as bringing emotional challenges. Experiencing a car accident can be both physically traumatic—injuries sustained—and emotionally traumatic—fearing you are about to die. You can also end up with a self-sustaining cycle: A physical trauma, for example, your Mitochondria not having sufficient energy to sustain your cells, can create emotional trauma. Think about the fear or frustration that your lack of energy causes you. This emotional response to the physical event, in turn, elevates your body's stress response, which, as we are about to explore, cuts your body's ability to function physically. That brings on more physical trauma, and so the cycle grows and grows. However, there is good news: You can break this cycle and reverse it! But, first, let's keep building up the full picture. This knowledge is what is going to empower you to begin that process of breaking the downward spiral.

ENERGY SAVING AID

These are the essential points that are helpful for you to take away from the following section:

- *The ground-breaking research paper, led by Dr. Robert Naviaux and Dr. Eric Gordon in 2016, uncovered something called the Cell Danger Response. This is the idea the body's cells have gone into an ongoing state of "hibernation" called dauer.*
- *This causes your cells to shut down and reduce the performance of tasks to an absolute minimum to keep you safe from a threat and allow you to survive, but this state does not support "thriving."*
- *The perception that you are under threat is coming from the central nervous system. The "threat" it is sensing is your stored trauma: physical, mental, and emotional.*

The Cell Danger Response

In my opinion, one of the biggest "breakthroughs" in understanding what may be happening in the body in CFS came from a team led by Dr. Robert Naviaux and Dr. Eric Gordon. You may have heard of this—or you may not. The Cell Danger Response. If you choose to delve deeper, you will find a lot of complex science behind this explanation.[44] For this book, I want to try to translate it into a simpler metaphor to help guide you. In their 2016 research paper, Dr. Naviaux, Dr. Eric Gordon, and a team of researchers found that CFS patients showed consistent abnormalities in twenty metabolic pathways.[45] For

---

44 You can start by exploring Dr. Naviaux's website: https://naviauxlab.ucsd.edu/
45 Here is the link to the paper: https://pubmed.ncbi.nlm.nih.gov/27573827/

anyone still thinking this illness is somehow "made up" or "all in the head," this is evidence to demonstrate it is very much in the body! To quote from the paper's abstract:

"Our data show that despite the heterogeneity of factors leading to CFS, the cellular metabolic response in patients was homogeneous, statistically robust, and chemically similar to the evolutionarily conserved persistence response to environmental stress known as dauer."

What does that mean? Basically, even though we are looking at a lot of different symptoms, when you begin to study the body at the level of its cells, Dr. Naviaux found all patients were exhibiting a set of behaviours—"metabolic responses"—that were identical. This pattern is similar to something called *dauer*.

I find it easiest to see the dauer response a bit like hibernation. In an attempt to preserve the life of the cell, the mitochondria instruct it to shut down or limit its activities. Think of this like a hibernating animal reducing its body functions to conserve energy and survive through a cold climate. Why is this a sensible adaptation? During the winter months, food is scarce, the weather is inhospitable, and basically the environment is extremely challenging for survival. So, rather than attempt to find the food necessary to keep the body warm enough to survive, the animal creates a cosy den and turns down its normal bodily functions to the lowest possible level where it uses minimum energy and doesn't require scarce food. Then, when the summer months return, weather becomes warmer, and food more plentiful, the animal can go back to living fully.

Is this sounding in any way familiar? What is your body desiring? Sleep, maybe? Perhaps a desire to avoid all types of exertion? Yet, this is not acceptable as a lifestyle for a human. Moreover, it is not fully a state of hibernation. The human body has not adapted to a place where it doesn't require food or water. It hasn't fully turned off its kidneys, liver, and bowels. Instead, you find yourself in an uncomfortable halfway house where you are not sufficiently shut down to survive without energy but, at the same time, have lost the resources to carry out the activities that keep your body energised and healthy. Not to mention, appealing as it may be to hibernate, it is not socially acceptable!

Another helpful analogy is the analogy of war. Imagine an army in battle, trying to protect a city from being invaded by the enemy. The army fights and fights and fights until the generals begin to realise they are running out of ammunition. Pretty soon, firing guns and trying to kill the enemy isn't going to be an option. So, what next? The best chance of survival may be to retreat back into the city and try to defend it as best they can. Between the battlefield and the city lay fields of crops. The retreat is going to need to be pretty fast. So, there isn't time to harvest all that food. However, if it's left in the field, the enemy will be able to eat it and strengthen their own army. So, what is the best idea for survival? Burn the crops so nobody can eat them.

So, when the research shows physical mechanisms either shut down or under-functioning, this relates to the Cell Danger Response. The brain is telling the Mitochondria the body is under threat, and they are bringing in the natural response, which involves either ceasing certain tasks completely or cutting tasks back to a bare minimum. From the perspective of explaining why the symptoms of CFS are so many and so varied, I believe the Cell Danger Response is extremely powerful. Think about it: This signal to shut down can be happening in any cell in your body. So, the cells in all the parts of your digestive tract are being signalled to shut down. Could this then lead to IBS? The cells in your heart are being ordered to shut down. Might this explain the lowered blood pressure, irregular heartbeats, or breathing issues?[46] Equally, it is possible the shut-down signal is only being sent to specific parts of

46 This is a logical hypothesis or speculation. I am not suggesting we have proven this is what is happening within the body, but the implication of all your cells being signalled to reduce their working rate is profound.

the body, not every single cell. That would explain why each person can experience a different set of symptoms and differing quantities of symptoms, as we mentioned at the beginning.

If we believe that this shut down can account for the symptoms, the next logical question would be: What is signalling this shut down? The answer: your central nervous system assessing your body and communicating to the brain you are under threat. That brings us to another question: What form is this threat taking? The answer: trauma—which is what we are going to explore in depth in this section. To give you a taste right now, I am defining trauma as unprocessed emotions inherited at birth—past-life or collective trauma—experiences from early life, and physical symptoms that result from physiological changes caused by your central nervous system never reliably returning to the rest and digest state.[47] Hopefully, in that brief overview, you can see we have elements occurring at each of the Four Levels of Creation we explored in the last section.

47 You can read more about this in the work of Benjamin Fry: https://www.benjaminfry.co.uk/post/4-why-the-body-cant-just-get-over-it/

> ***ENERGY SAVING AID***
>
> *These are the essential points that are helpful for you to take away from the following section:*
>
> - *A lot of researchers have focused on their field of expertise—understandably—and this has led to argument and debate about which is "the one" thing that causes CFS.*
> - *Taking a top-level perspective of all of those "causes," we can see they have a shared root. Each system viewed as being "responsible" for triggering or perpetuating CFS is controlled by the central nervous system.*

Taking Another Approach

Many of the research studies into CFS have focused on individual angles. So, we have hypotheses that CFS may be an auto-immune disease.[48] I have heard specialists talking about symptoms like brain fog and digestive issues being linked to problems with the gut microbiome.[49] We also have hypotheses that it is a purely Mitochondrial issue, in terms of the Mitochondria being unable to produce sufficient ATP to fuel the cells.[50] Could the illness be caused by a failure of the liver?[51] Too many toxins have been allowed to build up in the body. This could be the reason for issues with the gut, and it could also explain the auto-immune link. If the immune system is detecting toxins in particular organs, it may end up attacking those organs, but the

---

48 You may find this article from the CDC website https://www.cdc.gov/me-cfs/causes

49 Dr. Michael Ruscio is just one expert in this field: https://drruscio.com/blog/

50 Find out more about this here: https://www.drmyhill.co.uk/wiki/CFS_-_The_Central_Cause:_Mitochondrial_Failure

51 If you are interested in this angle, take a look at this article: https://www.theoptimumhealthclinic.com/blog/chronic-fatigue-syndrome-and-the-liver/

liver lacks the capacity to rid the body of the toxins.[52] So, where does that leave us? Are all of these individual things the problem, or are we missing something? I am not saying I have a definitive answer to that question,[53] but I would like to offer you an interesting perspective. There is a common link with all of these. I find it helpful to think of this a little like a river. The individual symptoms are "downstream." If you flow back "upstream," you arrive at an underlying connection with your central nervous system. In each case, the reason for the malfunction goes back to the signals coming from the nervous system, which believes it is detecting danger and is trying to react to keep you safe. As I said above, if you keep going back even further, you find the trauma response is the original trigger. We are going to unpack that response over the next few chapters. Before I take you there, I would like to invite you to consider another perspective.

---

52 Dr. Ameet Aggarwal has some beautiful explanations of these types of mechanisms: https://www.drameet.com/

53 For some individuals, the fatigue is 100% a physical issue. Addressing diet and lifestyle can create recovery for them. So, I feel it is great to explore that area as a starting point. Then, if that doesn't bring you the resolution you are seeking, be prepared to explore other levels.

> ***ENERGY SAVING AID***
>
> *These are the essential points that are helpful for you to take away from the following section:*
>
> - *I invite you to turn things on their heads. The central nervous system is sensing danger in its environment. It is signalling that danger to the cells, and they are reacting according to a system designed to keep you safe and allow you to survive. Logically, then, your body has not "gone wrong." It is doing exactly what it has been programmed to do. The problem is not with your symptoms; it is with the environment triggering that danger signal.*
> - *For me, letting go of the idea of trying to "get rid" of my symptoms and turning, instead, to working on ways of creating energy led to recovery.*
> - *We need to change our environment at the physical, mental, and emotional levels, which means addressing issues that sit in all layers of the Four Levels of Creation model.*

There is Nothing "Wrong" with Your Body

We all get drawn into the perspective when we are ill that our body is being attacked and the attack is causing it to malfunction. From this perspective, it is logical to look for a solution by trying to work out how to identify and then get rid of the threat. So, you might think of things like taking an antibiotic to kill the bacteria causing an infection. I'm not saying this is incorrect, or inaccurate, but in the case of an illness as complex as CFS, and where we cannot identify the single cause or attacking factor, might it be more helpful to view things from a different perspective? What if, instead of seeing this as the body "going wrong," we see this as the body adapting—perfectly—to its environment? So, rather than looking for a protocol that treats individual issues within the body, we start looking at the outside. If we take the perspective your body has made perfectly sensible adaptations to an unsupportive environment, it raises another interesting idea. Perhaps you can change your environment to one that promotes health—is supportive—and then allow your body to adapt naturally to that. Going even further, in the last section we spent time looking at the biofield, the creative process, and the idea your physical body is built upon a foundation of constantly flowing energy. So, in order to create this more supportive environment, we need not simply stop at the physical level. We can also work with the biofield and make adjustments at the "energetic" level: in other words, in your Psycho-Emotional or Intuitive bodies. Those will also feed through to correct the issues appearing at the physical level.

You might think this is a crazy idea, but this is the idea that lay behind the path I followed in order to regain my energy and quality of life. Instead of focusing on trying to "get rid of symptoms," I began working with a protocol based on understanding how we create energy. I hope you might be able to see the logic in this idea. I want to suggest we can route symptoms back to the central nervous system. Then consider your central nervous system is not "malfunctioning"; it has just learned how to adapt to a less-than-supportive environment. So, it is functioning perfectly by allowing you to survive. The trouble is, we all wish to thrive, not simply survive. Whilst your body remains in a state that veers between freeze and fight/flight, your cells are constantly receiving the message they are under threat. So, they are doing their job perfectly. They are going into hibernation/conservation mode to keep you alive. By focusing on what is "wrong," we may be able to identify issues like a leaky gut or low levels of vitamins or minerals. We may even have treatments and protocols for correcting these things. We can get pretty good at addressing the physical trauma—

Because you have these symptoms. The point Dr. Maté is trying to make is this is not an explanation of anything. It is a statement of relationship. It never really answers the question of "Why?" or "How?" in any meaningful way. So, unless you can explain where a set of symptoms originates, how can you hope to treat it in a way that truly heals? In other words, if you can't define and understand the problem, how can you find a solution? With this idea in mind, I invite you to continue as we begin to explore how trauma resides in the body and changes our biology. Let's examine whether that can provide a better answer to the questions of "Why?" and "How?" With those answers, we can start addressing the problem at its root, rather than trying to work with issues that are only really "side effects" or "correct" adaptations to the root problem.

ENERGY SAVING AID

Please complete the following practice. Answering these questions will provide you with critical information to help you create your optimal roadmap for recovery.

Your Invitation to Practice

Please grab your journal and write about how this new information is making you think and feel. It's OK if you don't understand everything here: we still have a lot more ground to explore. You may want to come back to this chapter after we have taken a look at more of your maze:

- Can you follow the logic of the argument I am trying to present?
- If not, which part isn't making sense to you?

- How is this information making you feel: what emotions are coming up as you read it?
- Is this bringing up questions for you? If so, write them down.

Chapter 10

Meet Your Central Nervous System

In the last chapter, I suggested that the many physical symptoms of CFS share a common thread: They can all be traced back to signalling from your central nervous system that causes physical adaptations to its environment. So, in this chapter, I want to introduce you to your central nervous system. We are going to explore some basic ideas about how it operates and how it responds to its environment, both physical and psycho-emotional. Now, some of the ideas here may, at first reading, feel a little like you are somehow at fault for your experience. Actually, nothing could be further from the truth. Yes, once you understand the connections here, you can become empowered to change your experience, but taking responsibility for making those changes is not the same as being to blame for your current situation. So, we are also going to explore that idea.

Before we start following that path, let me share another journal entry, reflecting my experience before I really understood what the psycho-somatic connection meant for me. If this entry resonates with you, and you struggle with the rest of the chapter, just hold onto the idea that I was once where you are now. Things changed for me, and they can change for you if you wish: this is just a process that takes a little time.

> ***ENERGY SAVING AID***
>
> *The following journal excerpt frames the discussion themes for this chapter, but it is my personal story, so it is not essential to read if you are low on energy.*

Journal Entry: August 2015

I haven't written in this journal all week. What does this mean? Did I relapse and find myself facing another few days unable to function? Or did I just lose the will to keep writing this? Actually, neither of those things occurred. My energy continued to move in an almost imperceptibly upward direction, and the "wired" feeling diminished a little. I am still not back anywhere close to my "best" energy level, but I have been able to function pretty well. So, I've spent the week trying to use my energy wisely. I've been taking regular periods of rest each day. On Tuesday and Wednesday, I deliberately kept my activities low to conserve as much energy as possible for teaching a workshop on Thursday. I knew that it was entirely possible that this would tip me back over the edge into "crash" on Friday, but I'm very happy to find that it hasn't.

So, how does one conserve energy or build it? You might think that lying on the couch in front of daytime TV is resting. It may be resting your body physically, but if you accept the idea that CFS is also brought on or exacerbated by mental activity or stress, then you also need to rest the body mentally. Before I go on to talk about that, this word "stress" is such a loaded term in our society, so I want to share some personal thoughts about it. For starters, it is imprecise. When someone tells you they are "stressed," what do they mean? Usually, they are feeling overwhelmed in some way. This could be they have too many tasks to accomplish in the time they have allotted. It could be they are feeling trapped by a situation; for example, being bullied by their boss and not knowing how to deal with the bullying and keep their job. Or it could be a more "positive" stress in that someone they love needs a lot of care or attention, and they are struggling to provide that. All of these things involve the emotional or mental side of life. People rarely, if ever, talk about being "stressed" by physical things. Yet, there are plenty of things we do that can place strain on the physical body. Wearing heels that are too high, sitting for long periods of time with bad posture, or carrying a heavy bag on your shoulder can place strain on the spine, but you never hear someone with back pain talking about their spine being stressed.

I personally find it strange and unhelpful that both society and the medical profession seem to set up this divide between "the body," meaning the physical things that we can see and touch, and "the mind," referring to the systems we can neither see nor touch. It seems to me that the assumption is: If you can see it and touch it, then someone else should fix it for you. If you can't see it or touch it, then only you can control it. In reality, we are now coming to understand that "the mind" is an incredibly complex set of chemicals, reactions, and conversations between neurons and transmitters. We are slowly beginning to find some ability to "see" these activities taking place through brain scans, but we still have very little idea about how they really work. It is also true that this divide between "body" and "mind" is probably totally unhelpful. The two systems are inextricably related, and each one impacts upon the other.

Had I known then what I now know about the central nervous system, my ideas about stress would have been very different. Once I began to understand what I am about to share with you here, I began to make real progress in my recovery.

ENERGY SAVING AID

These are the essential points that are helpful for you to take away from the following section:

- *Your central nervous system—CNS—is like the master controller for your body. The Autonomic Nervous System—ANS—is one of the oldest evolutionary parts of your brain, sometimes called the Reptilian part. Its sole purpose is to help you survive. So, it is constantly assessing your environment—external and internal—and communicating to your cells to let them know if they are safe or in danger.*
- *Modern life is complex: Emotional challenges are now more common than physical dangers, but your ANS has not adapted to understand that. So, a negative emotion can create as big a danger signal as coming face to face with a sabre-toothed tiger. The difference is the emotion won't kill you, but the sabre-toothed tiger might. However, your ANS doesn't understand that.*
- *As our brains evolved, we developed the mammalian systems wired for social contact and able to understand more of the nuances of life. If the ANS has already kicked in and fired off the danger warning, our access to the more conscious, rational, decision-making parts of the brain is shut down.*

Meet Your Autonomic Nervous System

Before any panic begins to set in, I am not about to give you a lesson in biology! What I want to share in this chapter is a conceptual understanding of how part of your central nervous system—CNS—works. This should help you understand how you can support yourself as you recover. I would like to introduce you to your Autonomic Nervous System—ANS. I like to think of mine as a cute little dinosaur. Now, I'm not asking you to return to primary school by creating this image of part of the body. I'm asking you to see your ANS as a "part" of yourself rather than as "you." That makes it easier to deal with any shame, powerlessness, or hopelessness that may be coming up. So, rather than feeling *"I am traumatised,"* which may feel like admitting you are weak, bad, or stupid, I want you to reframe this as *"My nervous system has experienced some Trauma."* Remember how I invited you to access the witness state, or your True Self, back in Chapter 2? Well, this is one way of doing that: to understand that you have a part that is deeply wounded, but not the whole—or even the core—of who you are. You can observe it without becoming it.

The stress response mechanism is one of the oldest parts of the human brain. It developed very early in our evolution and is sometimes referred to as the Reptilian part of the brain—hence my dinosaur image. This part is programmed to allow us to survive. So, your ANS has one hugely important job: your survival. Any time you start to analyse any of its decisions or adaptations, please remember that. They might now be causing you challenges, even pain, but they developed with your best interests at heart. At some point in your life, these adaptations allowed you to survive. So, thank your ANS for doing that.

One of the challenges we face in modern life comes from the fact that the part of the brain that is analysing our environment is still living in prehistoric times. It is using the earliest evolutionary parts of your brain: the emotions:

- Fear keeps you alive by allowing you to avoid danger.
- Anger protects your boundaries to keep you safe and whole.
- Love helps you connect to others to find safety and meaning as part of a group.

So, here we have a cute, well-meaning dinosaur that wants you to survive, but it hasn't really evolved to understand life in the twenty-first century. It sees everything in black and white: safe or dangerous.

In contrast, as the human species evolved, different parts of our brains evolved in response to our changing environment: We added the Mammalian layers that desire social interaction. So, alongside the parts of your brain that relate to your ANS and use emotions to analyse the environment, you also have a conscious mind. This may analyse your environment according to very different criteria: rational thoughts. This assessment may be more nuanced. For example, *"This feels unpleasant and is making me anxious, but I know it isn't going to kill me, so I can take a breath and work out how to react."* If you receive an unpleasant email, your analytical brain may know this isn't going to kill you, but your emotional brain might be feeling fear or anger, which signals that you are in danger. So, up jumps your little dinosaur to step in and keep you safe by activating your stress response. Not only can this lead to unhelpful behaviour—for example, you respond with a knee-jerk message, acting from anger, and the situation escalates. It can also lead to confusion in your mind. Your emotions are telling you you're in grave danger, but your rational mind knows it's only an email. Think of that old saying *"Sticks and stones may break my bones, but names will never hurt me."* Yes, your rational mind knows the email won't kill you, but your ANS makes no distinction between that email and a bullet fired from a gun. Both can evoke the exact same emotions and, hence, the same automatic response from your ANS. The critical thing is, this response is *automatic*. Telling you to ignore it is about as helpful as telling you to stop breathing. Unless you can slow down, step back, and assess, you are going to find yourself following that—possibly—unhelpful automatic reaction. That is your trauma response.

In the next chapter, we are going to explore trauma in more detail and highlight the difference between a "stress response" and a "trauma response." So, a stress response can be helpful. In this case, it might allow you to write a strongly worded email that defends your boundaries but doesn't escalate the situation any further. You end up resolving the problem, and all is well. However, a trauma response may mean you end up writing an aggressive email full of obscenities, escalating the issue to new heights and ending up causing serious harm. For example, this email conversation is with your boss and your response causes you to lose your job. So, what makes the difference? How can one person manage to take a breath and calm themselves before responding in a constructive manner while another person leaps in and turns the scenario into a nuclear-level disaster? This is where you need to understand what is going on in your ANS. Here we turn to polyvagal theory.[55]

55 This short, four-minute YouTube video shows Dr. Porges outlining a few key points about the Polyvagal theory: https://youtu.be/ec3AUMDjtKQ In my explanation, I've used different imagery to tie things together.

ENERGY SAVING AID

These are the essential points that are helpful for you to take away from the following section:

- *Your ANS has three possible states: rest/digest—parasympathetic or Ventral Vagal, fight/flight—sympathetic, and freeze—Dorsal Vagal.*
- *Ideally, you should be living in parasympathetic: in this state, your body is maintaining its systems, you are open to social engagement, and all is well. This state promotes health and healing.*
- *If your ANS detects a threat, it will take you up into the fight-flight state, signalling all your cells to prepare to either fight off an attack or run away to safety. In this state, essential maintenance tasks are temporarily suspended to focus all your energy on saving your life. This is supposed to be a temporary state, and it requires a lot of energy to sustain that state.*
- *So, if your body gets stuck in that state for too long, it will run out of energy to sustain the fight-flight state. If your ANS does not feel the danger has passed, it has no choice but to move into freeze. This is a low-energy state, but NOT a state of safety. So, in this state, you will be shut down, dissociated, and still not maintaining your organs and systems.*
- *Your body is naturally going to try to move down from this state back to parasympathetic, but for it to get there, it has to pass back through the fight-flight. If the original danger is still felt to be present, it will not manage to exit the fight-flight but will end up running out of energy again and returning to freeze.*

- *This can become a permanent cycle, which we term as a "maladaptive nervous system." In this cycle, your body is consistently struggling to maintain itself: this state does not promote health or healing.*

Understanding the Structure of Your ANS

When I originally learned about my Autonomic Nervous System, I learned it has just two states: at rest—"off"—known as parasympathetic, or under threat—"on"—known as sympathetic. Your ANS can only be in one state OR the other. So, it is either "on" or "off." It can never be both or somewhere between the two. Typically, the parasympathetic state could be described as "rest and digest." In this state, your body is in balance—homeostasis—and all your systems are busy maintaining themselves and supporting health. The sympathetic state can be described as "fight, flight, or freeze." In this state, everything is on high alert, responding to a threat. So, that means "maintenance" tasks are temporarily shut down to focus all the body's energy on dealing with the threat. That is part of what we explored in the last chapter when we looked at the Cell danger Response.

Now we come to Polyvagal theory. This explains how your central nervous system has three basic states. Your natural, safe state is called the Ventral Vagal. In that state, your cells are receiving signals that all is well, and they should be carrying out their duties. When a threat comes along, this moves you into the "fight or flight" state—your sympathetic nervous system. That fires you up to take action to evade the thread. You should then settle back down to the parasympathetic Ventral Vagal state—safety. This is the pattern of what I am terming the "stress response." So, that's a temporary elevation of energy to allow you to deal with the problem, followed by a smooth return to your maintenance mode. You also have a third state, called Dorsal

Vagal. This is the freeze response. Think of a small rodent about to be eaten by a bear. The rodent knows it can't outrun the bear or fight it off. So, instead, it plays dead, fooling the bear into thinking there's nothing worth eating, here, and keeping the rodent safe. Your nervous system can do something very similar. Instead of firing everything up, it can shut everything down to keep you safe. So, rather than running away, this reaction might cause you to faint in terror, for example, deliberately block out or forget a memory, or shut down an emotion. Again, when the threat has passed, or you come around from your faint, you should return to the parasympathetic ventral vagal state. To do that, you need to process the original threat, and that is something humans are frequently unable to do, as we will explore.

The critical difference between the model I originally learned, and the polyvagal model is understanding what can appear to be a calm state is not necessarily the healthy Ventral Vagal state. The "danger" response of Dorsal Vagal, which signals that the ANS is overwhelmed, unable to cope, and cannot see how to get itself back to safety may also appear calm. Yet that calmness is more like a preparation for death, rather than a state of embracing life. In terms of recognising what is happening, this can be confusing. For example, "people-pleasing" can be a trauma response that comes from the Dorsal "frozen" state. Yet, it might look and feel like a sign of social engagement you would expect in the "safe" state.[56] So, I now want to share an example to help illustrate what the transition between these states can look like in a real-life situation. As you are about to discover, the theoretical model of simply switching on and off between safety and danger can be seriously complicated once we understand the Dorsal state—the trauma state.

---

56 We will explore more about this nuance in a later chapter. For now, simply keep the idea in mind.

Your Central Nervous System Response

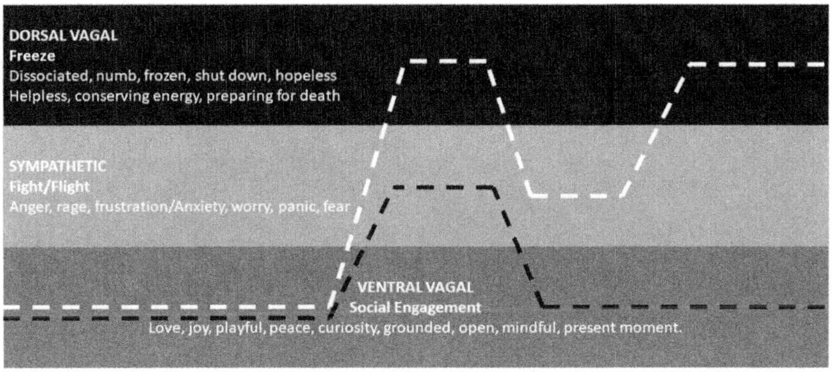

In this image, we have the three basic elements of the Polyvagal system:

- Ventral vagal. This is your state of safety, having the capacity for social engagement, growth, and health. Emotions associated with this state might include things like love, joy, openness, the capacity to play, and to be present.
- Sympathetic. This is your initial response to danger. Your body is primed to fight an attack—it may feel emotions like anger, frustration, rage, OR to run away to safety—it may feel emotions like anxiety, panic, fear, and worry.
- Dorsal Vagal. This is the freeze state. When neither fighting nor running away are working—or are options—your stress response escalates even further but your body has run out of energy, so freeze becomes the only possible escape remaining. This can bring emotions like feeling numb, dissociating from the events, and feeling hopeless and powerless or even that you may—or want to—die.

Using this model, a "healthy" ANS responding to a stress would move from the ventral vagal state into the sympathetic fight/flight state, allowing them to respond to the stress—black dotted line, and then return to ventral vagal. If the stress was extreme, the ANS may go into the dorsal vagal freeze state but would still eventually return to the ventral vagal state of safety.

An "unhealthy" response would mean that the ANS flies up into the sympathetic fight/flight state but cannot re-regulate itself—white dotted line. Eventually, it runs out of energy but still feels under threat, so it continues into the dorsal vagal, freeze state. At some point, it may try to exit the freeze state, but as it falls back into Sympathetic, it once again feels threatening emotions, like anger, and still lacks the capacity to deal with them, so it once more runs out of energy and ends up back in the freeze state.

ENERGY SAVING AID

These are the essential points that are helpful for you to take away from the following section:

- *It is really helpful to understand the emotional links. If we have trouble processing specific emotions—for example, anger—they can trigger us to become stuck in the loop of fight-flight-freeze-fight-flight-freeze.*
- *We will be elaborating on this idea in a later chapter, but it is important to remember none of this is your fault.*

Understanding the Emotional Links

I find this model really helpful because it focuses on the emotional links. Let's imagine you have difficulty processing an emotion like anger. Maybe, as a child, you learned it wasn't safe to express your own anger. Or maybe you witnessed someone else's anger causing harm to you or to one of your caregivers. Whatever the reason, when you meet a stress that causes you to experience anger, you have no capacity to deal with that emotion. So, instead of following the "healthy" ANS pattern of moving into fight mode—anger-processing it, re-establishing your healthy boundary, and returning back to safety, you cannot complete the processing part, you then run out of energy, and finally you end up in the freeze response. In this response, you feel "safe" because you are numb to the anger; you have shut down or dissociated. However, this state doesn't allow you to feel alive. In this shut-down state, you will struggle to engage with other people. So, at some point, your ANS is going to try to move out of this state and head back to its natural "safe" social engagement state. The problem is, as you do this, you open up to the anger once more. If you still lack the ability to process it, you won't make it back to safety because your ANS will sense it is in danger and begin the cycle over again. This is what it means to be stuck in a trauma state or what you may hear termed a *Maladaptive Stress Response*. In a later chapter, I want to explore how these emotions become "stuck," what that feels like, and what it may mean for your body. For now, we need to develop the images of the ANS further to give you another layer of understanding. These explanations may be ringing alarm bells in you. Perhaps you are starting to recognise you have difficulty with certain emotions or you are feeling shut down and distant from life. You need to understand this is not your fault. Your ANS is not inferior, wrong, or in any way to "blame."

ENERGY SAVING AID

These are the essential points that are helpful for you to take away from the following section:

- *There is another layer to this model. We each have a different Window of Tolerance. This is my way of describing the "bandwidth" of your parasympathetic state.*
- *If you have a low bandwidth—narrow Window of Tolerance, then a small incident can trigger a full trauma response. If your bandwidth is wider, then you have a greater capacity to feel the stress but also maintain access to the rational, thinking part of your brain, which can regulate your ANS back down to safety.*
- *It is important to understand that stress and trauma are not about the event itself; they are a description of how your body reacts to the event.*

Why None of This Is Your Fault

You might be sitting there thinking you are somehow at fault for not being able to control the way in which your ANS reacts. I mean, if it's as simple as understanding the three states, surely you can modify your behaviour to try to stay within the social engagement state as much as possible? If that's what you believe, but you can't seem to modify your behaviour, where does that leave you? Feeling hopeless? Feeling stupid or useless? Frustrated? Well, let me reassure you by bringing in the next layer. Do you remember when we were talking about the possible reactions to a nasty email? I asked how some people were able to take the time to calm down while others simply flew into a rage. Yes, in part, this may be to do with behaviour and habits. So, as I've just explained, it can be helpful to understand the structure and be aware of how you naturally react versus how you *could* react. You will hear a lot of self-help gurus telling you to just change your thinking. However, if you remember, I also explained that a large element of the reaction is *automatic*. So, it's not as simple as *deciding* to do something different. Why might that be? I believe the answer lies in your Window of Tolerance.[57]

In a moment, you will see an image to help you understand this, but basically, not every ANS is the same. I've labelled your social engagement/safe/parasympathetic state as your window of tolerance. As long as you are operating in that area, you are able to make rational decisions and engage socially in ways that are productive. In other words, when your boss annoys you, you recognise that shouting at him/her is probably not a wise course of action if you wish to keep your job. The point is, we all have a slightly different Window of Tolerance. I like to think of it in terms of width. So, think about someone you know who is really laid-back. Whenever something stressful happens to them, they seem able to just accept it and respond in a calm, sensible manner. I would say that person has a wide window of tolerance. Now, think about someone you know who is always in a state of stress. The smallest unexpected event sends them into a panic. You might think of them as a "drama queen," perhaps. Well, in this case, I would suggest you're looking at a person with a small window of tolerance.

So, bearing this in mind, let's consider the imaginary email we've been talking about. Imagine two people in the same situation both receive that same email. One person writes back, sorts the problem out easily,

---

57 In part, I intend this to be a conceptual idea that will help you understand what is happening in your body. However, I believe the concept is backed up by an area of scientific research that has been exploring the role of epigenetic expression of Cortisol Receptors. In other words, the genes responsible for your Cortisol Receptors can begin to express incorrectly, resulting in your cells becoming hyper-sensitive to even the tiniest level of Cortisol. This leaves your body open to "overreacting" to any stimulus, be it emotional or physical in nature.

and forgets it. The other person manages to turn it into a major drama. What is happening in each person's ANS?

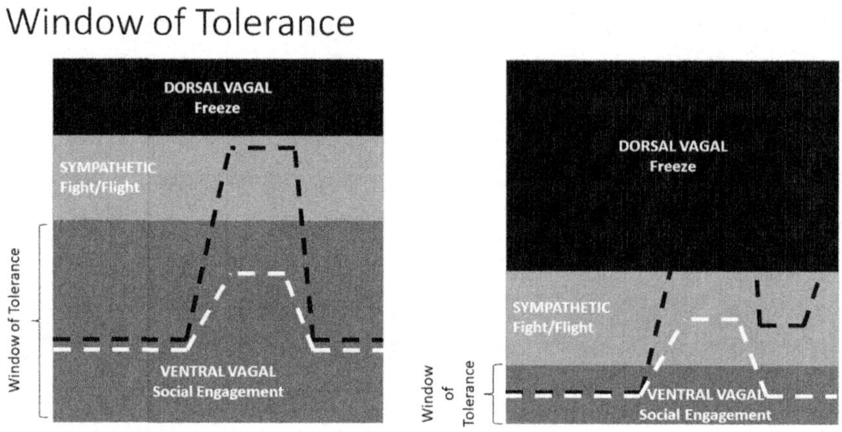

Going back to the image I gave you in the last section, let's develop this idea a bit further. Take a look at the two charts. The left-hand chart represents person one—the calm response. You can see the point at which they read the email. Their stress level—black dotted line—rose significantly, but they have a nice wide Ventral Vagal Window of Tolerance. So, even though their stress increased, it managed to move successfully in and out of the sympathetic state. In another situation, it might even remain within the Ventral Vagal state completely—white dotted line. They were able to formulate a response that defended whatever boundaries had been violated and also sorted out the problem, all without experiencing any significant issues.

Now, look at the right-hand chart. Notice how the Window of Tolerance—lower band—is a lot narrower. Also notice the email elicits the exact same level of response—the escalation of the black dotted line is identical. However, in this case, that black dotted line ends up hitting the "danger" area—sympathetic state. It is still escalating and goes into the top—freeze—state before it begins to flatten out. So, in this case, the cute little dinosaur wakes up and launches the stress response. Perhaps this person flew into a rage and emailed back a volley of abuse, escalating the situation. Or, possibly, they hit the freeze response before taking any action, and the action they ended up taking may have caused them more harm or trauma. Now, look at the white dotted line. Again, this is the same line—a response to a less stressful event. Even here, because of the narrower Window of Tolerance, this person's body experiences the stress response. In other words, their dinosaur wakes up and reacts. The point I want to make is the idea that "trauma" isn't the event; it is your body's ability to respond to the event. We will be exploring this in more detail in the next chapter. For now, just understand, in the case of someone with a narrow Window of Tolerance, a seemingly "small" event can be traumatic, whereas, the same event, in a person with a wider Window of Tolerance, is successfully managed or barely even noticed. So, the next question is this: what determines the width of your Window of Tolerance? Or, to put it another way, how and when is your nervous system "built"?

ENERGY SAVING AID

These are the essential points that are helpful for you to take away from the following section:

- *Your central nervous system develops in the womb and during your early life. It learns how to adapt to stressful events and how to reregulate itself from the mother and primary caregiver. If your early years were spent in an unsupportive environment, this has a lasting impact on your nervous system, setting up patterns that you will carry into adult life.*
- *It will also be affected by ancestral trauma: gene expression can be changed by experiencing trauma, and that altered gene expression can be inherited through multiple generations.*
- *The good news is you can repair your system and reprogram it, so it returns to supporting your health and healing. Trauma is your body's reaction to an event, not the event itself. So, whilst it would not be possible to "undo" the event, it is possible to heal the reaction.*

Developing Your Central Nervous System (CNS)

The CNS begins forming in the womb, and its formation is regulated by the mother. So, the amount of stress—or trauma—experienced by the mother is going to have a direct impact on the formation of the baby's CNS. Again, this is not about blame and shame. Your mother didn't "do this to you"; it's just how the body works. The second factor is inherited trauma. So, remember how we looked at the idea of ancestral trauma and how it can affect gene expression? That means if, for example, your grandparents experienced a lot of trauma, this would have changed their genes.[58] Those genes would be passed

58 Research into Holocaust victims has shown that the children of the survivors

on to your parents and then down to you. When I introduced the chapter concerning the Intuitive Level in the Four Levels of Creation, I talked about my surprising reaction to a mock air-raid shelter in a museum. Well, both sets of my grandparents lived through World War II, and they all experienced pretty serious trauma. One set of my grandparents lived in London, literally with bombs falling around them. My other grandfather fought on the front line and was captured and held as a prisoner of war for several years. We all knew how much that had traumatised him: He couldn't even talk about his experience. It might seem crazy to think about this, but all of those experiences were passed down to me, affecting my own CNS before I was even born. I also mentioned the potential third factor: trauma inherited from past lives. So, if you don't believe in reincarnation, you can set this to one side and work with the other ideas, but if you are open to the idea of reincarnation, this is a really important area to understand.

Then, we move on to a baby's early years. During that time, its CNS is developing and working out what is safe, what is dangerous and, most importantly, how to regulate itself back to safety when it experiences some kind of perceived threat. So, when a baby cries, it is signalling that it feels unsafe for some reason. Instinctively, the carer will pick up the baby and work out how to soothe it.[59] This process is teaching the baby's CNS how to regulate.[60] It is taking cues from the carer and

---

inherited genetic trauma patterns that could only be attributed to the Holocaust experience, according to 2015 research carried out by Rachel Yehuda, PhD, at Icahn School of Medicine, Mount Sinai.

59 Research into epigenetic expression of glucocorticoid receptors in the human brain that are affected by childhood abuse has found "In humans, childhood abuse alters HPA stress responses and increases the risk of suicide." *Epigenetic Regulation of the Glucocorticoid Receptor in Human Brain Associates with Childhood Abuse,"* McGowan, P., Sasaki, A., D'Alessio, A. et al., published in *Nature Neuroscience, 12,* 22nd February 2009, https://www.nature.com/articles/nn.2270

60 Remember how one of the Adverse Childhood Events was mental illness in a parent. This can be as "benign" as mild depression. A parent with depression will struggle to regulate their own CNS. If we factor in other traumas, it is probably fair to say most parents spend at least a portion of their life with a dysregulated CNS. So,

using those cues to learn. This process continues as the child grows up. Learning how to recognise and respond to its emotions sets up more patterns of behaviour. The Window of Tolerance will expand or reduce based upon how quickly and effectively the child learns to reregulate its CNS.

The key thing to recognise here is that the developing CNS doesn't have the ability to "learn" except by regulating itself against others. So, it can't sit there and say, "I don't feel safe here, but that's because I'm scared of the noise outside." All it feels is "I'm not safe." In a baby, that triggers crying. In an optimal situation, the caregiver will pick up the child, try to identify what is causing the crying, and take steps to soothe that. If the caregiver manages to soothe the child successfully, then the CNS has learnt how to regulate itself and, also, learned something new about its environment. In this example, "That noise isn't going to endanger me." However, if a child grows up in an environment where it never, or rarely, experiences safety, that sets up the CNS with a very, very narrow Window of Tolerance. This is something we are going to explore more fully as we continue travelling through this section. According to the work of Dr. Laurence Heller, we have five key areas that need to develop in a healthy way to allow a human to function within society—in other words, to be able to connect to others and develop healthy, fulfilling relationships. That connection process comes from the CNS. Dr. Stephen Porges talks about the parasympathetic state as the "socialised" state. In this place, you can assess your environment accurately and connect safely to others. So, when you meet a neighbour, you are able to read their face, recognise they are happy, and have a conversation with them, feeling safe and connected. How do you know this? Because as your CNS was developing during childhood, it was exposed to happy faces and learned that these were safe. However, if your CNS had little to no experience of safety, as an adult you may have trouble reading

they are then lacking the tools to teach their child how to regulate in a healthy way.

or sensing the environment around you. Coming from a place where your CNS is permanently in the trauma state—think of this as the long-term dorsal state—you may find the world around you confusing and unsafe. Perhaps you interpret a neutral face as being angry. So, when that person opens their mouth to speak, you expect them to shout at you, and you are primed to defend yourself. How do you think that conversation is going to go?

This may sound like a pretty bleak picture, but I do also have good news. Your Window of Tolerance is not fixed. It is possible to expand it. It is also possible to heal past trauma. So, we're not talking about going back in time and undoing things that happened. This is about understanding and developing awareness, and then using our adult knowledge to process whatever has lain unprocessed within the body up until now. As Dr. Gabor Maté has pointed out, since trauma is the reaction to an event, and not the event itself, we can heal. It is possible to reprogram the emotional and mental response to an event. Some might view this as rewriting the narrative. From the perspective of working with your biofield, we are removing the energy block or distortion that resulted from the traumatic experience.

ENERGY SAVING AID

Please complete the following practice. This is providing you with the self-awareness and information you will use to create your personal roadmap for recovery.

An Invitation to Practice

Once again, I would like you to take out your journal. Please answer the following questions:

- How do you *feel* about the information in this chapter?
- What do you *think* about it?
- Do you have any awareness of how your body changes state? For example, noticing when you move into fight/flight or live in freeze.
- Do you feel your emotions in your body? Are you aware of them coming and going?
- How much of the time are you aware of what your body is experiencing, and how much time do you spend in your head, thinking and analysing?

Please remember, there are no "right" or "wrong" answers to any of these questions. This is simply to build up information. So, if you do catch yourself judging your responses or wanting to judge your past life experiences, just notice this happening, make a note of what is coming up, and politely set those judgements to one side.

Chapter 11

What Is Trauma?

Having outlined the links between your CFS symptoms and a maladaptive stress response in your central nervous system, and having introduced you to your nervous system, it is now time to look at what can cause that adaptation: trauma. So, in this chapter, we are going to explore the difference between stress and trauma. I have already talked a little about how a stressful event will trigger your nervous system to move out of its "safe" state. So, now we need to understand how that survival system can end up adapting in ways that are constantly triggering your body, leading to physical symptoms. I am going to link this discussion to my own experience to try to illustrate how critical it was for me to understand the difference between stress and trauma to find my path to recovery. So, let me start with another excerpt from my journal.

> *ENERGY SAVING AID*
>
> *The journal entry sets the scene and shares more of my personal experience. It's not essential to mapping your recovery. So, if your energy is low or reading is a struggle, you can skip this section.*

Journal: November 2015

Ever since CFS was first given recognition as an illness, battle has raged between those who want to label it as a "mental" condition and those who want to demonstrate that it is "physical." Why is it so important to have it recognized as a "physical" condition? I think there are several reasons for this. "Mental" health disorders are treated with a certain amount of disdain: There is a long history of sufferers being treated as social pariahs, being locked away and subjected to treatments that are really tantamount to bullying. So, at all costs, you do not want to have a "mental" problem. Secondly, there is a common perception that if it's "physical," then it can be cured. We may not have the right drug available yet, but, one day, someone will find that drug, and it will all be OK. Thirdly, "mental" disorders are often seen as a sign of personal weakness: This taps back into those comments about "being lazy" or "attention seeking." We seem to have an unfortunate lack of understanding towards things we can't physically see. Fourthly, there is a huge difference in perceptions about responsibility and treatment. For some reason, we seem to assume if a problem is "physical," you can't control it, but if it's "mental," you can.

Wouldn't it be wonderful if we discovered that simply by changing the way we think, we can allow our bodies to heal themselves by changing the chemicals that the brain is generating? That is incredibly empowering. On the other hand, it also places a huge burden of responsibility on the person who is ill. For starters, there is the "guilt trip": the strong message you did this to yourself. You didn't approach life correctly, so look what you've done to yourself. Secondly, the level of responsibility placed upon you is simply enormous. If you don't start to heal, then, once again, it's your fault. You must not be following the treatment plan, or you're not doing it correctly. Then comes the sinister insinuation that perhaps you're doing this deliberately. Perhaps you don't want to be well; you like the attention or you're afraid to live life. Finally, just step back for a moment and think about what it takes to make that kind of epic lifestyle change. If you've tried to give up smoking or sticking to a diet, those are physical things we think should be easy to control. However, anyone who has tried them knows it's not. They also have a mental component. Why did you start smoking? Why do you persist in doing it even though you know it's doing you harm? Maybe because it makes you feel less stressed. So, therefore, the answer must be to remove the stress from your life. How do you go about doing that? Quit your job? Walk out of your marriage? Stop interacting with other people because they might say or do something that upsets you? Of course not. The idea is for you to modify your reactions and feelings in all of these situations. The next time your boss asks you to work late, you politely but firmly explain that this isn't going to be possible because you would like a life. The next time your spouse starts an argument, you calmly diffuse the situation by acknowledging you understand they've had a really bad day, and you're sorry about that. The next time your friend makes a sarcastic comment about your choice of clothing, you ask them why they said that, explain that you find it hurtful, and ask them not to do it again. Well, wouldn't it be lovely if life worked like this?

I'm not saying any of these things are bad ideas. Everyone can look at the lifestyle choices they make and the way they interact with others and find areas where they could do better. Are you going to do that in reality? Probably not; unless, of course, your health is dependent upon it. Then you really start to think about these things. I write all this with half an eye on Mickel Therapy[61] *and the claim on the website from a lady who had been suffering from CFS for 15 years and tried everything, then after just eight sessions of Mickel Therapy, she was cured.*[62] *For me, Mickel Therapy is*

---

61 Mickel Therapy is a talking therapy developed by a Scottish doctor specifically to treat CFS. It aims to address the maladaptive response in the central nervous system—CNS—by looking at how a patient deals with stress in their life and suggesting behavioural changes to help develop new ways of coping with stressful situations. By creating these new patterns, it is hoped that the CNS can be re-regulated. In my experience, this can be effective for some patients, but in my opinion, it doesn't address developmental trauma. So, for patients with strong trauma adaptations, the therapy may not be particularly effective.

62 This article is one of a series on the Action for ME website that takes a balanced

certainly one of the things I would point to as having a noticeable positive impact. Not least because it removed some of the anxiety by offering me a possible explanation for the way I was feeling. The Hypothalamus may be an area of the brain, but at least it seemed to offer an explanation with some positive actions I could undertake to control the symptoms. Yes, when pointed out to me, I could see ways I viewed life that I could change. Making those changes isn't easy, especially if they happen to involve relationships with other people. However, to suggest that this is a "cure" is something I find worrying. If you are facing an illness that has turned your life upside down, you are going to be in a very vulnerable position where any little chink of hope is something you will grasp with great eagerness. At the same time, it is likely you are going to be facing financial difficulties if you can't work, so any treatment for which you have to pay had really better deliver results. There are various treatments on offer on the private market: Lightning Therapy[63] *and Reverse Therapy are just two that immediately spring to my mind. I mean no offence to any practitioners in these areas when I say that, based on my limited knowledge, all these therapies are trying to achieve similar things, albeit in slightly different ways. They are all encouraging changes in lifestyle and thought patterns and promoting these as routes to health. I am open to new ideas, but after living with the illness for thirteen years, it is fair to say I have developed a "healthy" cynicism towards anything presenting itself as a "cure," or even just a treatment. The one critical factor that seems to be missing from all of these treatments is any statistical analysis of their effectiveness. I have been unable to find anywhere a report that looks at the progress of patients, immediately after treatment and one year or two years on. If you ask the practitioners directly for these kinds of statistics, I have found it impossible to get a straight answer.*

---

look at real patients' experiences of the various therapies: https://www.actionforme.org.uk/get-support-now/info-and-support-resources/interaction-magazine/managing-your-illness/

63 This is a similar article that looks at the reported effectiveness of the various therapies: https://www.actionforme.org.uk/get-information/managing-your-symptoms/complementary-and-alternative-approaches/

I picked that journal entry because it shows how much the idea of needing to work on my psycho-emotional state challenged me. I felt that argument was invalidating my physical experience and trying to push more blame and shame on to me. As a result, it took me a long time to open up to the idea of working beyond the physical realm. You may be in a similar position, so I want to acknowledge that and simply invite you to remain open and curious. I mentioned a little more about my experience of Mickel Therapy in my journal extract at the start of Chapter 4. So, as we progress through this chapter, I am going to use that experience to help illustrate why it is so important to understand what trauma really is and how it differs from stress.

ENERGY SAVING AID

These are the essential points that are helpful for you to take away from the following three sections:

- *For a long time, CFS has been viewed as a "stress-related illness." I resented that view because I had always seen myself as good at coping with stress—even thriving on it.*
- *Several therapies were developed to work with the psycho-emotional components of CFS. One of these was Mickel Therapy, which I tried on the advice of my doctor because he had seen it work "miracles" for other patients.*
- *It turned out that Mickel Therapy was another form of talk therapy focused on making behavioural changes to reduce the body's stress response. I found it interesting, but not the "miracle" I had hoped.*
- *This left me wondering what could be "wrong" with me. It further underlined my conviction that CFS is not a stress-related illness. It led me to reject avenues of exploration that*

> *would have been genuinely helpful to my recovery.*
>
> - *This establishes a common problem: lack of understanding about symptoms can lead to patients being directed towards treatments that aren't right for them or ignoring treatments that could be essential to their recovery.*

Looking at CFS as a Stress-Related Illness

Very early after my diagnosis, I remember people telling me that CFS was a stress-related disease. I strongly resented that assertion for two reasons:

1. It seemed to imply what I was experiencing was "all in my head"—a psychological condition rather than a physical issue. Indeed, this was backed up by the treatments on offer at the time, one of them being Cognitive Behavioural Therapy—CBT.

2. I knew for a fact I was very good at coping with stress. I was not an anxious person. My job had been all about meeting tough deadlines, working under pressure, and I felt like I thrived in that kind of environment.

So, these misconceptions stood in my way for quite some time. In fact, I even thought I had found "proof" that "stress" wasn't the key issue here. Let me share a little story.

A Story About Stress

In 2005, I went back to my doctor to report on some new, uncomfortable symptoms. It turned out that he had another couple of patients with CFS. One of them had walked into his office a few weeks earlier. Nothing remarkable in that, you might think. However, he explained, she had been bedbound and unable to ever visit his office. He had needed to carry out home visits to see her. So, as you can imagine, to find her walking into his office came as something of a shock. What had caused this miraculous change in her situation? A new treatment called Mickel Therapy, and that was what he told me about. Knowing nothing about it, as soon as I got home, I found the nearest Mickel Therapist and booked an appointment.

So, what was this "miracle treatment"? It turned out to be another talking therapy. A Scottish doctor had developed it directly in response to trying to heal his partner from CFS. So, it came with the "credentials" of being developed by a conventional doctor—but did it actually work? For me, no. However, the official Mickel Therapy website was full of testimonials from grateful, happy people reporting remission of their symptoms. So, what was going on here?

- Was the website lying?
- Did these remissions really last as long-term recovery, or were they just providing some sort of temporary relief?
- Did I somehow "do" the therapy wrong?
- Or did I have some kind of hopeless case that was "never" going to heal?

These were all the questions I was asking myself.

I'll give you my answer at the end of this chapter. Let's get back on track and answer the question you're probably asking—What has this got to do with stress? And why are we talking about stress in a chapter that I told you was going to be about trauma?

A Structure for Understanding the Stress Response: Mickel Therapy

So, to answer that first question, Mickel Therapy is based on an understanding of how the central nervous system works. Specifically, it focuses on the Hypothalamus Pituitary Adrenal axis—HPA axis. This system monitors your external environment, picks up on danger, and should respond to keep you safe. The Hypothalamus is the area of your brain that processes information about the environment. If it believes you are facing a threat, it will send a message to your Pituitary Gland, which then communicates with your Adrenal Glands and releases "stress" hormones. These are posted to all the cells in your body, signalling them to respond to the threat. What I am describing here is part of the *mechanism* through which the central nervous system functions to keep us safe. Basically, this is the ancient Reptilian portion of our evolutionary system, which I introduced to you in the last chapter: our survival mechanism. So, back in the early days of humanity, when your biggest threat would likely be a Sabre-Toothed Tiger, it worked perfectly. The signal from the stress hormones would trigger reactions like sending blood away from your stomach—digesting food isn't necessary if you're about to die—and towards your legs—having additional energy in those muscles will allow you to run faster and escape the tiger.

Basically, the system allowed you to run away or perhaps fight your threat. Having done that and survived, your Hypothalamus reassesses your environment. All safe now. So, it once again signals your Pituitary Gland, this time to say everything is OK. The Pituitary passes the message to your Adrenals, and those glands release a different set of hormones to tell your cells to return to their normal job. Your stomach goes back to digesting. Your arms and legs may feel rather tired from all the extra exertion.

So, putting that into the context of your central nervous system—CNS—response, your body is sitting in its social engagement—Ventral

Vagal—response when your Hypothalamus signals the danger. The hormones from your Adrenal glands escalate your CNS into fight/flight mode. You use that power to overcome or escape the threat, and you are safe to return to Ventral Vagal state and continue with your day. The problem isn't with this system but that it hasn't evolved to work well in a modern environment. You see, what your Hypothalamus perceives as life-threatening may not really be so. Now that we live more complex lives, we have more to worry about than Sabre-Toothed Tigers. So, that argument with your partner, your work colleague's bullying, and so on are all perceived to hold the same level of danger as the tiger. So, for many of us, between the constant stream of bad news in the media and the everyday stress of modern life, we may never move out of the "stress" response.

This was the thesis of Mickel Therapy. CFS stems, in large part, from a "maladaptive stress response," which means your cells are almost never performing their "housekeeping and maintenance" duties. So, over time, your body gets weaker and sicker. Hopefully, you recognize this is another way of looking at the Cell Danger Response we talked about in Chapter 9.

Mickel Therapy was designed to analyze a patient's life and develop strategies for dealing with stress more productively, gradually pulling the HPA axis back to a place of balance. The problem, in my case, was I really wasn't facing a lot of ongoing stress in my life. A course of Mickel Therapy was supposed to last for eight sessions. After five sessions, I was sent away because I had learned all I needed to know and, supposedly, had the tools to live a less stressful life and then heal.

I left this experience feeling like it had been interesting. I was grateful to finally have an explanation of the HPA axis and an understanding of how that could be impacting my body. I had greater awareness of how I dealt with stress. Yet my over-arching opinion was Mickel Therapy was something to benefit every human on planet Earth, rather than a "cure" for CFS. Once more, I felt validated in my belief that CFS was not a "stress-related" illness. Or, at least, not in my case. Interestingly, since my Mickel Therapy experience took place in 2005, the research findings from Dr. Naviaux, Dr. Gordon, and their team had not yet been published. That research paper, with its explanation of the Cell Danger Response, only appeared in 2016, and I didn't see it for another few years.

So, having gotten that sorry tale told, what can we learn from it? Well, let's turn our focus to defining what we mean by stress and trauma.

ENERGY SAVING AID

These are the essential points that are helpful for you to take away from the following section:

- *Trauma is not the "event"; it describes how the individual biology responds to an event. So, it is possible to experience the same event as either a "stress"—opportunity for growth—or a "trauma"—permanent adaptation of biological processes linked to the central nervous system. That same event may even register as "nothing at all" for another person.*
- *So, when we focus on identifying trauma in terms of events, we are missing the fact trauma is a biological response that can have far-reaching impacts on many different physiological systems and psycho-emotional behaviours, patterns, and beliefs.*
- *Trying to identify trauma as an event can also lead people to believe they haven't experienced any trauma simply because they are using a narrow definition of what constitutes a "traumatic event."*

What Is Trauma?

Trauma is an often-misused word today. Firstly, it is frequently used interchangeably with "stress," yet these are not the same things. Secondly, it has become a common figure of speech that can lose its meaning. For example, in a context like this: *"OMG, the heel broke off my shoe as I was running for the train, and I was so traumatized!"* Yes, that situation might have been embarrassing, annoying, and maybe even caused you pain, but was it really a trauma? Or was it simply stressful?

So, what does trauma really mean, and how is it different from stress? The first misconception many people hold is that trauma is an event. So, we might think of a war, a car crash, physical abuse, or sexual abuse. You might be wondering how that can be a misconception. Well, it is true all those events are traumatic, but the trauma—or, more precisely, its impact on your physical, mental, and emotional bodies—comes from your central nervous system's ability to process the events, not from the events themselves.[64] So, in that context, it is possible something as—seemingly—small as losing the heel of your shoe could be traumatic for one person but merely stressful for another, and even just plain annoying for someone else. That understanding could also explain why one soldier can come home from a war zone and return to civilian life with relatively few problems, whilst their colleague, who had the same experience of war, ends up with Post Traumatic Stress Disorder (PTSD).

Again, let me underline this point: stress and trauma are not events. They are the body's response to certain events. When an event occurs, its long-term impact on the person depends on what is happening in their biology. We are looking—broadly—at three possibilities:

---

64 This is a topic that Dr. Aimie Apigian has explored in great depth in her work, *The Biology of Trauma*™. Dr. Gabor Mate also talks about this concept in his books and interviews, which you can find online.

1. The CNS switches on the stress system I've just outlined and successfully switches it off again when the stressful/dangerous event is over.

2. The CNS has a sufficiently wide Window of Tolerance the person is able to respond to the event without even needing to go into a stress response.

3. The CNS has become so fragile, or the impact of the event is so huge, the person ends up shutting down completely and fails to process their experience, which leaves them trapped in a cycle of maladaptive stress response. In other words, they are stuck in a loop between fight/flight and freeze but never completely return to the social engagement state.

We began looking at what happens to physiology in the last chapter when we looked at the Window of Tolerance. I'm going to offer you another perspective in the next chapter when we explore different types of trauma. For now, I want to explain a couple more factors that suddenly make sense when you begin to see "trauma" as a response rather than an event.

> ***ENERGY SAVING AID***
>
> *These are the essential points that are helpful for you to take away from the following two sections:*
>
> - *When we explore trauma in the light of a physiological response rather than an event, we can develop a more helpful understanding of how and why a person may be exhibiting symptoms of a maladaptive central nervous system.*
> - *This new framework only began coming to light in 1997 in a study into obesity, which became known as the Adverse Childhood Events—ACEs—study. This study identified events that occur in childhood, many of which we would consider to be a "normal" part of growing up, can end up creating biological changes that have long-term repercussions for health. Literally, these events can end up creating a "signature" that leaves the adult body prone to a variety of diseases and even to premature death.*
> - *So, we may need to start addressing the impact of early life events to recover from health issues that appear to have started only in adulthood. In reality, their root causes may lie in our childhood experiences.*

Could You Actually Have Trauma After All?

You might not even consider that you have any trauma—I know I didn't. You may be sitting there thinking you didn't grow up in a war zone and have never experienced any form of abuse or life-threatening situation. Have you ever stopped to consider that something like bullying at school, having a parent with a mental health imbalance, or your parents' divorcing can have the same impact on your biology as the events we more commonly associate with the word "trauma"?

Well, if you haven't considered that, it may be a good time to think about it now.

The ACE Study

Between 1995 and 1997, the CDC—Centers for Disease Control and Prevention—conducted a study at Kaiser Permanente under the supervision of Dr. Vincent Felliti.[65] This study asked over 17,000 people to complete a simple questionnaire about their early life experiences. It has become known as the ACE study—Adverse Childhood Events Study. The study analyzed the correlation between the number of ACEs experienced by each participant and their health. What constitutes an ACE? I've given you the original questionnaire at the end of this chapter, but this is basically things like parents getting divorced, emotional or physical abuse, or neglect all taking place when the person was under the age of eighteen. And notice this: We aren't necessarily talking about *extremes* of abuse or neglect here. The belief that "traumatic events" have to be extreme is what can end up leading to confusion. The significance lies as much in the timing of the events. During childhood, the central nervous system may not have been sufficiently developed to process the event on its own. Unless adult intervention supported the child in dealing with the event and reregulating the nervous system, that unprocessed trauma can be carried

65 This article tells the fascinating story of how Dr. Felliti originally came to set up the study in his clinic. The CDC had tasked him with finding an effective protocol for treating obesity. He created a very effective program, but then he found some of his most successful patients dropped out just when they were losing the most weight. Curious, he asked some of these patients why this was. All came back with the same answer: losing weight made them feel unsafe. The obesity was a subconscious adaptation to help them deal with trauma. Taking this information, Dr. Felliti and his colleagues developed the questionnaire and shared it among a cohort of thousands of patients, all with different health issues. From those results, various studies have been able to come up with the types of statistics shared below: https://acestoohigh.com/2012/10/03/the-adverse-childhood-experiences-study-the-largest-most-important-public-health-study-you-never-heard-of-began-in-an-obesity-clinic/

through into adult life in the form of biological and psycho-emotional adaptations, which can end up leading to health issues. Although that may sound like a depressing, perhaps frightening, prospect, it is also another example of the brilliance of the human body. I now look back on my experience of CFS as a gift. It prompted me to look for answers, and that led me to address and heal those childhood burdens not serving me. It was like a "second chance." In childhood, I didn't have the capacity to process these experiences, and that was nobody's fault. However, it still resulted in them lying dormant in my system, slowly depleting my energy until I found myself forced to wake up and address them.

So, you might be curious as to what I experienced. Well, I grew up in what I perceived as a "normal" loving household, living in middle-class England, and I was lucky enough to enjoy a lot of privilege, as you will have seen from my story in chapter one. So, I never regarded myself as a candidate for trauma: I believed trauma had to include things like violent physical or sexual abuse. However, on taking the ACE study, particularly when the questions are broadened to include the wider social environment, I identified with four or five ACEs. It turns out I am not alone. Shockingly, in the original study, 69.9% of participants reported experiencing at least one ACE. Later, the study was expanded to include "community stressors" like bullying at school. In that study, the number reporting at least one ACE rose to 83.2%.[66] We shouldn't really be surprised. In our modern society, divorce is normal, mental health conditions like depression and anxiety are commonplace, bullying at school and on social media is rife, and these factors are widespread across all socio-economic groups. In a sense, our society has "normalized" trauma.

---

66 Figures taken from this article: https://nhttac-stage.acf.hhs.gov/soar/eguide/stop/adverse_childhood_experiences

So, what does this mean for adult health? Well, let's look at just a few statistics. Compared to someone reporting no ACEs, those with a total of four ACEs or more are:

- 240% more likely to contract hepatitis
- 390% more likely to suffer chronic obstructive pulmonary disease
- 240% at higher risk of contracting Sexually Transmitted Diseases
- Twice as likely to be smokers
- 12 times more likely to attempt suicide
- 7 times more likely to become an alcoholic
- 10 times more likely to have injected street drugs
- More likely to be violent, to have multiple marriages, suffer more broken bones, more depression, and more auto-immune disease.[67]

Ultimately, life expectancy can also be affected. Shockingly, these participants were not all from deprived backgrounds: they represented average Americans.

What is the point I am making here? Many events that we would not typically classify as "trauma" create a "trauma response" in a person's biology. Meaning that person's body is less equipped to fight disease and more prone to suffering many physical ailments. I talked above about the body never having the chance to "exit" the danger response.

67 Interestingly, a number of researchers have considered whether CFS is an autoimmune disease. Some patients suffer symptoms that do seem to correlate to autoimmune issues. To date, nobody has been able to demonstrate this is the single underlying cause of CFS. To me, this suggests there could possibly be a plausible train of progression from trauma to autoimmune to CFS.

Well, this isn't about ongoing stress; this is about early life experiences setting up the central nervous system so that it loses its capacity to deal with challenges.

Personally, I find Aimie Apigian's model very helpful. She talks about trauma in terms of depth and length. She defines it as anything that causes the nervous system to activate the stress response as a result of an event that creates too much stress too fast, or which offers too little safety for too long. In this model, a car crash would create too much physical damage and/or too many challenging emotions—fear—too fast. This would send the body and mind straight through the fight/flight and into overwhelm. In the other section of the model, something like starvation would create too little for too long. The human body can survive happily if it skips one meal, but if it receives no food for five days, that is going to set off a stress response which doesn't get resolved, so ends up with the nervous system in overwhelm. I find this model helpful because it covers both physiological and emotional stressors. It also moves away from the stereotypical idea of "Big T" trauma to illustrate everyday life situations happen to a lot of people and can cause ongoing dysregulation. I invite you to explore that idea even more fully in the next chapter. First, let's go back to where we started this exploration.

ENERGY SAVING AID

These are the essential points that are helpful for you to take away from the following section:

- *Stress and trauma can both lead to a similar initial response in the central nervous system. The difference is, stress is designed to create a growth opportunity—Hormesis—which means your system will naturally reregulate, and the stressful experience will bring you new or enhanced skills—e.g., a stronger immune system or a greater ability to set and maintain healthy boundaries in a relationship. Trauma occurs when the system becomes overwhelmed and gets stuck in a maladaptive response. So, instead of achieving growth, you may find your body adapts in ways that eventually lead to ill health.*
- *In my experience, Mickel Therapy seemed designed to help with managing ongoing stress. In my opinion, it is not a trauma therapy. So, if your health issues are being caused by ongoing stress, then it could be helpful, but if your issues are caused by early life trauma, a therapy like Mickel Therapy seems unlikely to address that sufficiently.*
- *This illustrates the importance of correctly identifying the underlying causes of the physiological and psycho-emotional shifts that lie behind your symptoms. Once correctly identified, you can use a healing modality that is suited to the specific problem. If you have been using healing modalities not directly related to the root causes of your symptoms, this could be a factor in what is keeping you stuck in the CFS maze.*

What Is the Difference Between Stress and Trauma?

So, let's come back to my original question. Trauma creates damage producing ongoing patterns that keep manifesting throughout a person's life and affecting their biology. Stress, on the other hand, should strengthen a person and make them more resilient, physically and mentally. It has a "fancy" name: Hormesis. This is the idea subjecting the body to something that challenges it will lead it to adapt and grow.

So, in emotional terms, take a "stress" like having an argument with your partner. In a well-adapted, healthy system, this situation is going to feel challenging, but it will be an opportunity for growth. The people involved will end up finding a way to sort out their differences, and the relationship will grow stronger for the experience. Whereas, in an already-challenged central nervous system, the argument will trigger old patterns of behaviour that relate to unresolved trauma in the past. Those triggers will cause an escalation in the nervous system, leaving a person unable to communicate effectively, and this can end up impacting the entire situation—perhaps, ultimately, leading to the end of the relationship.

So, how is this relevant to where we began? CFS as a stress-related condition and Mickel Therapy as a possible treatment? If you remember, I said I found Mickel Therapy interesting and informative, but found it did little to nothing to treat my CFS. Yet, I read glowing testimonials about other people being "cured," and I couldn't understand why this didn't work for me. Well, looking back, years later, everything fell into place. I was quite correct: I do have a good capacity for dealing with stress. My life experience has given me enough skills, in certain areas, to be able to thrive in certain stressful situations. However, I became aware my body is also carrying a lot of trauma. Not the "Big T" trauma that comes from living through a war or surviving child abuse. Rather, a dose of Ancestral Trauma, Past-Life Trauma, and Developmental

Trauma changed my biology and made me prone to the symptoms that correspond to the disease we call CFS. So, I have the capacity to put my body into certain situations and to deal with those as a "stress" and achieve growth through that. When I put my body into other situations, my system has little to no capacity to deal with them. As a result, it becomes very dysregulated, and a whole cascade of biological changes occur, leading to the symptoms I experience as illness. In my experience, Mickel Therapy was not designed to heal trauma, but more as a tool to manage stress. For some, simply managing everyday stress might be enough to reregulate their central nervous system and then allow the body to heal. For me, and others like me, something more is needed.

I have just mentioned three specific types of trauma, so let's continue with our exploration. In the next chapter, I am going to introduce you to some trauma types and invite you to consider whether they might be impacting you.

> *ENERGY SAVING AID*
>
> *Please make sure you follow this exercise. It is going to help you identify whether you need to focus on looking into trauma and addressing that as part of your recovery plan.*

Your Invitation to Practice

Before we dive into exploring different types of trauma, I invite you to grab your journal once again and consider how this chapter has changed your view of your body and your CFS experience. You can journal generally or use the following questions as writing prompts:

- Before you read this chapter, did you think you were carrying any trauma?

- How do you *feel* now? Do you *think* your body could be carrying some trauma?
- Has any of this information made you think differently about your CFS symptoms?
- Out of interest, I invite you to take the basic ACEs questionnaire: how many of the following did you experience while you were under the age of 18? Tick all that apply, and count up your total.
    - Did you feel that you didn't have enough to eat, had to wear dirty clothes, or had no one to protect or take care of you?
    - Did you lose a parent through divorce, abandonment, death, or another reason?
    - Did you live with anyone who was depressed or mentally ill or who attempted suicide?
    - Did you live with anyone who had a problem with drinking or using drugs, including prescription drugs?
    - Did your parents or adults in your home ever hit, punch, beat, or threaten to harm each other?
    - Did you live with anyone who went to jail or prison?
    - Did a parent or adult in your home ever swear at you, insult you, or put you down?
    - Did a parent or adult in your home ever hit, beat, kick, or physically hurt you in any way?
    - Did you feel that no one in your family loved you or thought you were special?
    - Did you experience unwanted sexual contact?

Chapter 12

Identifying Different Types of Trauma

Having established that trauma is not the event itself, but the overwhelm it causes in the central nervous system, I want to introduce you to some different types of trauma common in our modern world. These may or may not relate to your life experience, but for me, discovering trauma is not what I thought it was and seeing how early life experience framed my later life were critical steps on my recovery path. The first small glimmer of that understanding came in August 2016 when I first saw the specialist who carried out the blood tests that highlighted my Mitochondrial issues. He was the first person to explain something of how biology and lifestyle interact and how my childhood experiences could still be impacting my adult life. In case you think I have always been strong and resilient in the years spent living with CFS, this extract also illustrates some of my struggles, and it may even correspond more closely to your current situation.

> ***ENERGY SAVING AID***
>
> *The following journal section is here to set the scene and share my personal story. It is not essential for understanding recovery, so you can skip it if you need to conserve your energy.*

Journal: August 2016

Today is a particularly bad day, mentally and emotionally. I don't have enough energy to do anything much, but at the same time, I have too much energy to do nothing. I am too aware of everything I can't do: I don't know when, if ever, this is going to improve, and I resent having to live like this, but I don't know how to change it. I'm bored. The beading that is my creative outlet isn't really cutting it at the moment—I can't seem to feel any satisfaction in what I'm creating. I've been watching good films and reading good books, but right now I'm finding it very hard to appreciate any of that. I have too much time to think, which is never a good thing. My thoughts are a circular process: question after question all related to the grand theme of what is happening to my body, why it's happening, and what I can do about it.

The reality is, I'm doing as much as I can. I saw the specialist: He proved very kind and very positive, so I have been started on a range of supplements—part homeopathic, part vitamins and minerals—designed to try to do three things: support my mitochondria, support my adrenal glands, and help my body to begin absorbing nutrients properly once again. I was told that I could start to see improvement in about three weeks. I have now been taking them for ten days, so, yes, it's too early to expect results, but that is also frustrating. Every day seems like an eternity at the moment. Yet in the grand scheme of fourteen years and counting, three weeks is such a short length of time. I still have no answer as to how much I will improve—I guess that is a question only time will answer.

I do have a clearer theory as to how and why this could have happened. It's not a great theory, to be honest, although it isn't entirely new. It goes something like this: Some stuff that happened in my childhood put my body under a huge level of stress for many years. My adrenal glands reacted as they were designed to, but of course they are not designed to react this way constantly. My body got used to this and began to see this adrenal workout as "normal," so I got used to operating well under pressure, maybe even seeking it out, as this felt normal. It took me through six years at Cambridge University.

I'm going to take you on a brief digression here: A lot of people have the impression that Oxford and Cambridge are playgrounds for the rich and spoilt. The reality is, the opportunities to over-indulge in drinking and partying are no greater there than at any other university, but the press do enjoy regaling the general public with tales of drinking societies and outrageous "public school" dares, as if this kind of behaviour isn't happening every Friday and Saturday night in London or any other city you care to mention. On the other hand, the academic pressure is enormous: Everyone around you is incredibly, brilliantly clever. The entrance process for getting there is really, really hard and every place is hard-won, so you had better demonstrate why you deserve to be there. For me, studying history, this meant writing a 3,000-word essay every week, for which I had to read, absorb, and understand ten to twelve academic books. I think the most extreme module I took was studying historical philosophers—brilliantly interesting, but an unbelievable amount of work. One week I had six days in which to read Hobbes Leviathan—a mere 1000 pages!—Locke's Two Treatises of Government, plus half a dozen modern historians' learned tomes about these two philosophers, and then turn all that into a 3000-word essay. Day seven, I had a one-to-one tutorial to discuss my essay and set the essay for the next week, and so it all began again. In addition to all this earnest study, I did my fair share of partying and a lot of ballet classes. It may have been an accepted fact my dream of becoming a ballerina had long since gone, but that was no reason to stop dancing. The local ballet school in Cambridge was a brilliant school, so I soon found myself taking three or four classes a week with daily practise to keep me in shape. I took five ballet exams and danced in several shows during my time in Cambridge, all requiring extra rehearsals and practice. As you may imagine, this lifestyle did not leave room for the recommended eight hours of sleep a night; certainly, it practically never involved going to bed at a "decent" time, and it is fair to say that students are not known for their healthy eating habits. All added up to a lot of "stress" and a continual workout for those adrenal glands.

I followed this up by moving into Strategy Consultancy and soon found myself working eighty hours a week, consistently. I began to think that Cambridge had not so much been an intellectual training as a training in how to deal with stress and how to perform mentally on no sleep at all. For the last year to eighteen months, I found myself working all night about once a month. That meant forty hours non-stop working on computer spreadsheets, presentations, and attending meetings. When I finally collapsed and my doctor diagnosed me with exhaustion, it came as no surprise.

Six months later, that diagnosis turned into CFS simply because I had not recovered, and they could find nothing else wrong with me. My personal search for answers has already led me to understand that this lifestyle had put my body under so much stress it was bound to give up. I had flogged my mitochondria to death and drained my adrenal glands. The specialist I have just seen explained there is another factor that may explain the timing. As children and teenagers, we have high levels of Human Growth Hormone—HGH—that allow us to grow and develop. This means any damage we do to our bodies at that time of life will heal faster because the body is able to regrow faster. So, whatever damage I was doing by pushing my mitochondria and adrenals beyond their limits was healing fast enough I didn't notice a problem. When we reach maturity, the levels of HGH drop dramatically because it is no longer deemed necessary for growth. However, my use—abuse? —of adrenals and mitochondria did not drop, so my body just failed to keep up with the same rate of healing, until eventually it broke completely, in effect.

This makes perfect sense, but it leads me to a few more questions. Still the question of why did this happen to me? I am not alone in having experienced bullying—at school—as a child. I am one of thousands of Cambridge students, and I did not live a crazier life than anyone else there. Happily, there were many ways I could have abused my body, but didn't: I've never smoked, didn't do drugs, and didn't even drink excessively. Similarly, I may have been slightly unlucky in my work projects, but there are hundreds of other management consultants both in my old firm and in others who were "enjoying" similar lifestyles to me. In fact, as I look around at the people I know, I can reel off a list of people who have high-pressure jobs and travel consistently—so much, in fact, I doubt their bodies even know what time zone they're supposed to be inhabiting, get no sleep because they have young children, eat unhealthy diets, and generally fall prey to a lot of stress. What I am describing is basically modern life, and it seems to have become a badge of honour to live as fast as you can for as long as possible. That old adage of "live fast, die young" no longer seems true because we all "live fast," but relatively few "die young." So, why have my mitochondrial and adrenal and all the interconnected systems broken down? The only rational answer is genetics. Something in my make-up means I'm effectively not "fit for purpose" in today's modern world. That would be me and at least a quarter of a million other individuals in the UK alone. I say "at least" because CFS is just one of the manifestations of this inability to deal with stress. I was recently reading an interesting scientific paper that looked at the relationship between adrenal stress and diabetes. There is a whole school of thought that sees cancer as the body's failure to adapt to modern stresses. We are all familiar with the connection between heart attacks and stress. The conclusion is I can do nothing about my genetic make-up and nothing to change the age into which I have been born. Frustrating as it may be, it is a case of learning to accept I am unfit for everything that society regards as "normal" and learning to adapt my life to that for which I am fit. Whilst I may be pretty good at rationalising myself round to a more positive frame of mind, this does not entirely silence the feeling of failure. Ridiculous as it may sound and actually be, there is a part of me feeling a "failure" for not managing to live the life that modern society seems to expect and demand.

On the other hand, there is a compelling argument I keep coming across, but which governments and mainstream medicine would like to silence. Nobody is fit for purpose in this modern society. If the links between stress and cancer, heart disease, diabetes, and Alzheimer's are correct—and why not?—then I am, in fact, probably very lucky my genetic make-up dictated CFS for me. I hate the fact that CFS hit me so young, and it leaves me with a feeling I've missed out on some really important things in life—not the career: I would much rather be doing what I am than what I used to do—but the chance to marry and have a family. Although maybe it is wrong of me to blame the CFS for the loss of those things—maybe they just weren't ever in my life's plan—just been watching "The Adjustment Bureau"—a film I love and highly recommend! There are also days when I hate that CFS isn't fatal, just an endless unfurling of struggling through life without energy to do things I would like to be doing. Yes, I know I need to work on my "Pollyanna" skills to see and appreciate the good in the small things and focus on that instead of looking at the missing pieces. I do manage that well most of the time, but I guess there are going to be slip-ups and today is just one of them. So, back to curling up under the duvet and just crying.

In the last chapter, I introduced the seminal ACEs study that began to draw attention to the fact our childhood is not a "one and done" event: It is setting up our biology for life. In that extract, I had a few insights into some of the ways in which my lifestyle had changed my biology. Yet it took me a few more years before I learned about Developmental Trauma. So, yes, my genetic make-up is certainly a factor, as were my pre-illness lifestyle choices. What I had not fully appreciated was the extent to which early life experiences set up the parameters that helped me make some of those lifestyle choices.

ENERGY SAVING AID

These are the essential points that are helpful for you to take away from the following section:

- *Childhood Emotional Neglect—CEN—is, sadly, a common fact of life. It doesn't come from unloving or abusive parents. It is simply a reflection of the caregiver's ability to recognize and validate the child's emotions.*
- *Without recognition and validation, a developing brain learns patterns of behaviour in regard to the emotions. It may learn that certain emotions are unacceptable and need to be suppressed. Or it may learn to act out certain emotions in ways that are not productive.*
- *The patterns become unconscious behaviours in adult life and can trigger the nervous system or be linked to other trauma responses.*

Childhood Emotional Neglect

I want to focus on one of the ACEs: emotional neglect. At first sight, that might seem puzzling to you, or you might see it as some form of extreme neglect like a mother who cannot feel love and constantly rejects her child. However, the work of Dr. Jonice Webb and others has found this can be a much more "normal" and common phenomenon. It "involves overlooking and dismissing some or all of the emotional needs of a child—whether deliberately or inadvertently."[68]

68 Quote taken from this article, written by Hope Gillette and medically reviewed by Akilah Reynolds, PhD: https://psychcentral.com/health/emotional-neglect-childhood

In other words, this is not just "bad" or abusive parents. This can be an excellent, loving, caring, devoted parent. The problem may not be a lack of love or lack of compassion. It can be a lack of time or lack of understanding. To illustrate this, let me use a story. Annabel is a sensitive, shy six-year-old. One day in class, she finds herself sitting next to a little boy called Benjamin. Now, Benjamin was rather bored and thought it would be an excellent game to start throwing Annabel's pencils on the floor repeatedly throughout the entire lesson. Annabel found this very upsetting and annoying. She asked Benjamin to stop, but he just laughed. As soon as she had picked up her pencils, he simply began throwing them on the floor again. Anyway, at the end of the day, Annabel went home and told her parents about this. One parent—Parent One—just laughed it off as a silly little thing and told Annabel she just had to put up with annoying people. Annabel's other parent—Parent Two—put themselves in her shoes and understood that, silly as this might be to a grown-up, it was a big deal for Annabel. So, they helped her process the emotions she was feeling and work out a strategy for dealing with this.

Now, Annabel's parents certainly loved her, and they certainly did what they felt was best to help her. Each of them approached this from their own point of reference. So, Parent Two, who noticed her emotions and tried to work with them, was able to do this because they were emotionally aware themselves. Parent One, who suggested she just needed to understand stuff like this happens in life, was also giving her good advice: yes, stuff like this does happen, and we need to find ways to deal with it. However, they lacked the emotional awareness to help her learn *how* to manage a situation like this. Perhaps something in their background had dampened their capacity for empathy, meaning they genuinely couldn't see the issue from the perspective of a six-year-old. Or perhaps their background had led them to reject their own emotion of anger, or they had never developed their boundary-management skills. In other words, this was not deliberate neglect; it reflected a lack of skill. As an adult, how are you going to teach a skill that you do not understand or possess?

So, what may happen to Annabel? Well, if Parent One had been the only one from whom she sought help, she might have grown up learning when she finds herself in a situation that makes her angry, where another person is harming her in some way, she is powerless to do anything about it. Moreover, she may have learned it's not OK to feel angry about this: We just have to accept the situation and bury our emotions. Yet, as she also had advice from Parent Two, the more emotionally aware parent, she learned it's OK to feel angry when someone violates you in some way. She learned there are things we can do in response to keep ourselves safe without needing to act out the anger in an unhealthy way. Now, there are always going to be times when, for one reason or another, a child doesn't have their needs met. So, does that matter? Well, the human body is set up with windows of tolerance and also safety mechanisms. In other words, it's OK for things not to be perfect. However, let's take a look at what happens when the child's needs are unmet or neglected for too long or to too great a degree.

ENERGY SAVING AID

These are the essential points that are helpful for you to take away from the following section:

- *Developmental Trauma relates to a very specific pattern of trauma hard to spot because it takes place during a child's early years.*
- *The work of Laurence Heller, PhD, has identified five critical areas we need to develop if we wish to navigate adult life. These developments take place during the first few years of*

life and in relation to the way we are treated by primary caregivers.

- *First, Connection. This is the ability to connect to our own body and emotions and the capacity to be in connection with others. Trauma in this area leaves us moving through life feeling disconnected from our bodies and emotions and unable to form meaningful connections with others.*
- *Second, Attunement. This is the capacity to attune to our needs and emotions and recognize, reach out for, and receive physical and emotional nourishment from others. Trauma in this area creates difficulty in knowing what we need and beliefs our needs don't deserve to be met.*
- *Third, Trust. This is the capacity for healthy dependence and interdependence. Trauma in this area can leave us feeling unable to depend on others and feeling the need to control through power or manipulation.*
- *Fourth, Autonomy. This is the capacity to set appropriate boundaries, say no, and speak our minds without guilt or fear. Trauma in this area creates resentment and difficulty saying no or setting boundaries.*
- *Fifth, Love-Sexuality. This is the capacity to live with an open heart and integrate a loving relationship with a vital sexuality. Trauma in this area creates a feeling that self-esteem comes from perfectionism and performance.*

Developmental Trauma

I want to introduce you to some ideas from Dr. Laurence Heller's work on Developmental Trauma.[69] Small children do not have the capacity to work things out for themselves or fix things. The areas of the brain that are built to analyse and problem-solve don't even come online until the age of about seven. So, prior to that, children are totally reliant on the caregivers around them to teach them how to navigate life. Dr. Bruce Lipton talks about this as being like downloading computer programs we automatically run throughout our life without thinking. So, in the example above, Annabel could have downloaded a program that tells her she's powerless to defend herself. As an adult, she perhaps becomes very submissive. Whenever anyone challenges her, she just backs down without attempting to defend herself. More importantly, because she downloaded this program at an early age, it is second nature to her. So, as an adult, she barely even notices this is what she's doing, and she certainly isn't aware there could be another way to deal with this type of situation.

In addition to the automatic nature of these programs, the pain that they create becomes lodged in the Energy body. That means the triggers for the trauma response are sitting within a person's subconscious. Children lack the capacity to appreciate they are "good" people in unsupportive environments. They take on the belief they are "bad." So, the Energy body ends up carrying emotions like powerlessness, worthlessness, self-hatred, and survival fears. When those emotions are triggered, they are simply too painful to tolerate, so the protective nervous system brings in learned coping strategies. These might be seemingly innocent behaviours like people-pleasing, or possibly "bad habits" like smoking, or maybe addictions—either socially acceptable or not—and even escalating to physical self-harm. The extremity of

---

69 *Healing Developmental Trauma: How Early Trauma Affects Self-Regulation, Self-Image, and the Capacity for Relationship*, Laurence Heller, PhD and Aline LaPierre, PsyD

the behaviour is likely a reflection of the intensity of the pain felt when this type of trauma is triggered.

As I hinted above, it is normal and natural for all of us to pick up certain patterns that may not always serve us. A few here and there probably won't have a big impact on your life, but when these types of neglect, or the number of unhelpful patterns, are large in number, it can create real problems. This is where we can move into the territory of Developmental Trauma. In the words of Dr. Laurence Heller, *"It is the experience of being in connection that fulfils the longing we have to feel fully alive. An impaired capacity for connection to self and others, and the ensuing diminished aliveness, are the hidden dimensions that underlie most psychological and many physiological problems. Unfortunately, we are often unaware of the internal roadblocks that keep us from experiencing the aliveness and connection we yearn for. These roadblocks develop in reaction to developmental and shock trauma and the related nervous system dysregulation, disruptions in attachment, and distortions of identity."*[70]

Dr. Heller's work highlights five areas of childhood development critical to creating the connection that provides us with the stability to thrive. Yet, for most of the population, one or more of these areas are operating in unhealthy patterns or have simply not been developed at all. So, the common adult experience is feeling like you are operating with certain parts of you missing. This can also be very difficult to recognise: It may be easier to notice something being done to you than to notice something simply lacking from your environment. This feeling of being "incomplete" is hugely traumatic. As I said above, this is a part of you: There is no escaping this felt sense of being. That has great implications for your central nervous system's ability to regulate itself effectively. It goes beyond an emotional or psychological state. This type of trauma feeds into your biology, creating long-term

---

70 *Healing Developmental Trauma*, Laurence Heller, PhD and Aline LaPierre, PsyD.

biological changes that can manifest in various types of disease. So, let's take a look at these five stages of development.

We are talking about development that takes place primarily under the age of seven—the first three stages all take place between conception and age two. As adults, we have no conscious memory of those years, so our conscious minds don't remember the missed connections. Yet, they are stored in our unconscious and in our bodies—both physical and Energetic. This means they are constantly brought out in the form of behavioural patterns and belief systems for which we have no explanation. When any of these behaviours manifest and we experience undesirable results, we simply feel we are inhabiting an unkind world. This is being done *to* us, it makes no sense, and we certainly have no power over it—or so we believe. In fact, becoming aware of what this Developmental Trauma feels like and where it originates empowers us to change and to heal.

The first type of trauma is something Dr. Heller has called *Connection Trauma*. This relates to the formation of a healthy bond between the soul and the physical body, and it should take place in the womb or the earliest months of life. As with all these trauma types, *Connection Trauma* creates a tension wherein the natural, healthy, supportive state is effectively reversed. So, instead of feeling connection to oneself, an adult with *Connection Trauma* may be very connected to other people. Those who identify as empaths may relate to this. They have a powerful ability to tune into what other people are feeling, perhaps picking up the emotions or even physical pain of those around them without any deliberate attempt or desire to do so. At the same time, they may struggle to feel grounded within themselves, living with a sense of being scattered and "out there," rather than feeling safe and present.

The second type, called *Attunement Trauma,* occurs between birth and two years old. Healthy attunement comes from being able to identify your own needs and emotions and the emotions of others. It comes from caregivers who are able to support the baby emotionally. So, when the baby cries, the caregiver is able to identify and respond to the baby appropriately. This includes obvious things like feeding and changing, but it also includes simply "holding space" for the baby. When we were looking at how the nervous system develops, I mentioned a large part is in learning how to co-regulate. So, a baby may feel distress that comes more from an emotional level rather than a physical place. As well-meaning adults, we see the distress, look through our checklist of hunger, thirst, and wet diaper, and then we panic because we cannot identify the problem. We then try to distract the baby back into calmness by pulling strange faces or waving a toy in its face to try to force a smile. Whatever need or emotion the baby is experiencing, the "program" it learns is that this thing is unacceptable and must be squashed and ignored. When this is a repeated pattern, the ability to read, react to, and process the emotion has been programmed out of the developing brain, meaning throughout life, every time the nervous system picks up on this emotion, it runs a program of suppression. Locking away emotions, instead of allowing them to flow, simply creates blocks that inhibit the body's flow of Energy.[71] If those connections weren't comprehensively made at the appropriate time of development, they are carried through to adult life unconsciously. Once we become consciously aware, we can break and correct these patterns, but we first need to identify that they exist. In adult life, *Attunement Trauma* can create a conflict between being able to identify one's own needs and subjugating them to the needs of others. You may struggle to identify your needs or believe those needs don't deserve to be met. In place of working with your own needs and emotions, you may find safety through helping others.

The third area is *Trust Trauma*, which evolves from the child's needs being attacked, manipulated, or used against them. This is not

---

71 This type of process and reaction is beautifully described by Karla McClaren in the book *The Language of Emotions: What Your Feelings Are Trying to Tell You*

necessarily malicious or even conscious. Experiencing this type of trauma can lead to unconscious feelings of powerlessness, helplessness, and vulnerability. As adults, this may translate into feeling the need to control others or seek power over others to feel safe. As with the other trauma types, it creates a complex push-pull relationship. We all need to be able to call on others at times, whether that is within a friendship or relationship or in wider society. Yet, with *Trust Trauma*, the pain of doing that can be so great, individuals avoid it altogether. Instead of seeking co-relationships, they only feel safe when they feel in control of those around them.

Next, we move on to *Autonomy Trauma*. This is most closely related to what is happening in the child's life around the age of two. We all witness the toddler phase of "no." In essence, the part of the brain that has recognised the child is separate and able to do things differently has come online. This can manifest as "the terrible twos," where children seem to be throwing tantrums and refusing all reasonable cooperation. Whilst that may be challenging when you're the one trying to care for the child, it is also a very necessary growth phase. At this stage, the developing brain and personality are learning how to set boundaries and ask for their needs to be met. So, when that process is thwarted—however well-meaning that opposition may be—the child grows up with a sense their needs cannot be stated. As an adult, this translates into extreme anxiety around setting boundaries and having difficulty saying "no." This anxiety comes from another underlying push-pull resentment. On the one hand, it feels unsafe to ask for your needs to be considered. On the other hand, constantly living according to someone else's rules brings up anger and resentment. Attempts to speak up can lead to simultaneous fear, guilt, and shame. It is a no-win situation, which feels deeply uncomfortable and is constantly triggering the nervous system.

Lastly, we have *Love-Sexuality Trauma*. At first glance, you might be expecting me to say this is related to abuse. In fact, it is much broader than that. The basic intention of this connection is to be able to live with an open heart and integrate love with healthy sexuality. From a developmental perspective, this trauma type is most often triggered either around the age of four to five or during teenage years. It can be triggered by the relationship with the opposite-gender parent—not explicitly sexual—meaning the degree to which the child feels seen, appreciated, loved, and valued. Or, especially in teenage years, it can be triggered by the relationship with peers, and this could be both in the context of feeling appreciated and valued and also in the context of beginning to develop adult sexual relations. As an adult with this style of trauma, relationships can feel extremely confusing. Again, we end up with a tension: perhaps feeling sexually attracted to unavailable people where no true love is going to be possible.

As you may have noticed, there is some overlap between the different stages. In a sense, one stage of development should naturally lead on to the next. It is possible to experience trauma across all stages or just one or two. Again, I need to emphasise all of us may identify with certain parts of each developmental trauma style.[72] The key factor is the degree to which the adaptations we made as children trying to survive go on to impact our adult lives. Also, the reason so much of this goes unnoticed is because the adaptations take place in early years. So, in a sense, they are adaptations away from the "ideal," rather than adaptations away from a previously established level. We have no idea we made any adaptation because we have no experience of life being lived another way. So, this is very different from a trauma occurring in adulthood where we may have a conscious sense of being changed.

---

72 Dr. Gabor Mate, in his book, *The Myth of Normal*, talks about the degree to which modern societies have normalised trauma adaptation styles. So, yes, we can be living in a society where we are all traumatised, but because we are all alike in this, we see it as normal and lack the awareness that brings the desire to change.

Before you begin to panic, I also have good news. Yes, most of us may be walking around carrying some degree of developmental trauma, but it is possible to change and heal it. However, the tools and approaches we might need for that are going to be a little different from the tools and approaches we can use to work with other trauma types. So, if you are beginning to identify yourself in any of what you have been reading, don't worry. In the next section we're going to get on to what you can do to work with any trauma patterns causing you problems.

ENERGY SAVING AID

These are the essential points that are helpful for you to take away from the following section:

- *Ancestral Trauma originates in changed gene expression inherited from our ancestors. For example, the grandchildren of Holocaust survivors exhibit gene expression that makes them more susceptible to triggering the nervous system.*
- *Collective Trauma is linked to Ancestral Trauma, but it relates more to the information and awareness of collective memory; for example, tapping into a belief system that sees women—or another minority group—as secondary and deserving of abuse.*
- *Past-Life Trauma relates to the Karma brought in by the soul when it incarnates into this human body in this lifetime.*

Ancestral, Collective, and Past-Life Influences

The first of those relates to what we inherit—or bring in with us when we are born. As I mentioned earlier, we now have some fascinating research that has shown how traumatic experiences cause gene expression to change. This new gene expression can then be passed down through multiple generations. This is what I am terming Ancestral Trauma.

Closely linked to that is another type of trauma: Collective Trauma. In part two of this book, I introduced you to the idea of your biofield. We also looked at the Four Levels of Creation. All of that work is linked by the understanding of Energy fields. In essence, this is a "space" in which information is guiding the particles to create a particular outcome. We can talk about Morphic Fields. Simplistically, this is a field relating to some sort of group or activity. We each have our own personal Morphic Field, and we also access more general Morphic Fields. So, as a woman, I would be accessing the Morphic Field for women: in other words, all the information that has been recorded as relating to women. I like to think of this a bit like an encyclopaedia. So, I can—metaphorically or at an "Energetic" level—access this information to discover what we know about a particular experience or situation and apply that to guide my behaviour. So, let me develop this example since it is one that I have personally experienced. The information in that field includes all the ways women have been disempowered, disenfranchised, and abused AND all the ways they have fought back, owned their power, gained enfranchisement, and so on. I have the capacity to tap into all of it and use the information to guide my own current life and experience. So, which pieces of information are going to guide me? If I am aware of this, I may wish to consciously choose: I may be inspired to follow the example set by a successful, powerful woman. However, because this also works at an energetic level, my personal frequency is going to determine a lot of what happens. If my frequency is operating at a lower level (e.g., holding a belief I am inherently unworthy), it may be difficult to simply mimic the actions of an inspiring woman and replicate her success. Why? Simply, I am acting only at a physical level, without having altered the energetic frequency being carried in my Psycho-Emotional Body—the inherited and developmental trauma—nor having addressed any of the Karmic influences being carried in my Intuitive body. If I wish to replicate the example, I need to raise my frequency—by processing stuck negative emotions—to match the higher level, as well as replicate the physical acts of the woman inspiring me. Again, all of this can be addressed, but it requires different tools at different levels.

So, let me briefly mention Past-Life Trauma. This relates to the Karmic debts we explored in Chapter 6. Although some people have memories of past lives, most of us don't. In fact, I believe only around 50% of people in the Western World even believe in reincarnation. So, if you don't believe in—or don't know anything about—your past lives, does this matter? No. You don't need to be able to name or remember any of this. Whatever you need to be addressing is going to be coded in your biofield, which means you are naturally going to attract people and circumstances that open up ways to address it. You see, we think of trauma as a terrible thing. Yes, it feels awful when you are experiencing it. The circumstances and events that produce trauma responses can be horrific. And yet, it is also an invitation. You don't get to choose what you experience—at least not consciously; your Soul has made that choice, and you have forgotten all about it—but you do get to choose how you respond to it. Does it break you, or do you find the path to experience post-traumatic growth? Before we move on to consider how you get onto the growth path, I want to finish by addressing the most widely discussed type of trauma.

> ***ENERGY SAVING AID***
>
> *These are the essential points that are helpful for you to take away from the following section:*
>
> - *PTSD is the most commonly referenced form of Trauma. I am defining it as a reaction to a specific event rather than an ongoing lived experience.*
> - *Treatment of PTSD may require different tools and methods from treatment of the other types of trauma discussed in this chapter.*

PTSD

When I talk about PTSD, I am talking about a trauma response to a specific "big" event that is life-threatening—for example, being in a car crash. If you don't fully process your experience, you may suddenly develop symptoms like anxiety when you have to get in a car or if you hear a sound that resembles something you heard in the crash experience. Basically, a specific event has occurred. After that event, you develop symptoms you didn't have previously, and they correspond to the event in some way. So, what happens is your body and mind didn't fully process the event at the time. Some parts of them are still stuck in the state of feeling under threat. Every time you get a reminder of the event, it triggers your central nervous system to flare up again. This is in the hope, this time around, you will finish processing the event and can fully return to "safety."

This is different from the other types of trauma we have been looking at because the event is discrete and identifiable. Interestingly, it is also possible to develop PTSD-style trauma in reaction to a smaller event. For example, the challenges of living with CFS may create experiences that feel traumatic to you and can create a trigger that will later need addressing. We might refer to this as "small T PTSD." This is different from Developmental Trauma, which has led to certain parts of you shutting down, getting lost, going offline—or never coming online in the first place. This has become a part of your identity and creates subtle differences in the way these traumas become triggered and need healing. So, the way in which you would treat PTSD is different from how you would go about treating Developmental Trauma. We are going to explore more about this later. I will briefly mention that there is one area in which we see some overlap: Complex PTSD. This occurs in adulthood and relates to a situation where you face a series of ongoing discrete events; for example, living in an abusive relationship. So, it bears similarities to Developmental Trauma in that we are dealing with a gradual or ongoing change in state. Having Developmental Trauma can also predispose you to other types of trauma because you lack the innate resources to form healthy connections with others.

ENERGY SAVING AID

These are the essential points that are helpful for you to take away from the following section:

- *The reason we would want to identify different trauma types is because they all come together to create the nervous system response driving the biological changes creating the symptoms of CFS. By understanding the origins of these, we can move towards using appropriate treatments and tools to address and heal them.*
- *Although the landscape of trauma is complex, it is not necessary to precisely pinpoint or identify every single traumatic event to heal. Simply becoming aware of triggers and working with them will allow the original unprocessed trauma to come to the surface and become integrated, returning the body to a state of flow and ease.*
- *This information is not intended to be overwhelming or fear-inducing. It is empowering, giving you a framework for understanding your experience and looking for solutions that will support true healing and recovery from CFS.*

What Is the Significance of These Ideas?

We have covered a lot of big ideas in this chapter, so let me try to bring it all together and place it in the context of your experience of CFS. So far, in this section, we have looked at CFS symptoms tracking back to the nervous system. We have explored how the nervous system is set up, how it is triggered, and what happens to your biology when trauma is created and triggered. So, hopefully, you are beginning to see that finding resolution of your physical illness has a lot to do with identifying and working with the trauma patterns keeping the nervous system stuck in—or close to—fight/flight/freeze state. Now, when I first heard mention of the word trauma, I thought it simply meant the "Big T" events like car crashes and operations, and, yes, maybe my experience of CFS counted. I had no idea that a lot of trauma is brought in with us and also created in our early years. So, we are constantly stuck in a world of non-specific unsafety, which keeps the nervous system in that hyper-vigilant triggered state.

So, let me take my own example to try to explain how all these different areas link together. My soul, when it decided to incarnate into this human body in this lifetime, had a mission. Part of that involved addressing Karmic debts I had incurred in past lives. When I began working on healing my trauma, I began to remember small parts of some past lives, so I had a sense of some of the trauma my soul had experienced. Most of us don't have any memories, and we certainly don't have any sense of what our soul decided it wanted to achieve in this lifetime—but that's OK because the soul is going to incarnate into a human body that will bring about opportunities to complete its mission. So, my human genome contains some trauma inherited from the genetic expression changes induced by my ancestors' experiences. I have awareness of some of them through looking back at what my parents and grandparents experienced in World War II. This would relate to both Ancestral and Collective Trauma. My soul incarnated into a female body, so I am—unconsciously—tapping into the Collective female trauma patterns held in that Morphic Field. None of this had anything to do with my physical experience in this current lifetime. Yet, it brought me in with a set of information in my biofield, which made me susceptible to adapting in particular ways as I was developing during my early years. So, as I bring this all together, I can see patterns emerging. Perhaps we might argue that women are generally more likely to develop *Autonomy Trauma*. Throughout many, many generations, women have been encouraged to suppress their own needs to fit into society. Perhaps we might also argue that men are more likely to develop *Trust Trauma*. Again, the social constructs of multiple generations may have left men feeling manipulated by women and seeking to wield power for that reason.[73] Basically, there is a lot of complex interplay taking place. In my case, whatever I brought into this life set me up with a greater propensity to developmental trauma in specific areas. In essence, this magnifies the patterns my soul wishes to heal. So, as I progress through life, I am attracting situations that invite me to explore and heal the trauma. For me, although there have been many individual circumstances and events, my experience of CFS crystallised everything and paved the way to experience incredible deep-rooted healing and post-traumatic growth.

On the one hand, this may be a very frightening or depressing realisation. If you believe what I have shared here, then you may be feeling quite overwhelmed and hopeless or helpless right now. This is not what I intend by sharing this information. In fact, as you begin to understand there are levels you haven't even begun exploring yet, this is great news. If you are like I was in 2018, at a point where you've already tried a lot of different CFS treatments, and you're still experiencing debilitating symptoms, this is intended to bring you hope. Everything I have shared here can be treated. It takes time, though. You may also be feeling this is incredibly complicated. Yes, it is very complex. I am sharing this to help you become aware there are multiple layers at play in multiple ways, but you don't need to be able to pinpoint and identify the individual pieces of trauma to recover. You can trust, every time you are triggered, or a challenge emerges, this is your invitation to simply work with that trigger or challenge, learn from it, and grow. In essence, this is what trauma healing is

---

73 These ideas about the predisposition of certain genders towards particular types of Development Trauma are entirely my own speculation. They are not based in any research of which I currently have awareness.

about: witnessing, accepting, and allowing the return of flow. This idea will make more sense as we explore where and how trauma is stored in the next chapter.

> *ENERGY SAVING AID*
>
> *Don't skip the following section. This is the part that will help you map your personal recovery path. It's OK if you don't have the energy to answer all the questions in one go—you can journal entries over time. It's also OK to keep your answers short, but please don't miss this opportunity to get in touch with how you honestly think and feel about your situation.*

Your Invitation to Practice

Once again, I invite you to take out your journal and reflect upon the information in this chapter. As always, I have offered you some writing prompts in the form of questions. Or you can simply journal more generally to bring awareness to your developing understanding of trauma.

- How do you feel about these different trauma types in relation to your own experience? Do you feel any of them may affect you?
- What do you think about the information in this chapter? Where do you agree, or disagree, or simply not understand the relevance?

The following questions may help you to identify areas of developmental trauma.[74] Remember, though, we all carry some of this, so identification with the trauma type may or may not have a significant bearing on your symptoms of illness. Please also note how much of the time any of these things apply to you: never/occasionally/most of the time/always.

- Connection Trauma Indicators: which of the following apply to you?
    - Feel terrified and inadequate
    - Feel shame at existing
    - Feel like you never fit in
    - Feel like you are always on the outside looking in
    - Feel like you're a burden on others
    - Identify yourself based on your role in life, e.g., I am a mother, a husband, a teacher, etc.
    - See yourself as rational and non-emotional and feel this is a good thing
    - See yourself as spiritual and above the trappings of "this world"
- Attunement Trauma Indicators: which of the following apply to you?
    - May be needy

74 This is not intended to be an official diagnosis of Developmental Trauma. I have put together these questions based on some of the more common ways in which people with these trauma adaptations identify. If you wish to get a diagnosis, please consult a qualified profession NARM—Neuro-Affective Relational Model—Therapist.

- Feel unfulfilled and empty
- Feel like your happiness is dependent on getting something outside of yourself, e.g., your career or relationship or recognition, etc.
- Feel you don't have your own needs or don't need others
- Identify as the giver or helper and enjoy feeling needed by others

• Trust Trauma Indicators: which of the following apply to you?

- Experience difficulty in asking for help directly
- Feel small and helpless
- Feel used by others
- Feel betrayed
- Feel powerless
- Feel weak
- Take pride in being strong and in control
- See yourself as successful and proud of that
- Try to be larger-than-life
- Betray other people
- Use or manipulate other people

• Autonomy Trauma Indicators: which of the following apply to you?

- Feel afraid people won't like you if they really know you
- Have difficulty expressing any views you feel could cause conflict
- Feel angry—even if you don't allow yourself to show it
- Feel rebellious, but don't necessarily act this out
- Feel resentful of any type of authority
- Take enjoyment from behaving in ways that other people don't expect or in disappointing the expectations of others
- Feel burdened
- You are always seen as—or try to be—the nice/sweet/compliant person
- You are the good boy/girl
- Fear of disappointing others
- Feel proud of being able to take on many things—I can carry it all on my shoulders.

- Love/Sexuality Trauma Indicators: which of the following apply to you?
    - Feel fundamentally flawed or wrong
    - Have constant underlying feelings of hurt
    - Feel rejected
    - Feel unloved and unlovable
    - Are determined to never let anyone hurt you again

- Reject others before they have the chance to reject you
- Self-esteem is based on your appearance and image
- Is important to be perfect and for everything in life to move seamlessly

Chapter 13

Where Is Trauma Stored in Your Body?

It may seem as though this section is entirely separate from the last section, in which we were exploring the Levels of Creation. So, in this chapter, I want to bring the two sections back together. We are going to continue our exploration of trauma. So far, we have explored what it is and the different forms it can take. We have physical biology, thoughts, and emotions involved in this exploration. Now it's time to look at where trauma is stored in your body. As you probably guessed, this brings us back to our Four Levels of Creation. Just as your body consists of different layers, the impact of trauma is going to leave scars at different layers. Why is it important to understand this? Because, in the next section, we are going to take a look at treatment options and the recovery process. Rather like trying to build a house, if you don't understand what you are trying to treat, and which tools you need for that purpose, the end result—your recovery—is not going to go as smoothly as it might. Before we get to that point, let's explore how we store the trauma that we have accumulated. Let me set that up with another early journal entry.

> ***ENERGY SAVING AID***
>
> *The following journal section is here to set the scene and share my personal story. It is not essential for understanding recovery, so you can skip it if you need to conserve your energy.*

Journal: November 2015

One of the big problems with this illness is that there is absolutely nothing visible to show for it. I eat incredibly healthily, and I try to get eight hours of sleep a night. In fact, everything about my life is set up to be so "healthy" that I seem like a paragon of virtue. Consequently, I look incredibly healthy: my skin glows, my hair shines, I'm slim, and the only tiny, tiny thing you might spot if you know me well is the tiredness in my eyes on a bad day. In full crash phase, my skin looks a bit washed out, but unless you live with me, you're never going to see me in full crash phase.

It would be really helpful if I started to turn blue or something when symptoms occurred. Or maybe I should turn a different colour for different symptoms. Maybe I could turn an increasingly vibrant shade of blue according to how tired my body was feeling, then perhaps come out in pink spots as my throat started to hurt, maybe add in some yellow spots as my lymph glands swell, orange stripes as I begin to feel nausea, a white flash as I experienced a dizzy spell—and that would at least cover the most common symptoms. I could document these clues, and then the entire world would know as symptoms were coming on, and they might be able to help. Instead, nothing happens when the symptoms occur.

My Mum has lived through all this with me, and she can detect when something is wrong, but she still doesn't know what, unless I tell her. She worries about me constantly. If I'm out with friends and start to feel I've had enough and need to go home and rest, there is no visible sign and, often, there is no compulsion on my part to tell my friends. If it's really bad, I might make my excuses and leave, but mostly I don't want to do this. I don't want to miss out on more fun, and I know the symptoms will pass, so I'm very good at blotting them out.

I don't want to talk about this illness because I don't want it to define who I am, and I don't want to be "that bore" or "that hypochondriac" who has nothing else to talk about other than how they feel. My immediate family has stood by and watched all of this struggle from the side-lines, unable to do much to help, other than look after me on the really bad days and offer support. My friends have continued to ask how I am, to invite me out, even though there were periods when I was turning down invitations far more often than I was accepting them. Or worse still: when I was accepting invitations to "big" events like weddings and "significant" birthdays, then having to miss the events when they came around. OK, so this happens to everyone: things crop up and life gets in the way sometimes, but not with this regularity, unless you're just a "flaky," unreliable person. I'm not, and I don't want to be thought of in that way. So, basically, anyone who knows me also has to come with a huge level of trust that when I say I can't do something, it's not because I don't want to, but because I really don't feel well enough. That's a big ask.

The net result of all of this is isolation. There is the physical isolation that comes from not being able to leave the house during bad spells. The bigger problem is the mental isolation: the fact nobody else can make this better for me, that however much they love and support me, at the end of the day, this is my battle and the only person who can fight it is me. I can't show anyone how much pain, anger, and frustration I feel and, unless you have experienced this or something similar, it's almost impossible to understand not just the emotions of the illness, but the emotions that result from other peoples' attitudes. There's the fact nobody can categorically tell you, "This is what is wrong with you, and this is what you need to do to make it better." There's the fact some people choose to deal with that by accusing you of faking it, of being lazy, or of attention seeking. In another quirk of fate and TV, as all these feelings were washing over me again, I found myself watching "Philadelphia" for the first time yesterday. It may be a film about the prejudice surrounding AIDS and homosexuality, but so many of the issues it raises also apply to CFS: the lack of understanding, the blame games, and the fact as if fighting a terrible illness isn't bad enough, on top of that, you're constantly facing judgements and having to justify yourself. Don't get me wrong. I don't particularly care what strangers think of me, but those judgements have a real impact on a lot of practical aspects of my life, and that can be hard. It's no wonder there is such a high suicide rate amongst CFS sufferers: the temptation to make a final way out of this is almost overwhelming at times.

In the days when I was writing my journal, I had no idea about trauma. So, I picked that entry to illustrate one of my dilemmas: personally understanding, then being able to communicate my symptoms to others. The material we are going to explore in this chapter is not about visible symptoms, but I hope it will be a useful tool you can begin using to unravel some of what you are feeling inside.

ENERGY SAVING AID

These are the essential points that are helpful for you to take away from the following section:

- *Unprocessed emotions are not simply a "theoretical concept"; they are tangible, and we can measure their effects even when we cannot see them.*
- *From the perspective of your Energy body, your emotions are energetic frequencies. You may be able to sense them in a person's Energy Field—Aura—even if you cannot directly see them.*
- *They have a visible impact on your physical body, creating observable changes in appearance, hormones, and immune response. Such changes may be observed fleetingly as an emotion flows through—e.g., blushing with shame. Or it may cause a long-term change when an emotion becomes stuck—the science of psycho-neuro-immunology is exploring this.*

Unprocessed Emotions as an Indicator of Trauma

I want to take you back to our exploration of the states of your central nervous system—CNS. We looked at how your ability to move smoothly back to the "safe" ventral vagal state reflects your ability to process an event. This ability is what determines whether you process a stressful event and grow from it, or whether the event remains unprocessed and turns into a trauma imprint that affects your body. We also, in that chapter, touched briefly upon the idea of emotions. So, if you remember, we looked at the different emotional states that correspond to the different states of your CNS. Now, let's start bringing that together with some of the ideas about trauma types we explored in the last chapter. If your early life didn't teach your CNS how to process certain emotions, then this has a serious impact on its ability to regulate its different states.

Now, the next point I want to address is what we mean by "unprocessed emotions." Is this a theoretical construct? If not, then where do all these "unprocessed emotions" sit in your body? Hopefully, after considering the biofield and the Four Levels of Creation, you may even be ahead of me here. Perhaps you are already beginning to see where emotions might sit in your body. Well, firstly, let me emphasise that this is "real," not theoretical. You may not be able to see your emotions, but that doesn't mean they don't exist. We may not be able to see them as physical objects in their own right. However, we can observe them as physical effects. For example, shame or embarrassment might cause someone to go red in the face. This effect can be felt by the person experiencing it and seen by others observing that person. Many of us are familiar with the feeling of butterflies in our stomach or nausea in response to feeling nervous. An outside observer may not see this, though.

We are now aware these physical sensations can match with changes in physiology. For example, with the release—or blockage—of specific hormones or changes to the immune system.[75] So, in theory, that can be measured. However, these changes may be fleeting in nature, and therefore it is not always easy to take the measurement at a time that shows the change occurring. MRI scans can also look at the brain and see particular areas light up or shut down in response to triggers. This could be memories of an event,[76] but we are only ever measuring and observing *responses*. We don't yet have a test or some kind of machine that can look and see an object we can label as "love" or "fear" or "anger." Or *do* we? If emotions are not physical objects, yet we know that they exist in some form, what are they? The answer: energetic frequencies and informational imprints in your Biofield.

We are aware of the physical elements of our body. Yet, we are less aware those physical elements are really energy compressed so tightly it moves from its state as a particle, to a wave, and then takes on physical form. Our basic five senses cannot detect the particle or wave state, only the physical form. Yet, some of you may have a sense of something more than your basic five senses. You might call this a sixth sense or an intuition. You might be aware of using it when you meet people and get an immediate "sense" of their emotional state. For example, you might say someone gives you a "good vibe," meaning you feel safe and happy in their presence, even before they have said or done anything. You may also sense other people who give you a "bad vibe," meaning you immediately feel unsafe when you meet them. Then there are the confusing instances where you feel a "bad vibe" from someone, yet their actions or the words they speak could

---

75 I have heard Dr. Christiane Northrup talk about the increase in the Cytokine IL6 in connection with the emotion of shame. The—relatively new—branch of scientific study called Psycho-Neuro-Immunology studies the links between the mind, nervous system, and immune system. We are beginning to understand that these systems are deeply interconnected.

76 A great book to read is *The Body Keeps the Score*, by Bessel van der Kolk. It is a brilliant explanation of how trauma gets stored in the body, and is also a really entertaining read.

be described as "good." This may or may not resonate with you. If it doesn't, don't worry. Simply set aside whatever you don't understand and remain curious and open to receive what does make sense to you right now. If this does resonate with you, then what you are most likely assessing is a person's energetic body. As we mentioned earlier, this is the newest direction that the field of health and healing is starting to explore. We are starting to see machines that can measure and assess the energetic body, which you may see termed the human body field or biofield. An EEG is doing this in a very specific way. It is measuring the electro-magnetic waves around the heart. The NES scanning equipment I am certified to use is reading the biofield as a whole and also the smaller individual fields. A Reiki practitioner will be reading the body's Energy field. So, why is this of any relevance to trauma? In order to answer that, we need to start looking at where trauma is stored in the body and how it is read by the nervous system.

ENERGY SAVING AID

These are the essential points that are helpful for you to take away from the following section:

- *All emotions are an Energetic Frequency, and all Energy is in constant flow: It cannot be created or destroyed, it can simply change state. So, you cannot "remove" your emotions, but you can cause them to stop flowing freely by creating resistance to experiencing them. This is going to result in inefficient or slow Energy flow in your biofield. So, this is one area in which we "store" unprocessed emotions.*
- *This then feeds into the physical body. Specifically, muscles and fascia can record the unprocessed trauma emotions, leading to pain and stiffness.*

- *Polyvagal theory is based upon studying the Vagus nerve, which is a major communication system between the brain and body. This nerve assesses both the state of the body and the state of the mind, communicating between the two. So, when you are asked to make a decision, you are not simply calculating in your mind—you are also receiving information from the signals in your body via your Vagus nerve. This can lead to conflict, leaving you confused and uncertain and reducing your capacity for fulfilling social interactions.*

Exploring Where Trauma is Stored and Interpreted in the Body

A few paragraphs back, I asked where unprocessed emotions are stored. The first part of the answer is in the body's electro-magnetic field. All emotions have a particular Energetic Frequency, and they are designed to be in constant flow. Our emotions are ever-present: We simply become more or less aware of them according to the situations in which we find ourselves. Emotions are the signals that guide us into particular behaviours. They are their own set of information, guiding the particles in our Biofield. When we block—or attempt to block—that flow, we are simply creating resistance. We cannot make the emotions go away: You cannot create or destroy Energy, simply change its state. So, by trying to ignore or block them we are changing their state from flow to frozen. This blocks or disrupts the natural, optimal flow of energy, but the energy will still flow—just at a slower, less efficient rate.

The second part of the answer lies in how that disrupted flow then manifests in our physical body. So, let's turn to look at the body's muscles and fascia. Someone with a lot of stored trauma—trapped, unprocessed emotions—may find it difficult to relax. Their muscles may feel permanently tense, and their body may lack flexibility.

Interestingly, as a side note, this lack of physical flexibility is like a mirror for lack of mental flexibility. In a trauma state, you lose the capacity to create and adapt to situations. Instead, you are more likely to run automatic patterns of thought and behaviour: the patterns that allowed you to survive traumatic situations in early life. In other words, your conscious, creative mind goes—temporarily—offline and your subconscious mind, with all its automatic programs, comes online to take control of the situation.

Returning to your CNS, and specifically to Polyvagal theory, I want to briefly explain something critical. Polyvagal theory is not a theoretical concept. It is based upon observing part of your body's physical anatomy: your Vagus nerve. This is the main nerve that runs between your brain and your gut. It is the main highway of communication for your CNS. It has links to most of the major organs in your chest and abdomen, as well as fascia, muscles, and skin. So, it is picking up and carrying messages to and from many areas of your body. According to Polyvagal theory, about 80% of the Vagus nerve fibres are "afferent," meaning they signal from the body to the brain. That leaves just 20% signalling from the mind to the body—"efferent." This is relevant when you are making decisions and not simply thinking and assessing with your mind. You are also assessing with your body.

So, let's pull this into a real example. Imagine your best friend calls and asks if you want to go and meet for coffee at the local coffee shop. Your mind may be consciously thinking that you don't have anything planned, and it would be lovely to have a catch-up with your friend. So, it communicates a "yes" to your brain's decision-making centre. At the same time, unconsciously, your Vagus nerve is assessing your body. Your muscles are holding a lot of stored images from an incident that happened and remained unprocessed. This incident took place in a social setting, similar to a coffee shop. So, the idea of meeting for coffee out in a crowded place feels very threatening. Your body is feeding back a "no." What answer do you end up giving your friend? Do you find yourself with a sudden, inexplicable desire to spring clean your house, which would mean you really don't have time for coffee right now, so you say no? Or do you agree to the meeting, and then wonder why you're feeling anxious? Looking for an explanation for that sensation, you blame it on the fact it's really hard to find a parking space near the coffee shop, and you're wishing you had asked to meet somewhere different. Basically, two parts of you are giving your brain two opposing messages, and your conscious mind is left there trying to rationalise and explain this because you aren't aware of this conflicting messaging: you simply feel an inexplicable sense of confusion and need to create a story to explain that in some way.

Incidentally, understanding this relationship between mind and body and the balance between what the body is messaging versus what the mind is messaging, is key in another area. If you have ever tried following any sort of self-help advice that tells you to simply change the way you think, you may have found this didn't work for you. Perhaps you have layered on more shame because you were "too stupid" or "too weak" to be able to control your thoughts. Understanding how the Vagus nerve communicates, in my opinion, explains why it is rarely as simple as "just" creating a different thought pattern. Unless you change your biology as well, your body is going to continue to sense danger and signal that to your brain.

If you're finding this fascinating, but wondering what it has to do with CFS, don't worry—we are getting there! I just want to take this in baby steps so you can gain a really thorough understanding of what is happening in your mind and body. That understanding is what is going to empower you to read your symptoms better and find solutions that work for you, rather than constantly falling down rabbit holes that lead nowhere fast. So, let's continue, and explore how this stored trauma may appear in your life. In the rest of this chapter, I'm going to be giving you several different metaphors to help you understand what we mean by storing trauma and how that could change your biology and behaviour. We are dealing with a lot of different angles here, so I am inviting you to explore these through different metaphors. You may see connections between some of them. Some may look like different aspects of the same thing. Or, this may just feel like a jumble at the moment. That's OK. There is no need for you to take all of this on board at once, or even to understand it all. Just knowing that things exist can be helpful. If you don't know what to do with the information right now, just sit with it, and there may come a time in the future when it suddenly makes sense and becomes helpful to you.

ENERGY SAVING AID

These are the essential points that are helpful for you to take away from the following section:

- *The first metaphor for what trauma stored in the mind/body looks like is a memory bank. This sits in the subconscious mind and is basically all the programs you learned in early life. These programs kept you safe when you first installed them, but they may not have been the wisest behavioural patterns.*
- *This lack of wisdom may become apparent when, as an adult, you are repeating unhelpful patterns on autopilot and facing challenges as a result.*
- *The solution is to access the subconscious mind and reprogram the responses that aren't serving you in your current stage of life.*

Behavioural Patterns: Creating a Memory Bank

Earlier, we looked at the idea that your CNS learns from experience. It stores those experiences safely in your subconscious mind so it can bring them up again and reuse them in similar situations in the future. I want to give you a metaphor to help explain what is happening here.

Imagine a threat comes along. Your CNS identifies this thing as something that could kill you, but it can't work out how to deal with the thing. At this point, your little dinosaur is terrified and overwhelmed. However, it is also a brave, determined little creature, and it will do anything to keep you alive. So, if there is an adult on hand to step in and sort out the danger, all is well—but if nobody is around to help, your little dinosaur will do the best it can. In other words, it will practice trial and error until it stumbles upon a behaviour that allows you to survive. The behaviour may cause you pain, and the experience may be painful. Yet remember, this is about surviving, and sometimes the act of surviving doesn't feel good.

To give a concrete example, if you are a small child in the playground at school and a larger child comes up to you and threatens to hit you, your CNS will automatically move into assessment mode. Can it see a teacher, or even another child who could help you? No. Then it escalates the situation, and it may direct you to run away—moving into fight/flight response. If the larger child chases you and catches you, you are still in danger. So, your CNS learns that behaviour wasn't helpful in this situation. Your CNS needs to look for another way out. Maybe it now decides to try fighting, even though the odds of you managing to fight off the bully are small. It's running out of options, but it is determined to make sure you survive. When, predictably, the first punch you land does nothing to help but ends up with you being hit harder, your CNS is forced to try another approach. It may now believe your only option for staying alive is to submit to being hit and hope for the best—you're now moving into freeze response.

So, you stop trying to run or fight and instead, crouch down to try to shield yourself from the blows. Guess what? The older child stops hitting you. They found it fun to torment someone in fear, but when the person submitted, they had no interest in doing anything more. What has your little dinosaur learned? That help wasn't available; it can't stay safe by trying to run away or by fighting. However, when it submitted, it survived. So, that's a great result. It has just worked out a pattern of behaviour it can use in response to a particular threat to keep you safe. It's going to store that knowledge in your subconscious memory bank like a computer program. The next time the bully comes up and threatens you, it's just going to pull out that program and run it automatically, and all should be well.

Fast-forward thirty years, and you're walking down the street one evening. A man comes up to you, threatens you, and demands you give him all the valuables you have with you. What's happening? Your little dinosaur wakes up. Danger! It overrides your adult, rational conscious mind and searches its memory bank in your subconscious mind. It remembers it has a strategy for dealing with this type of situation. So, out comes the program for submission, and you just hand over your money, credit cards, watch, mobile phone, etc. The man runs away, and you've survived. Your CNS is pleased: It has done its job successfully. However, your conscious mind comes back online and realises this doesn't feel like a great result. You feel violated, angry, and ashamed. Because, guess what? The adult "you" is a black belt in martial arts and has just realised this "man" was a teenage boy who was smaller and weaker than you were. You could have run away or fought this boy off instead of giving him all your worldly goods and now having to sort out the mess that loss has created. The more you think about it, the more you realise you're not going to be able to tell any of your friends because they're all going to think you were really stupid for just submitting. So, what do you do? Act out the anger? Keep rerunning the situation over and over in your head? Tell the police? Go and get blind drunk? Well, that depends on which other patterns of behaviour or beliefs you have developed. We'll get on to that next part in a moment.

First, I want to step back and take a look at your memory bank. Earlier on, I mentioned that we can end up feeling conflict between our rational mind, which assesses a situation in one way, and our CNS, which is reacting on autopilot based on the lessons it learned as it was developing. So, the adult "you" is aware you could have engaged in a different behaviour. You—and others—may be critical of the way you handled the situation. Yet, remember, when the CNS is activated, it is "reacting" rather than "acting." It is playing what it believes to be the most appropriate program for the situation. That program—the behaviour you followed—did manage to keep you alive. In fact, I could argue, even though you might be fully capable of defending yourself in this particular situation, your automatic response was the wiser, safer option. If the attacker had been carrying a knife or gun you weren't aware of, then fighting them might not have been wise if you wished to survive. The point is, if you decide the old program didn't serve your purposes as an adult, you can't beat yourself up for following it. You will follow it again the next time you come up against a similar situation. The only way to change behaviour that isn't serving you in adult life is to go back into your memory bank and rewrite the program. We will talk about how you do that later on, but, for now, let's look at the next area.

ENERGY SAVING AID

These are the essential points that are helpful for you to take away from the following section:

- *The second metaphor is the boulder. This represents your core beliefs. Again, these may have their origins in childhood. Like behavioural patterns, we build them up in response to the lessons we learned and the things we observed as we were navigating the world to survive.*
- *We are not always conscious of our core beliefs. Like boulders, they will suddenly appear in the middle of the road, blocking us from seeing clearly or moving forward with ease.*
- *Again, as these are held in the subconscious, they tend to come out automatically in reaction to events. As we react to these core beliefs, we often find them being reinforced because we are getting the same results that caused us to develop the beliefs in the first place. So, it may feel comforting to hold onto them because they create a sense of security, even if their results are not what we truly desire.*

Core Beliefs: Boulders

These individual programs begin to accumulate and even join together to form a set of beliefs. I like to think of these as your core beliefs. So, in the example above, that small child in the playground may have learned he or she was worthless and powerless. People "always" see them as a target—worthless—and they can "never" do anything except submit to the bullying—powerless. The thing about these beliefs is they vary in size and density. So, if that occasion in the playground had been the only time the child was attacked, it might rate as a single incident, a vague memory. However, if it happened over and over again, maybe not just at school but in other situations, too, each of those individual incidents joins together. Instead of being a single memory, this becomes a pattern, then a belief. I like to think of it like little stones being glued together until they eventually form an enormous boulder. This boulder then acts like a block in your system. Remember, we talked about your parasympathetic state being the place you felt safe and able to connect? Well, in that space, you are free and able to adapt. When you aren't feeling threatened, you can be creative and enjoy new experiences. If your space is full of enormous boulders, it is only a matter of time before you come across one of them. Then what happens? You stop short in your tracks, sense danger, and remember your core belief. For example, "I am powerless." Instead of continuing to move through your new adventure, you begin backing off. Your little dinosaur is alert and looking for danger because it believes if you face a threat, you will be powerless to do anything about it. The thing is, none of this is happening on a conscious level. At some point, you may become consciously aware that whatever you're doing isn't fun anymore. In all likelihood, this will be a "feeling," and you may not be able to identify what triggered it. Your conscious mind may begin to try to construct a story to justify the feeling. Again, this is all happening at the subconscious level. So, some helpful friend or therapist or self-help guru coming along and telling you to "think differently" isn't going to work. You need to go back in and begin to dismantle that boulder until it becomes small enough to stop getting in your way.

ENERGY SAVING AID

These are the essential points that are helpful for you to take away from the following section:

- *The next metaphor comes from the saying "Lock it up and throw away the key." This is dissociation. It relates to the emotions we have no capacity to process, so, rather than remaining in the pain they cause, we find ways to ignore them and avoid seeing them as a part of ourselves: we become fragmented.*
- *In truth, these parts cannot be eradicated. They need to be processed, which involves feeling the emotion and learning the message it is trying to communicate.*
- *We may develop very effective adaptations for losing awareness of these parts, but they remain and will always try to come up for release. This is what we are sensing when someone or something triggers us. It is rather like that imprisoned part knocking on the door of our conscious mind and asking to be seen and healed.*

Dissociation and Fragmentation: Lock It Up and Throw Away the Key

The next image I want to give you deals with the idea of fragmentation. Another strategy employed by your CNS is to lock away or try to discard parts of you that are linked to trauma. I feel like this links back to the area of Childhood Emotional Neglect. Going back to the example with which we've been working, I asked how the adult version might react to the assault. All the emotions I listed—anger, shame, relief—would likely be brought up in this type of situation. However, depending on how the child developed, some of those emotions may have been shut down and locked away. Let's imagine a scenario where a child learns anger is never appropriate. All small children go through a phase of getting angry and throwing tantrums. If the carers in their environment react by locking them away until the anger has passed, this could mean the child's CNS learns anger is a dangerous emotion. If they experience anger, that leads to "neglect" or being cast out of society. So, the CNS reacts in the best way it knows how. It tries to shut down the anger. Think of this like locking anger into a tiny box, putting that box in another locked box, and another, and storing all those boxes in a room deep within the subconscious, then locking the room and throwing away the key. Now the CNS can feel safe because anger is out of the way—except you can't just lock away a part of you. Anger still exists. It is just trapped.

The key to processing any experience is to feel all the emotions and allow them to pass through. Some of them may be scary and unpleasant, but they don't last forever—unless, you lock them all away. In that case, they do last, and they grow, and they like your core beliefs can become another set of boulders that block you. They can also become like screaming children wanting to be heard. In some cases, they manifest as physical pain.[77] Again, it is important to remember none of these parts is *trying* to harm you. Each simply wants to be seen and processed. Until you manage to reintegrate the parts back into yourself, it is going to feel like your body is at war internally. This adaptation means your CNS is always going to struggle to feel safe. Somewhere inside of you, it is aware of those locked-up emotions, memories, and experiences trying to get out. So, although in the moment that they occurred locking them away was the best course of action, keeping them locked up forever is simply draining your body.

---

77 I have certainly discovered this to be true much to my surprise! For a more scientific perspective on this, you might want to investigate the work of Dr. Richard Schwartz, developer of the *Internal Family Systems* model of healing. In this model, these different parts may be seen as being at war with one another. Each wants to keep the body safe, but the conflict comes from each part's beliefs about the best way of achieving that goal.

What is the solution? Finding a way to process the emotions you are keeping locked up.

ENERGY SAVING AID

These are the essential points that are helpful for you to take away from the following section:

- *The final metaphor is the one that encompasses all the previous images. Each of those adaptive styles has caused a part of us, a part of our Energy Field, to become frozen and resistant to flow.*
- *When that happens, your nervous system is sensing the resistance, interpreting this as danger, and signalling this lack of safety to your body. In turn, your cells are responding by turning on the Cell Danger Response, and physical discomfort results. This may end up with the diagnostic label of CFS.*
- *All these beautiful, clever adaptations you developed to keep you safe are resulting in blocked flow, and your physical, mental, and emotional symptoms are simply invitations to process the blocks and open up to an efficient flow.*

Lost Social Connection: Frozen

Let's bring in the final metaphor. We have already spoken about how CNS cannot sustain the sympathetic state for too long. When it lacks the safety to return to the parasympathetic—rest and digest—state, it falls into the dorsal—frozen—state. This is the resting place of trauma, a place where you feel stuck, frozen, and cut off from yourself and others. It may not have occurred to you before, but your body's very existence is based upon flow. Breath flows in and out. Your blood flows around your body, circulating oxygen and nutrients to all the cells. Your lymphatic system is constantly flowing to help drain toxins from your body. Your nervous system is in a constant state of flow, assessing your environment, reporting back to your brain, and then instigating whatever actions need to be taken to keep you safe. Your "energetic" body—the biofield—is constantly picking up invisible signals from the environment and passing that information to your cells. Your cells are responding to all of that information as well. That is the process of constant creation that we explore through the Four Levels of Creation. So, if you have a system designed to function by flowing, what happens when it freezes?

Yes, you guessed it: Your body begins to slow down, struggle, and malfunction. Or, to be more accurate, your biology *adapts* to deal with this frozen environment. So, the end result may feel very uncomfortable to your conscious mind, wanting to enjoy a full life, but your central nervous system has put these adaptations in place to keep you safe. From a physical perspective, this may lead to your diagnostic label of CFS. Remember, at the beginning of this section, we explored how your physical symptoms track back to the nervous system as the body's control centre. Whilst your nervous system is in its frozen state, it is signalling the body to behave in ways that it has learned in order to survive. So, whilst these behavioural states and belief systems may be "normal" to you—even "normal" to wider society—they are not "natural".[78] More and more scientific studies into specific symptomology are linking the patterns of chronic disease with what they term "stress," or, as I have been suggesting, ongoing nervous system adaptations rooted in developmental, ancestral, collective, and past-life trauma.

---

78 Gabor Mate's book *The Myth of Normal* explains how we have come to normalise trauma across society. This is no longer an unfortunate situation that affects a few people. It is commonplace and is reflected in the plethora of chronic health conditions we are seeing, not to mention the huge increases in diseases like cancer and heart disease.

ENERGY SAVING AID

These are the essential points that are helpful for you to take away from the following section:

- *In summary, what may look and feel like an inexplicable, frustrating set of symptoms is a clever survival adaptation. It developed as the best way to survive in an overwhelming environment. The key word is "survival." For most of us, this is not enough—we have a desire to thrive.*
- *In fact, the very essence of our soul is about evolution and growth. It is seeking to understand, overcome, and learn from the challenges we face.*
- *When we made these intelligent adaptations to survive, they were designed to be temporary, rather like putting off a task you cannot complete in the present moment—but the task doesn't go away.*
- *As Energy Beings, we operate under the laws of Energy. So, all those unprocessed—trapped or stored—emotions are held as a particular frequency in the Energy Field. They naturally attract energies of the same frequency, not because you are being doomed to a life of misery, but rather as invitations to understand, grow, and heal.*

Bringing It All Together

I want to take you back to the top: you as an Energy Being; your physical body as the central—visible—portion of your entire Energy Field. That Energy Field contains the particles compressing together to form your body and the information—your human blueprint—guiding that process. Then, we bring in the soul: the part of you that has a reason for being here. Fundamentally, that reason is to grow, evolve, and learn. So, when your experience offers up a challenge you do not have the skills to process in that moment, the unprocessed emotions create a temporary freeze in your Energy flow. The survival skills you employed to move around the challenge become automatic behaviours and beliefs your subconscious mind will bring out any time it senses you in a similar situation. Because, when faced with a distressing situation, your conscious mind may end up going offline and unable to make conscious decisions that create a different behaviour.

Now, this all sounds—and will feel—pretty horrific. That is until you begin to understand the process. Your soul, seeking growth, is going to be seeking to process and learn from each of these distressing situations. That means seeing, feeling, and letting go of the emotions that are trapped. The principles of Energy are also at play here. So, any emotion has a frequency. It will attract situations—events and people—that match that frequency. This is not to keep you stuck and in pain but to invite you to grow and evolve and to heal the trauma and move into post-traumatic growth. If your biofield is carrying a lot of low-frequency *unprocessed* emotions, it will attract a lot of invitations for processing. I emphasise the *unprocessed* because this is not about getting rid of emotions. Emotions are the signals we need to help us navigate through life. They feel unwelcome or uncomfortable simply because we don't know how to read them and allow them to flow.[79] None of them are "better" or "worse" than any other, and we cannot dispense with any of them if we wish to thrive. However, as we have been exploring in this chapter, we end up adapting to challenges by trying to ignore, dismiss, and avoid the emotions we don't understand.

---

79 Two excellent books that explore this idea are: *The Language of Emotions: What Your Feelings Are Trying to Tell You*, Karla McLaren, and *90 Seconds to a Life You Love: How to Turn Difficult Feelings Into Rock Solid Confidence*, Joan I. Rosenberg, PhD.

That results in the stuck Energy, maladaptive nervous system, or however else you wish to term the trauma we are carrying around.

So, hopefully, you are following me this far. The process of healing—that's really healing, not simply "managing"—starts with beginning to process and let go of the trauma. As you do this, your system will thaw, your boulders will reduce in size, and your memory bank will be reprogrammed with automatic responses that keep you in flow and open you up to thriving. How do you achieve this miracle? Well, in the next section, we are going to look at that. We will be exploring the types of treatments available, how they work—and when they don't—and also the very important topic of what it is going to feel like as you begin healing. Before we get there, let me invite you to reflect on what you have learned in this chapter.

ENERGY SAVING AID

Don't skip the following section. This part will help you map your personal recovery path. It's OK if you don't have the energy to answer all the questions in one go—you can journal entries over time. It's also OK to keep your answers short, but please don't miss this opportunity to really get in touch with how you honestly think and feel about your situation.

Your Invitation to Practice

I'm sure you know the drill by now! Yes, it's time to take out your journal and begin exploring your reactions. As always, let me provide a framework you can use if you find it helpful. Or, you can simply journal "free-form" if you prefer. For those who like the framework, I invite you to consider the following questions:

- What do you *think* about this chapter? Explore your mental reaction to the ideas I have presented.
- What do you *feel* about this chapter? Explore your emotional reaction to this material, both as it relates to you and maybe as it relates to me as well. Perhaps it brings up feelings of shame or confusion towards yourself or maybe feelings of anger towards me. Hopefully, some more comfortable emotions also come up—maybe gratitude, hope, and empowerment.
- Try an exercise of self-exploration. Can you identify an emotion you try to avoid feeling or expressing? With that emotion in mind, answer the following questions:
    - Try to think of one to three recent situations that have caused you to feel that emotion.
    - For each situation, how did you react? Maybe you acted out the emotion, or maybe you suppressed it. Perhaps you engaged in some kind of behaviour to distract yourself from feeling the emotion or addressing the situation. Or did you do something else?
    - For each situation, how did you feel afterwards? What happened with your physical symptoms? What thoughts went through your mind? What other emotions did you feel? Did you learn any lessons? Did you get any "aha" moments or new revelations? Did this reinforce things you already believe about yourself, the other people involved, or the world around you?
    - Would you have liked to do something differently? If so, what? How might that have looked and felt to you?

Part 4

Preparing for your Escape from the Maze

Chapter 14

Treatment Options

Welcome to the final part—the exciting moment you begin to plot your exit from the maze. In this chapter, we are going to take a look at treatment options. This is not going to be a list of treatments and an assessment of their benefits but rather a guide you can use to apply to any treatment options that come your way now or in the future. Hopefully, by now, you are starting to recognise the value in working with all the different layers of your body. If you have been stuck in the maze seeking a way out for some time, you may have tried a lot of different treatment options already. If they didn't provide the benefits you hoped, you may have drawn some conclusions from that experience. Perhaps you are feeling there are no solutions. Or perhaps you are still hopeful of finding "the one" you need. I have been in both places. The lessons I learned come back to my original concept: the maze. I do not believe there is "one thing" that will bring you full resolution of your symptoms unless, of course, you are prepared to see that "one thing" as a system that brings healing to all parts of you. That means working with the physical, psycho-emotional, and intuitive layers. Or, in other words, your physical, mental, and emotional bodies. In my experience, all of this can be enhanced when we bring in the concept of the soul and connect consciously to the field of Unity Consciousness. So, my journal entry to set up this chapter is going to take you beyond the point of my recovery and into my own "next layer" as I began to find meaning in my experience.

ENERGY SAVING AID

The following journal section sets the scene and shares my personal story. It is not essential for understanding recovery, so you can skip it if you need to conserve your energy.

Journal: Reflecting on My Practitioner Training

I reached a momentous realisation today. Before I share that with you, I want to take you through some of the reasoning that has led me to this point. I feel like the completion of my own post-traumatic growth story comes from finding meaning and purpose in my experience. For sure, I could simply go back to my old life. Throughout many years of my illness, I thought that's what I would do when I recovered. I used to picture myself going back into the corporate world, climbing the career ladder, getting married, and having children—until my journey lengthened and lengthened and gradually those options seemed to fall off the table.

I certainly never expected to find myself at the point where I am right now, in 2023. At the end of last year, I completed my certification as a NES health practitioner and took the first steps to set up my own business with the intention of helping others. When I finally reached that magical endpoint of "recovery," I felt my Soul had been guided to explore all of this terrain in order to chart it and share my findings. So, with that ill-defined sensation, I decided that in order to fulfil that mission, I needed to get a certificate telling the world I was qualified to do this. What should that certificate reflect? Well, obviously, the endpoint—root cause—of my healing journey, a modality that works at the Intuitive Level in the Four Levels of Creation model. So, I followed my intuition and trained with NES. I loved the training, I love the system—its elegance and its power to open up so many layers of the biofield for exploration. I was all set, apart from those nagging doubts.

You see, the prospect of being here to help others is all at once mystifying, humbling, and terrifying. I can't explain the drive telling me to do this. I would dearly love to reject that drive. I have never seen myself in any sort of role that might be described as a "healer." I still don't wish to use that label. To me, it feels supremely arrogant to put myself out there in the guise of someone offering a solution to—well, anything, really! As I began to consider this feeling and break it down to its roots, I recognised that my desire to reject this path is about a fear of letting others down. I remember being in that space of anger and resentment as I struggled with my body. I desperately wanted solutions. The more I tried and failed, the more resentful I became of anyone who came along and suggested they might be able to help me.

So, rather than digging deeper, I decided I was feeling this way because I didn't have "enough" qualifications or certifications yet. The solution? Get more certificates! So, I spent 2023 signing on to more training. Now, I reasoned, I needed to certify in something that would help address issues at the Psycho-Emotional Level, too, so I could begin offering a more comprehensive coaching package to anyone willing to work with me. Again, I felt intuitively drawn to another course. This time, Neuro-Linguistic Programming—NLP—and Life Coaching. Again, I loved the course, and I have certainly gained powerful tools to help myself and others.

Yet still that nagging doubt: Who am I to do this? Still, I saw my potential clients as versions of myself, desperately grasping onto me—as coach—and demanding I become their saviour, and then feeling desperately angry with me when I didn't save them. Isn't it interesting to note my reasoning in there? First, I assume everyone else will be like me, but they're not. Although, maybe some are, and maybe some people will reject the idea I might have something to offer them. Second, I assume, even though I'm feeling driven to help others, I am also incapable of doing it. I am assuming I will fail in my attempts. Guess what that revealed? Yes, more trauma patterns! So, these may not be triggering my nervous system and setting off the mitochondrial dysfunction in the same old way. To put that more clearly, my CFS hasn't relapsed, but this approach to life is still depleting my energy and resources and impacting my ability to follow my desire to be of service.

So, let's bring this back to where I started—my revelation. Since I noticed these patterns coming up and, more importantly, since I registered they were keeping me stuck, I've been practicing my own advice, using the tools in which I've certified, and working on multiple levels to understand what kind of trauma imprint this is and how to integrate it. So, here's the big reveal:

Nobody else healed me. I facilitated my own recovery. Other people supported me. They offered me wisdom and guidance. I chose to take those and follow them, or reject them and ignore them, or return to things I had previously rejected and re-examine them from a new perspective. Every single individual who has recovered from CFS—or any other kind of illness—has also done it themselves. Yet, each of us has attributed our recovery to something—or someone—specific. Or maybe to a set of specific things. Many people have then taken the lessons shared with them by others, added their own particular twist reflecting their personal experience, and begun offering that to the world, either by practicing in an existing treatment modality or perhaps creating a brand-new modality—all in a bid to be of service. In each case, those modalities and treatments help some people immensely, do a little for others, and nothing at all for the remainder. Depending on your personal experience, you will label each practitioner or modality as "amazing" or "rubbish" or "maybe helpful."—and you are right—and so are the people who hold a different view about that same treatment. You see, each of us has our own experience. We take what we need and use it at the right time. Typically, the final thing we try, we then equate to "the cure." Yet, in reality, our recovery came from simply walking our path and that "final thing" just happened to be the last piece of a complex jigsaw puzzle that came together in some magical way. So, for me, now, on the other side of the equation, here's the lesson. I am not going to bring recovery for anyone. Some of what I share will help some people. In some cases, I will be the "final step," and for those people my coaching will seem like "the answer." For others, my experience will appear to do nothing, and those people may wish to get angry and label me as another money-grabbing charlatan taking advantage of the vulnerable.

I realised today that everything is inside me. The people who oppose me, in whatever form, are mirrors of my internal critics, inviting me to work on integrating more of myself. The people who derive benefit from my experience are also reflections of the parts of me I succeeded in reintegrating. At the end of the day, we are all one, and we reflect one another in ways perfectly designed to allow the Universe to keep expanding. My experience is no more or less important than anyone else's. My ability to help others is no greater nor less than the next practitioner. I'm just another puzzle piece. If I can remember that, I can keep growing and serve with integrity.

I chose that journaled reflection as a way to frame the rest of this chapter. I am going to be exploring different treatments for trauma. You might be asking why I'm focusing just in that area. Well, I hope you have begun to see your symptoms are tracking back to what is happening in your nervous system. So, the fastest, most direct way to calm that is to address the things triggering the nervous system—your trauma. That isn't to say your physical symptoms don't need physical support. In some cases, you may need to do the physical support first. Get your vitamins and minerals into sufficient balance to allow your body to begin producing a little energy. That energy, though, is going to be used up on the recovery journey about to unfold. So, don't panic if that level of physical support doesn't immediately transform into you running marathons! That's an angle we're going to explore more deeply in the next chapter. For now, let's get on with the task in hand—addressing trauma.

ENERGY SAVING AID

These are the essential points that are helpful for you to take away from the following section:

- *The place for you to begin is by identifying whether you need to recover from PTSD or Developmental Trauma—or both.*
- *The tools for treating these types of trauma are different. PTSD relates to a single life-threatening event, and it is linked to an external trigger or triggers. It can be treated successfully. EMDR has a particularly good track record for this type of trauma.*
- *Developmental Trauma occurs as a result of ongoing deficits in your relations with key caregivers in early life. It creates a pain-body held in your Energy field, and the trigger for this type of trauma is you! You will be living day to day with emotions like powerlessness, worthlessness, self-hatred, and survival fear, and you may not even be consciously aware of this if you have never known anything else. Addressing this type of trauma requires tools that work with frequency and resonance for day-to-day management, and tools that work with Geometry or information if you are seeking full recovery.*

How Do We Treat Trauma?

For me, understanding I might have some form of trauma and then putting that together with the Cell Danger Response answered so many questions. For one thing, it seemed to explain why I had reached a ceiling in my healing journey. As I began to ponder these ideas more, I realised it might also explain why particular treatments hadn't been working for me. Or had perhaps given me some help, but not the "cure" they promised. I open with those words to give hope to anyone else who has already been down several rabbit holes and still finds themselves living in some kind of nightmare we call CFS.

Assuming you are still with me, hopefully you have come to consider the possibility you might have some trauma stored in your body and addressing this trauma might be a key factor in finding your energy and vibrancy once more. So, if that is true, how would you go about treating trauma? In my opinion, the best answer to that question can be found in another book, *The Body Keeps the Score,* by Dr. Bessel van der Kolk.[80] So, if you would like to gain awareness of different modalities, I invite you to consult that. As we explore the implications for treatment, based on the models I have been sharing with you, I will mention a couple of modalities, but this is not an exhaustive list nor a recommendation for what is best for you. My experience has led me to become "trauma-informed," but I am not qualified to diagnose or treat you, simply to share information.

So, let me begin by underlining the importance of recognising all trauma is not the same. PTSD and Developmental Trauma are very different things. They may end up having a similar impact on your nervous system, which can then feed down into physiological symptoms, but the ways you need to treat them are different. So, your first step would be to identify whether you have PTSD. This is diagnosable as a mental health condition. It would relate to a specific, single, life-threatening event, and it creates a specific trigger that originated outside of you. It is treatable: The most effective treatments available at present are EMDR—Eye Movement Desensitization and Reprocessing—and somatic body therapies and EFT—Emotional Freedom Technique. Just a little note: EFT— also known as Tapping—is something you can learn and practice on your own. However, if you wish to use it to recover from PTSD, you will need to work with a qualified EFT

---

80 This is according to the work of one of the world's leading trauma experts, Dr. Bessel Van Der Kolk. I highly recommend his book, *The Body Keeps the Score*. It powerfully explains the science in a way that is accessible to anyone.

practitioner who specialises in working with PTSD. All of these modalities are designed to reset the nervous system in response to a specific, discrete event.

Developmental Trauma is not a specific event. It reflects poor relationships with key caregivers. Again, I need to emphasise, this is not deliberate: the bottom line is, very few people are walking around experiencing unconditional love. So, how can you pass on something you haven't experienced? Dr. Laurence Heller's work points out that children do not have the capacity to see themselves as good people in poor environments. In fact, it would be dangerous to do so. If, as a tiny child, you try "calling out" your parents, they have the power to remove the things required for your survival. More than that, how can the child even know there is any problem to "call out"? Unless the child enters this life with an understanding of unconditional love, how do they know whether or not someone else is showing them that type of love? All of this comes together in a pattern of ongoing programming that creates your memories, beliefs, identities, and trapped emotions. This is what Eckhart Tolle refers to as the "pain-body." This is comprised of emotions like powerlessness, worthlessness, self-hatred, alienation, feeling lost, despair, a chronic sense of unsafety or survival fears, and rage. Because these things have grown over time, with you, they are a part of you. So, the trigger is "you." Every second of every day, you are walking around with some sense of feeling one or more of those emotions. In other words, your nervous system is constantly receiving messages from your Energy field that you are not safe.

You develop strategies for dealing with these challenging emotions: perhaps numbing out or distracting through behaviour patterns—these can become the things we label as "addiction"—really, they are more like self-medication. These emotions also create internalised beliefs, which determine how you react to external events and people. The pain-body does not exist in the brain, nor specifically in the physical body, although the emotions it carries can manifest as physical pain or toxic thoughts. The pain-body is held in your Energy body—the biofield we explored in part two. As you learned in that section, some of these emotions may originate from experiences you inherited from your ancestors or brought in from your past lives, in addition to events that have occurred in this lifetime. These emotions are Energy frequencies stored as information in your biofield. So, if they are not held in the physical body or the brain, modalities that work with the physical body or the mind may provide you with symptom relief, but they will not change the frequency of the emotion. To change the frequency of the emotion, you need to work with Energy tools: frequency and resonance. This will allow you to manage your experience and work through emotions as they arise.

As we explored in the last chapter, these emotions act like blocks or boulders. They distort the messages your cells are receiving and, ultimately, that can translate into symptoms in your physical body. My experience has led me to believe this is why it is so difficult to understand how to reregulate the nervous system and fully switch off the Cell Danger Response. We are dealing with a state of being that has never been experienced in any other way. Consequently, many people may not even recognise they feel powerless or worthless—at least, not in a way they can verbalise. Without the awareness you could experience something different, how would you even know to begin changing that aspect of yourself? Even if you do have an awareness of feeling self-hatred, how do you change that? Some might suggest spending time doing affirmations about self-love. In my experience, that has little impact unless you are also breaking up the boulders that make up your pain-body of self-hatred.

The process of fully healing or integrating the parts of you that create the pain-body will require you to turn to tools that correct the information in your biofield. As I write this book, I know of three options for working at that level: full spiritual enlightenment,[81] the NES health system, and the Biogeometry of Dr. Ibrahim Karim. Now, none of these systems is going to be listed or approved by institutions like NICE or the FDA. Dr. Karim's work has probably been subject to the most scientific study, at present, but it has not been specifically tested on CFS. The NES system is being studied by independent researchers at UCLA and comes with the credentials it was developed on the experiences of one of its founders—Harry Massey—who had spent seven years living with severe CFS. So, it can address CFS specifically, as well as other forms of disease. The evidence for healing through spiritual enlightenment is anecdotal, and this will be something to which some people are drawn and others are not.

81 If you wish to explore the above, I recommend visiting the following website: https://nikiskye.com

ENERGY SAVING AID

These are the essential points that are helpful for you to take away from the following section:

- *The tools of frequency and resonance work on the principles of physics. The types of emotions held in the pain-body vibrate at a low frequency. If you can expose them to high frequency, they will shatter. It is the same principle as an opera singer hitting a high note and shattering a glass. Developmental Trauma essentially stems from a lack of unconditional love. Exposure to unconditional love—from within yourself—can heal this type of trauma. That is the principle.*
- *In practice, effective modalities include NARM Therapy—NeuroAffectiveRelationalModel, EFT—EmotionalFreedom Technique, EMDR—Eye Movement Desensitisation and Reprocessing, Sound Therapy, Bioenergetics, NLP—Neuro Linguistic Programming, and more.*
- *Where people can end up "going wrong" is in underestimating the amount of time it takes to heal Developmental Trauma. So, it is important—at least helpful—to find a practice that you can also carry out in your own time, at home.*
- *Dr. Bruce Lipton's research indicates that 95% of our genes can be switched on and off in response to our environment. Part of that environment comprises the pain-body that results from Developmental Trauma. So, working in this area can create beneficial changes in your epigenetic expression as well.*

The Tools of Frequency and Resonance and Understanding the Process of Recovery

I could take you on a long journey through some principles of physics here. This is what I studied as I was becoming certified as a NES Bioenergetic Health Coach. In fact, the simpler way of explaining the principle is through an analogy. Maybe, at some point in the past, you have heard stories that opera singers can shatter glass simply through hitting a particular note? Or, were you aware a battalion of soldiers marching in time could end up shattering the bridge over which they are walking? In each case, the act of singing or walking creates a sound that vibrates at a very high frequency. This creates an oscillating wave pattern, which will disrupt the wave pattern of a frequency it doesn't match—something lower frequency in this case. That disruption in the wave pattern will break up the physical matter formed by the compression of the low-frequency waves—the glass or the bridge.

When we bring this into the realm of emotions, love is the highest-frequency emotion. When you can expose low-frequency emotions, like those contained in the pain-body, to the high-frequency emotion of love, over time the low-frequency emotions are disrupted and shatter. What that means in practical terms is, working with modalities that employ frequency or work on the Energy field can dissolve the pain-body. In turn, this will change the danger signals reaching the nervous system, and that will feed through to the cells, creating a resolution of physical symptoms. In the words of Professor of Medicine Dr. Dean Ornish, *"People who are lonely and depressed are three to ten times more likely to get sick and die prematurely than those who have a strong sense of love and community. I don't know any other single factor—love—that affects our health—for better and for worse—to such a strong degree."*

So, does that mean if you can work out how to experience unconditional self-love and compassion and how to integrate into an unconditionally loving and compassionate community, you could recover from CFS or other chronic disease? Hypothetically, yes. Honestly, I don't know the answer to that, and perhaps it isn't something we could study until we have brought more unconditional love to planet Earth. More practically, are there any helpful modalities if you wish to address symptoms of Developmental Trauma? Yes. Dr. Laurence Heller has developed a modality called NARM—Neuro-Affective Relational Model—specifically to work with reregulating the nervous system in response to the five areas of developmental trauma he identified. This has helped me greatly on my recovery path. EFT can also be helpful for working with the emotions present in your pain-body. Anxiety is possibly one of the most widely discussed emotions and, in essence, this is a downstream effect of underlying survival fears. So, yes, you can use EFT to keep working on anxiety patterns as they arise. Over time, people do report increased energy. Sound Therapy is also helpful. We have been talking about resonance and frequency, and I gave you examples of these relating to sound. EMDR and pulsed electromagnetic frequency can also help. So, too, can NLP and, of course, the bioenergetics in which I trained. As I have just mentioned, there may be a difference between symptom relief or ongoing management of a condition and full recovery or healing. Yet, here we stray into the territory of anecdotal evidence. So, I offer that as an idea for further exploration and consideration.

The thing is, the process of working through Developmental Trauma takes time. The good news is, you don't necessarily need to heal it completely to find relief from chronic fatigue. Most people on the planet right now are walking around with some level of Developmental Trauma, and not all of them develop chronic fatigue. So, this comes back to the idea we do not have to be perfect in order to thrive. This idea of time is significant, though. As we will explore in the next chapter, for some people, underestimating the time required to recover can accidentally block recovery. Also, it is important to understand you will need to take responsibility for practicing with tools on your own. So, you will want to look out for modalities that offer the opportunity for you to practice alone at home rather than things that can only be done with a practitioner. If I hadn't supported my recovery with practices like EFT, journaling, NLP tools, and meditation, which I could use on my own, I would have been paying millions in practitioner fees! Even if you are willing and able to pay, you will not find a practitioner who has the time to devote to treating you alone: a good practitioner will have a large number of clients and only so many hours in their working day. It is important to understand you will only get out what you put in on your recovery journey, so the more you can commit to your chosen process, the sooner you will experience recovery.

Now, you may also be asking about the role of your genes in all of this. We've looked at the idea that trauma creates changes in the epigenetic expression passed down through multiple generations. So, how does this play into things? Well, according to Dr. Bruce Lipton, less than 5% of all illness is caused by genes. In the case of the remaining 95% or so, the genetic expression might be contributing to the disease, but that genetic expression can be switched on or off according to its environment. This is the science of Epigenetics. The pain-body we have been discussing here is a large part of that environment. In other words, once you begin breaking up the low-frequency Energy of the pain-body, the frequency of the entire biofield increases. That higher-vibrating environment can signal a problematic genetic expression to switch on or off. Once that happens, the cells that work from the gene expression receive the signal to change their behaviour, which will result in the relief of physical symptoms. Now, I cannot say for sure whether you are one of those unlucky people who has incarnated with a genetic expression that sits within the 5% we haven't yet worked out how to change. All I can say is that the odds are in your favour. So, before you start creating a story about recovery being impossible, make sure you have given yourself the time and made the commitment to recover.

These ideas, so far, have been focusing on the Energy field. If you are coming to recognise the power of working at that level, where does that leave your physical body? Well, in my experience, powerful as the Energy field is, you are still a physical expression at the centre of that field, and that physical expression does need the support of its physical environment. So, let's take a quick look at what that means.

ENERGY SAVING AID

These are the essential points that are helpful for you to take away from the following section:

- *In order to derive benefit from any sort of treatment, your body needs a basic level of energy to support it. That foundation is laid by focusing on your physical environment—what I call the "basic pillars of health."*
- *This includes adequate nutrition, water, light, air, and movement. You can create this foundation through lifestyle changes that are free to implement. If you need more details about how to do that, please visit my website: https://www.findmyenergy.co.uk/the-basic-environment-for-healing-and-supporting-cfs/*
- *At some point, you are likely to need more targeted support from a trained nutritionist who is able to assess your specific needs. This will save you money in the long run, as you won't be wasting funds on supplements that don't support your body.*

The Foundations of Human Health

Even though you might be using effective modalities at the Psycho-Emotional and Intuitive levels, it is important to lay the foundations to support you in the Physical realm. That means creating a physical environment conducive to healing. So, we are talking about eating a good diet, getting adequate sleep, movement, light, and water. These are the things that support all human health, regardless of whether or not you have become debilitated by any symptoms or labelled with any diseases. The best part is you can address this foundational layer on your own and, largely, for free. Or, more precisely, the tools for creating that environment can be free, but you may wish to invest in the odd book or expert course to help you put them in place. You can also head over to the Find My Energy website to read my blog series that covers the basics.

Before I embarked upon my recovery journey through the Optimum Health Clinic, I had already learned how to create a more supportive environment for myself. In essence, I may not have learned much about self-love yet, but I had gotten pretty good at self-care. I had already found a Paleo diet agreed with my body. I focused on eating organic food, minimising the amount of chemicals I was receiving through my diet. I also learned about circadian rhythm and adopted habits like going outside first thing in the morning to help set my natural body clock and not looking at blue screens late at night. Further along my journey, I learned more about breathwork techniques to calm or energise my system.[82] I was using yoga to give my body healthy movement at a level compatible with my energy at that time. All of those things, in their different ways, brought me small improvements in my energy.

---

82 Ari Whitten has conducted a huge amount of research into the basic pillars for human health and energy creation. He has some brilliant self-study courses on his website, https://theenergyblueprint.com, and I found them helpful in my own journey.

By 2017, I realised I had gone as far as I was able on my own. So, that year, I began working with a nutritionist at the Optimum Health Clinic. She was guiding me deeper in all the areas on which I had begun working. Critically, she was also using lab tests to work out and correct my nutritional imbalances. Although I was able to put a lot of basics in place for myself, I did need to work with a qualified nutritionist when it came to honing my diet. I would recommend the same for you. The reason for doing this is to save you money! You may be tempted to read articles, follow research, or listen to what fellow CFS patients are doing for supplement support. However, although particular supplements may be helpful in general, they might not be what you need. Or, possibly, not what you need right now. So, this is less about doing you harm and more about making sure you're not paying out for things your body doesn't need to be taking.

So, given all these options, which treatment is best for you? Well, the truth is, you are the captain of your own ship. Other people can advise you about the tides or weather forecast or how your ship is supposed to be operated, but as you make your voyage, you are the only one who can work out how to navigate the experience in a way that keeps you safe and takes you where you wish to go. However, I am not going to abandon you. Let's take a look at some pointers for working out how to navigate your voyage.

ENERGY SAVING AID

These are the essential points that are helpful for you to take away from the following section:

- *No single treatment is "better" or "worse." It very much depends on your personal needs.*
- *Some treatments have undergone more research than others. That doesn't mean they are necessarily "better"—just better researched.*
- *Each of us is different, so it is hard to be guided by what works for other people. Something may work for you and not others or vice versa.*
- *When you are researching different options, try to tap into your intuition as well as your logical mind. So, how is your body responding to reading about this type of treatment? Do you feel drawn to it? Does it feel good to you and make logical sense?*

Working Out Which Treatment Is Right for You

Ideally, you will want to use a combination of approaches to ensure you are supporting your physical body as well as addressing your pain-body, but which ones? Well, in most of these areas, we have very little comprehensive research. EFT and EMDR have been the most thoroughly researched, to date, and the research is largely positive. So, does that mean they are "better" than other options? Not necessarily. You have to remember that a lack of research doesn't necessarily mean a lack of benefit. It simply means we don't yet have answers. I believe it is also worth remembering that any research is only as good as the questions it asks. So, if you are reading a research paper that demonstrates a particular treatment is effective, check some basic things. Ask questions like effective on what? Knowing that 90% of patients with depression reported a 50% reduction in symptoms is great, but if you don't have depression, then those research findings are irrelevant for you. I think it is also worth noting that your response to any treatment is going to be very individual. So, just because it provided a breakthrough for someone else, it doesn't necessarily mean it is going to be right for you. Or, conversely, just because someone else felt no benefit from that treatment, it doesn't mean you won't benefit. So, annoying as this may seem, the best way to work out what is most effective for you is to be open to trying different things. Happily, that doesn't mean you necessarily have to spend a fortune on different therapists. Many of these treatments have some kind of free trial available—for example, a webinar that allows you to learn more about the practice, hear from other patients, and perhaps experience a short session. Or, even if you cannot find such a comprehensive free trial, just reading the literature about each treatment will give you a good sense of whether this might be a good fit for you.

As you are making this assessment, yes, use your rational mind. Does the "logic" work for you? Also remember to tune into your intuition. If you're reading an article or watching a video, what is happening in your body? Are you feeling compelled by this? Do you sense some excitement—perhaps a feeling of "I want more"? Crazy as this sounds, this is your body's way of communicating "This feels good to me." Sometimes, that may conflict with your mind, which may be pigeon-holing the information as "woo-woo." It is also possible your body's reaction is not simply a reaction to the treatment but a reaction to the practitioner offering it. Again, that may sound a little strange, but perhaps you have already had this kind of experience in the conventional world. If you saw a doctor who seemed to pay you little attention or treat you with minimal care, did you feel like the treatment they were recommending was going to be helpful?

Conversely, if you saw a different doctor who seemed to understand exactly what you were experiencing and feel compassion for you, and they recommended the same treatment, did that change your expectations of how powerful the treatment could be? You may not get it right the first time. You may also find you end up needing a combination of different things. So, one treatment may lift you to a better level, but you require something different to get yourself to the next level. We'll come back to discuss this in the next chapter. First, I want to mention two interesting factors that can have a huge impact on whether a treatment helps you or not.

ENERGY SAVING AID

These are the essential points that are helpful for you to take away from the following section:

- *Research into the placebo and nocebo effects has demonstrated that our minds have the power to create physiological changes in our bodies.*
- *Believing that a treatment will—or won't—be effective for you can create powerful impacts on the outcome of the treatment.*
- *The practitioner offering the treatment can also create a placebo or nocebo effect in you. For example, do you trust them and feel they understand your situation and the illness?*
- *Understanding this potential can empower you to support the efficacy of any treatment through what you believe it to be capable of doing. It can also explain why certain treatments may not work. If your existing trauma is creating mental blocks to healing, addressing those specific blocks may be a necessary foundation for you.*

The Placebo and Nocebo Effects

I expect you will have heard of the placebo effect. This is a beneficial effect produced by a drug or treatment, which cannot be attributed to the properties of the treatment itself. The patient simply believed the treatment worked. So, for example, I gave you a lump of sugar and told you it would cure your illness, and you ate it and began to feel better. Noticing this positive effect, you asked me for an ongoing supply of this magic pill, which I gave you. You proceeded to recover completely and put your recovery down to my "magic pill." Yet, all scientific tests proved there was no way a lump of sugar could have had any beneficial effect on your body, let alone have cured your illness.

The placebo effect is "real" in the sense it can cause actual, measurable, physical improvements. For example, if you are given a pill and told it will make you feel happy, and you believe this will be the outcome, your body may produce increased numbers of endorphins so you do then feel happy. The outcome is real and physical, but it was not produced by the pill, only by your mind inducing the change in your body.[83] You may already be making a connection here, but in case you aren't, let me note how this links back to the model of creation and the idea that changing what is happening at, say, the Psycho-Emotional level, will naturally feed down to the physical level, even though no actual change was made at the physical level. That's pretty powerful stuff. So, why are we still taking pills, shots, potions, and other medications? Why are we not all being taught how to believe that our health outcome is going to come to pass and then watch it happen? Quite simply, we don't yet understand enough about how this

---

83 One such example may be found in this study, results published in 2015. **References:** Association Between Placebo-Activated Neural Systems and Antidepressant Responses: Neurochemistry of Placebo Effects in Major Depression. Peciña M, Bohnert AS, Sikora M, Avery ET, Langenecker SA, Mickey BJ, Zubieta JK. *JAMA Psychiatry*. 2015 Sep 30:1-8. doi: 10.1001/jamapsychiatry.2015.1335. [Epub ahead of print]. PMID: 26421634.

works. We cannot detail the steps required and the physical processes that are happening to create a placebo response. Research to date has also found this response in some types of conditions but not all. Part of that is down to a lack of research. For example, we have anecdotal stories of cancer patients claiming to reduce a tumour through thought or energy healing, but we don't have enough scientific understanding to draw concrete conclusions.[84] So, what about the other side of the coin? If you can believe yourself back to health, could you also stand in the way of your healing?

The answer is yes. This is the nocebo effect.[85] It is essentially the same as the placebo effect but in reverse. If you believe that it is impossible to heal your illness, then even if I give you a treatment that has been tested multiple times in every single lab in the world and proven to have a 100% success rate in every single test—even if I share all that data and explain how the pill works—it is not going to work on you because you do not believe it is possible.[86] This scenario would relate to a patient with a powerful pre-existing belief, but a doctor can also create a nocebo effect simply by listing the potential side effects of a drug or by telling a patient to expect a negative outcome to their disease.

In 2011, Penny Sarchet won the Wellcome Trust's winning science writing essay with her research into the nocebo effect.[87] The most

---

84 If you wish to explore this more, a good starting point is the book *Radical Hope* by Kelly Turner, PhD.

85 Here is one meta-analysis of ten studies into the nocebo effect. Petersen GL, Finnerup NB, Colloca L, Amanzio M, Price DD, Jensen TS, Vase L. The magnitude of nocebo effects in pain: a meta-analysis. Pain. 2014 Aug;155(8):1426-1434. doi: 10.1016/j.pain.2014.04.016. Epub 2014 Apr 26. PMID: 24780622; PMCID: PMC4213146.

86 In the Framingham Heart Study, women who believed they were prone to heart disease were almost four times as likely to die—from heart disease—as women with similar risk factors who didn't believe. Voelker R. *Nocebos contribute to a host of ills*, published in JAMA, February 7, 1996

87 You can read a summary article here: https://www.theguardian.com/science/2011/nov/13/nocebo-pain-wellcome-trust-prize

extreme case she documented was reported in the Southern Medical Journal in 1992. It detailed the case of a man who, in 1973, was given a diagnosis of cancer and told he had just months to live. A few months after the diagnosis, he died, as predicted. However, the autopsy carried out after his death revealed the cancer on his liver hadn't grown. His medical doctor didn't believe the cancer had killed him but speculated perhaps his belief he was going to die had led to the outcome.

Further research into the nocebo effect, carried out by Irene Tracey and others, used MRI scans to show this belief about pain activates the pain circuits in the brain.[88] In other words, the expectation of pain activates the physical circuitry of the brain. As a result, the body feels pain. Earlier in this book, we explored how the mind and body are connected and how our thoughts, beliefs, and emotions create physical symptoms. This is just one example of this process. So, on the one hand, your mind has the power to create a positive outcome from a fake treatment. On the other hand, your mind has the power to create a negative outcome from a proven cure. Fascinating as this is, how does it relate to choosing the best treatment for recovering from trauma or CFS or any other challenging symptoms?

You may be finding this little nugget of information challenging to hear or, indeed, believe. This is going to be particularly true if you have experienced a lot of people telling you that CFS is somehow not a "real" illness but something made up. I know I didn't want to embrace the mind-body relationship for a very long time. The power in this understanding is in recognising there is a pattern to the apparent madness of CFS. When you can recognise the pattern and begin to work with it in a more supportive, aware, conscious way, then you can begin to recover. Why had nutritional support on its own not led

---

88 *The Effect of Treatment Expectation on Drug Efficacy: Imaging the Analgesic Benefit of the Opioid Remifentanil*, published in Science Translational Medicine, 16th February 2011, Volume 3, issue 70. https://www.science.org/doi/10.1126/scitranslmed.3001244

to recovery for me? Because it wasn't addressing the stored trauma. It was addressing some of the downstream symptoms like leaky gut. Unless I also addressed the root cause, I would be left "managing" an illness rather than "recovering" from it. Why had meditation not helped me? Because I introduced it at the wrong time. I hadn't set up any foundation for supporting my nervous system. As the meditation opened me up to what was stored in my subconscious mind, it simply retraumatized me because I had nothing in place to process the effects within my body. As for other modalities that I tried and found unhelpful, what was happening there? Sometimes it was the wrong thing at the wrong time. Other times it came down to the fact that unhealed trauma was in effect causing a nocebo response: survival fears were obscuring my desire to truly embrace life.

ENERGY SAVING AID

Don't skip the following section. This part is going to help you map your personal recovery path. It's OK if you don't have the energy to answer all the questions in one go—you can journal entries over time. It's also OK to keep your answers short, but please don't miss this opportunity to really get in touch with how you honestly think and feel about your situation.

Your Invitation to Practice

As usual, I would like to invite you to journal about your response to the information you've just learned in this chapter. What do you think about it? What emotions has it raised in you?

In addition to that "normal" practice, I am going to invite you to start on a slightly longer-term project. I would like you to begin creating a list of possible treatment avenues. This is going to become ongoing research you can use to begin guiding yourself towards creating a personalised program to address your needs. So, you can start by working through the following questions:

- What treatments for CFS have you tried in the past—or are you undertaking now? List each one.
- Against each of those listed, please answer the following questions:
    - Has this treatment been effective for you?
    - Based on what you have been learning in this chapter, and earlier in the book, why do you think that might be? I mean, why was it effective, if you derived benefit, or why wasn't it effective if you didn't derive benefit.
    - Let's look at your expectations with regards to this treatment. Often, our assessment of the benefit of a treatment is coloured by our expectations of what it would bring us. Were you expecting the treatment to give you a complete cure? If so, then in what timeframe did you expect that to take place? If not, then were you expecting the treatment to deal with a specific symptom—or set of symptoms—and did it do that?
- Now, I would like you to make a list of treatments that you haven't yet tried. Start with the treatments listed in this chapter. Add in any others that you have come across as being either recommended for CFS specifically or for trauma more generally.
- Over time, I want you to begin researching each of those treatments. For each one, answer the following questions, as best you can:

- Does the treatment—logically—sound like it could help you, based on your understanding of your own symptoms and experience?
- Do you feel drawn to the treatment?
- What is preventing you from signing up for this treatment right away?

Chapter 15

Getting Realistic About the Recovery Process

Having reached the exciting prospect of having so many different options for treatment, does this mean you now have the green light to speed out of your maze? Well, if you have been in this maze for a while, there is every chance you are not currently thrilled with me. You may have already tried plenty of treatments. If they didn't provide the benefits you hoped, you may have drawn some conclusions from that experience. Perhaps you are feeling that there are no solutions. Or perhaps you are still hopeful of finding "the one" that you need.

I have been in both places. In fact, my journal entry comes from when I had spent several months and invested a lot of money—and hope—in a new treatment, only to question whether it had created any improvement at all. That was a low point in my journey. However, once I had gathered myself up from the disappointment, it also proved to be an amazing learning experience. So, I will be sharing those lessons with you in this chapter. This is going to fortify and empower you on your journey through your personal maze.

> ***ENERGY SAVING AID***
>
> *The following journal section is here to set the scene and share my personal story. It is not essential for understanding recovery, so you can skip it if you need to conserve your energy.*

Journal: February 2017

This could be my last entry. I am not about to report a full recovery. In fact, I have grown steadily worse over the past four weeks. Last Thursday, I tried to go to the ballet for the first time since that unfortunate episode at the Proms back in August. Having just said I have been slowly deteriorating, you may be wondering why I thought this was a good idea.

The answer is a combination of factors. I have been following a regime of thirty minutes of yoga per day since I last wrote—on "prescription" from the specialist. I am enjoying this: I have always enjoyed yoga and enjoyed the sensation of physical activity to strengthen my body. Hence, I really miss ballet classes. On the one hand, I realised my muscles are not weak. On the other hand, I have been struggling to complete the thirty minutes, and I wasn't recovering, so by the following day I was starting from a lower base of energy. After two weeks, I finally succumbed and decided to miss a day and do every other day.

The other factor was that, instead of adding yoga into my day, I have had to cut out some work in order to achieve it. As energy levels have dropped, that has meant cutting more and more work until I find I'm having more days of doing no work at all than doing some. Days on which I do some, it is only two hours. If you ask me what I have accomplished each day, at the moment it is frequently difficult to list more than "cook healthy food"—less than an hour's activity—and watch a bit of TV—if you rate that as an accomplishment. Hours pass with me lying on my bed or the sofa, too tired to move or do anything, or possibly wandering aimlessly through the house, thinking I should be doing something but not able to summon the energy to actually do it.

The bizarre thing is yoga made me realise there is some strength there, so it felt like maybe I should be doing something physical. At the same time, my mental energy has disappeared. Normally my head is buzzing with plans and things I want to do. Right now, I can't be bothered. There is literally nothing I "really" want to do, and I'm wondering why I'm even bothering to fight this.

Put these two facts together, and I thought maybe getting out of the house would help. I thought I obviously did have the physical energy to make it. My brother kindly gave me a lift to the station. I sat down there while I waited for the train. I sat on the train for thirty minutes. I then took a taxi to the theatre. I ate lunch, but I also started to realise my energy was ebbing a little. Nothing catastrophic yet, and I determined I could do this. I really enjoyed the first act, sat quietly in my seat for the interval, and enjoyed the second act. Then, I had to go out for something to eat in the second interval. I bumped into a lot of people I know, all of whom wanted to talk to me. I was with my Mum and, despite her best efforts to shield me from this, it is impossible to make people understand, although I'm looking really well, I am only there balancing at the edge of my limit and about to topple off the cliff any second. I do not mean that to sound ungrateful: I realise I am lucky to have so many people in my life who do care. Unfortunately, those conversations sapped my last vestiges of energy. Longer-term, it adds to the psychological mountain, but I will come back to that.

So, I enjoyed the first part of the third act, but then I started to feel nauseous. This feeling increased and was soon accompanied by heart palpitations. I knew there would be a pause while they changed the set between the last two acts. Did I use this opportunity to leave the auditorium, or did I try to stay and hope I could calm myself and make it through the last act? I decided to leave, knowing I could lie down outside the auditorium. So, I left my Mum to watch the last act while I lay down. Luckily for me, the theatre has a policy of refusing to allow late-comers into the auditorium until a break. In order that such unlucky people don't completely miss the show, there is a large screen that shows what is happening on stage. It's not the same as being in the auditorium, but it is pretty good. So, I was able to watch the final act whilst lying down. This allowed me to recover just enough to limp my way home without further catastrophe. Longer term, it sent me back over the edge into a crash, from which I am still trying to emerge.

I mentioned the psychological effects. I am so, so very angry. I feel the specialist doesn't really understand and isn't really listening to me. I am sorry I am failing to fit into his nice potted journey of recovery, but it feels as though he dismisses that inconvenient fact. If I'm saying I feel like my body isn't building energy, then I am dismissed as not knowing how to read my body. Sorry, newsflash—I am actually very, very good at reading my body. The yoga that was prescribed focuses a lot on helping the student to identify how they "feel," where particular muscles are, and how to feel and use them. I like this, but it's not teaching me anything. I have been learning how to identify and use remote muscles since I was six years old, in ballet class. I have learned how to distinguish between different types of pain, how to work out which is "good" pain—i.e., a muscle complaining as it gains strength or flexibility—versus a "bad" pain—i.e., an actual tear or some other unwanted damage. I have an iron will that allows me to push through physical pain, even when I shouldn't. The upshot of all this is I feel I have spent several thousand pounds on treatment that hasn't taken me further than I managed to get on my own in this timeframe back in 2002-03. I have written to say I am ceasing treatment.

Going out into society and meeting friends at the moment leaves me feeling like a total fraud. Once again, that "you look great" comment, fighting with the "I feel [insert your choice of expletive]." Not to mention feeling so rubbish is a perfectly normal state of affairs. I'm beginning to question whether my quest to "not feel rubbish" is nothing more than seeking a pot of gold at the end of a rainbow. Somehow, sometime in my life, I managed to buy into a fairy tale, and I'm looking for a mysterious thing called "energy," which, in fact, doesn't really exist. I've built my life on seeking this promised reward, and it's never going to be forthcoming. Suddenly, I have just become an adult, reality has kicked in, and perhaps I need to stop looking for energy and start figuring out how to live without it. Except, that's just what I've been doing these past fourteen years—somehow trying to forge a life without the thing I need whilst simultaneously seeking it. Then the little voice in my head tells me I haven't done enough to seek it, so I've failed. Meantime, that has been distracting me from doing other "living," so I've failed in that too. All of it has been such a mammoth effort, and I've got no fight left in me and really can't for the life of me see what I'm fighting for anyway. My preferred option would be to just quit altogether. I wish nature would give me a way out as soon as possible. Even writing this seems utterly futile, since who is going to listen to me? Who will actually understand?

Oh my gosh, as I revisit my younger self and all she was experiencing back in 2017, I feel such compassion. I can also remember the anger, frustration, helplessness, and hopelessness. I applaud the fact she managed to regroup and continue seeking answers. In fact, that challenging experience became a catalyst for huge growth. I ended up moving on to work with the Optimum Health Clinic and continue addressing my physical needs. I expanded out to address trauma, using psycho-emotional tools and then Energy healing. I eventually learned the value of patience, and here I am today to share all those lessons and insights with you. So, let's get started.

ENERGY SAVING AID

These are the essential points that are helpful for you to take away from the following section:

- *We tend to have a pre-conceived idea about what it feels like to recover from an illness. That idea often comes from a much simpler type of illness—for example, a common virus like influenza.*
- *Recovery from a chronic complex illness like CFS is altogether different. It does not follow a smooth linear path. Instead, it will feel like a rollercoaster of improvements and setbacks.*
- *This is because you are working through multiple layers, rather like peeling an onion. So, each layer will be moving you forwards, but it may not always feel like that.*
- *One of the main reasons people remain stuck in CFS is they don't understand that idea. So, when the recovery path gets bumpy or seems too slow, they interpret that to mean recovery isn't possible for them and just give up. In reality, the final layer might be the next one you remove, but you won't discover that if you lose faith and stop too soon.*

Analogies to Understand the Recovery Process

I want to begin by alerting you to a critical fact. It has been my experience that the usual recovery process for illness doesn't apply to CFS. When I say "usual," I am thinking about recovering from something like the flu. The illness typically takes a course where you feel absolutely terrible at first. Then your body manages to overcome the worst of the symptoms, and you start to feel a little better, but it still takes a while to regain your full energy. The time spent on this process can vary from person to person, but it is generally linear and, usually, you feel better day by day.

The recovery process for CFS is nothing like this. When you think about the model we have been exploring, we have looked at multiple layers in your body and highlighted possible issues at all levels. We have also seen that the range of symptoms can be huge and affect many different systems in your body. Even though I have suggested these multiple systems can be traced back to the nervous system, they still all need to recover individually. So, this is a process. Rather than a smooth linear curve, it is going to feel like a rollercoaster. I like to use the analogy of an onion. You are peeling back layers. Each time you peel back and release one layer, you feel an improvement. However, that feeling of improvement can be short-lived. You soon lose track of how ill you were previously feeling. Although improved, you do not yet feel "recovered." So, your awareness of your continuing discomfort continues until you peel back that next layer of pain. Again, you experience another improvement, but only to reveal—yes, you guessed it—another layer. For me, this was a process that took several years to complete. At any point, your level of discomfort can still be quite high, and it is easy to lose track of whatever progress you have made or are making. So, it is easy to give up.

Back in 2017, as I was writing that journal entry, that was really my first shot at treatment with a specialist who knew about the biology of CFS, had a concrete plan for recovery, and was very optimistic about my prognosis. The part that was "off" was the timing. My expectation that one four-week course of a protocol would correct a set of biological adaptations, in place for—at that point—fifteen years, "may" have been a little optimistic! That is one way of looking at the situation. Another way might be to question the likelihood of a single protocol—even if I followed it for a longer time period—being the answer to this complex set of symptoms. So, that leads me to my next discovery.

ENERGY SAVING AID

These are the essential points that are helpful for you to take away from the following section:

- *The recovery process will require you to layer up protocols or treatments. So, don't make the mistake of doing some nutrition work, recognising you haven't recovered, and then stopping the nutrition to try something else instead. You need to maintain the nutritional foundation and then add the next benefit on top. It's rather like building a house: you need foundations AND walls AND a roof, not just some of those elements.*
- *You also need to make sure all parts of you are in alignment. If you are providing your cells with great nutritional support through supplements—for example—but your nervous system is still running a trauma pattern, your cells will be receiving mixed messages. The physical support is prompting them to maximise their energy. The nervous system is signalling it is unsafe to operate fully in the world. So, you need to address both issues and bring everything into alignment, so your cells get one clear, congruent message.*

Healing ALL Your Bodies

As we explored near the beginning of this book, the division between your physical, mental, and emotional bodies can be unhelpful. Yes, it can make life simpler to try to understand when we break things down. At the same time, it can create an illusion of "this or that."

Your symptoms are emotional, *or* physical, *or* mental. In fact, the healthy human is a wondrous orchestra of all these bodies working in harmony. Focusing on understanding just one element or trying to heal just one element can only get you so far. You really need to focus on everything together. So, I believe that breaks down into two areas:

- Understanding that you need to "layer" different treatments together
- Making sure you are bringing everything into alignment so all your bodies can work together

Let's explore those two ideas, starting with layering treatments.

When I described focusing on nutrition, then turning to the mind-body piece later, I need to make something clear. I did not shift to mind-body *instead of* nutrition. I added it *on top of* the nutritional foundation I had already built. I established a foundation and then added another layer on top of that. If you don't understand the need to proceed in that way, that is one reason why you may end up stuck in illness. To give you a metaphor: the process of recovery is very much like the process of building a house. Imagine if you laid your foundations, then stepped back to admire your work and recognised that you hadn't built a house. Maybe this causes some disappointment. If you take out the foundations and, instead, start to build a wall, your wall is going to be unstable. If you then realise your wall isn't holding up, so you knock it down and try to add a roof, you still don't have a house. Recovery is a process. It requires patience, and it requires you to understand and work with all aspects of your body, which brings me neatly to the second idea: getting everything into alignment.

Not only do you have to build a solid structure, but you need to make sure everything is in alignment. This is really where understanding the nervous system and trauma comes into play, alongside the concept of your physical body, your biofield, and the model of Four Levels of

Creation. Let's imagine the major symptom you are experiencing is a digestive issue. Let's imagine you find a brilliant nutritionist who does all the right tests, interprets the results correctly, and puts together an amazing protocol to repair and support your stomach, intestines, liver, and so on. Yet, somehow, even though you make some progress, you either hit a ceiling, or you relapse. What is happening? Has the nutritionist missed something critical? Is nutrition not enough for you? Or could something else be going on?

Well, let's imagine you experienced a lot of trauma—not necessarily anything "big"; it could just be a lot of little things—as you were growing up. This has lain unresolved in your body and created a subconscious belief it isn't safe to fully participate in life. Every time you try to go out in the world—literally or figuratively—your nervous system is on hyper-alert because it has learned danger lurks around every corner. Now, let's assume this hyper-alert nervous system is activating the Cell Danger Response. The cells in your digestive system are all receiving the message that the body is under threat, so they should be taking appropriate action to safeguard themselves. In this state, they are not going to be able to process all the beautiful nutrients your nutritionist has guided you to take. In a sense, these cells don't want to be "healthy" because they believe they are under threat. "Health" is irrelevant if they can't survive.

In other words, all your bodies are not in alignment. Your conscious mind is wanting to heal. A part of your—unconscious—nervous system is seeing "health" as dangerous, and the cells in your digestive organs are thoroughly confused because they're receiving mixed messages. The end result is going to be you hit a roadblock. I like the image of a river. Your mind is trying to flow downstream. Your trauma patterns are like a rock that's in the way. So, your nervous system, via the Cell Danger Response, is pushing your digestive cells upstream in order to avoid crashing into the rock. What is the solution? To get everything in alignment. In simple terms, you need to provide your nervous system with a sense of safety so it can get on board with the idea of moving back into a full and active life. This might be as simple as learning to be aware and finding ways to keep your nervous system in the parasympathetic state as much as possible. However, if you are carrying a lot of trauma, trying to force the nervous system into safety is rather like trying to persuade someone to walk into a burning building. Before you enter the building, you need to put out the fire. So, the solution is to start healing the trauma.

By the way, this model can also work the other way around. So, you might have done a lot of work to heal your trauma, creating a sense of safety for the nervous system from an emotional/beliefs perspective, but if you are still eating a diet that is full of chemicals and lacking in supportive nutritional elements, your digestive tract is not going to be supported at the level of the physical body. So, this would put you in a situation where the mind is heading downstream towards recovery. The nervous system is supporting this from an emotional standpoint, but the digestive cells are now signalling, "We have a problem here." This also would stimulate the nervous system to raise the red flags and signal danger. So, once again your cells are receiving mixed messages. They may appreciate it is safe to experience life, but they aren't being given the nutritional support to maximise their energy. In this instance, the solution would be to focus on putting in place the nutritional support to get your physical body into alignment with the movement towards recovery already in place in your mental/emotional body. All aspects of your environment need to be in alignment, supporting your body to rest in its natural balanced state. Or, to put this back into the more metaphysical model of the Levels of Creation, you need to be addressing the issues or misinformation at every single level of creation in order for that creative flow to result in the physical experience you are seeking.

ENERGY SAVING AID

These are the essential points that are helpful for you to take away from the following section:

- *This section is about getting real with you. The way in which we experience life has a lot to do with our expectations. So, if you set expectations and then the reality doesn't match up, you may experience disappointment. This is another common pitfall on the CFS recovery path. You have a set of expectations that don't materialise, so you turn it into a story that tells you CFS is for life and recovery is impossible.*
- *Secondly, get real about the idea of setting intentions. I'm sure you do intend to recover, and that intention is necessary and powerful, but don't get sucked into the idea it is enough all by itself. Your intention needs to be backed up by concrete, consistent action.*
- *The recovery path is rather like running a marathon. I have been using these pages to share my experience with the intention of being a good friend to you. Some of the messages I have shared may not be what you wish to hear. However, hearing the truth, however undesirable, is going to support you far better than someone telling you what you wish to hear. Like a real marathon, recovery is a process, it has challenges, and there will be times when you question yourself, your choices, and even your desire to recover. I can also testify that the euphoria of making it out of your maze and opening up to all the possibilities of life is well worth all the challenges and doubts.*
- *Lastly, there is no obligation to recover. You may simply desire to reach a place of greater comfort and rest there—and that's*

> *OK. You choose how far you go and what you are willing to experience. In order to facilitate that process, you really want to learn how to cultivate acceptance of where you are right now, on each and every day. Remember, you may not have much choice over the level of pain, but you have complete choice over how much you suffer with that pain.*

Understanding What Healing Feels Like

Now, the other big area where many people fall off the recovery path relates to their expectations and intentions. So, let me begin by asking you a question: if you reflect across your life and your experiences, which felt most enjoyable?

- The experiences you had been anticipating for months, and around which you have built up huge expectations about what they would bring you or feel like?
- The experiences that came out of nowhere and brought you joy you hadn't been looking for or planned on finding?

Just consider that for a moment, while I take you on a short diversion to look at your intentions.

This book has been all about taking a journey: specifically, a journey of recovery from chronic fatigue. Now, any journey begins with the same first step. Deciding where you are going. So, regardless of what treatments take you there, your first step is going to be setting the intention to seek recovery and defining what that means to you. The word intention is an interesting word. Depending on your background and exposure, it can mean many things. I have been inviting you to recognise you have a physical, emotional, and spiritual body. In the spiritual context, the word intention can take on some specific meanings. You will find a lot of people in the spiritual community talking about setting intentions and manifesting miracles. You may even have tried this yourself. Commonly, they will tell you to do something like get into a calm, relaxed, almost trance-like state and imagine every detail of what you wish to experience. Imagine the sights, sounds, smells, and tastes and get as much sensory detail in there as possible. Then, bring yourself back to reality and wait for your glorious image to manifest. Maybe you have to do this exercise regularly for a period of time, rather than just once—but if you have faith and follow the instructions, you will get what you desire.

Well, I am not here to criticise anyone, and I am not suggesting the method doesn't work. Maybe it does work for others. If you feel drawn to try it, then I say, "Go for it." However, that has not been my experience. I will explain why that is, and what my experience looked like. First, this manifestation through energetic intention alone does have merit, and it does link into the Four Levels of Creation model and into a worldview that brings in higher consciousness. However, it can often forget that action is also required in order to bring an idea into physical reality. So, if you are currently doing nothing to support your physical body, no amount of good intention is going to create the miracle you seek. Yes, the intention will inspire and maybe speed up your physical action, but you need to work on all levels of creation.

Now, let's return to my opening point. So much of human experience ends up disappointing us because we created an expectation, and then the reality didn't match up. Occasionally, the reality exceeds our expectations, but very often reality falls short. So, when that happens, how does that affect our experience? It's hard to be grateful or notice the positive things when you are trying to compare them to an ideal. The reality feels rather second-rate, and we may be inclined to view it with negativity instead of gratitude. I hate to break it to you here, but if you set expectations that turn out to be unrealistic, this can end up getting in the way of your progress along the recovery path. If you are expecting the healing to be linear and straightforward, and then you discover there are times when you feel like you're making no progress, this can lead you to give up too soon. If you are expecting a single treatment to manifest miracles and it doesn't, this may lead you to abandon something that was providing your body with an essential foundation for recovery.

Before I explain the reality of what you are likely to experience, let me draw your attention to another idea that might be new to you. When you are ill and experience unpleasant physical symptoms, what meaning do you attach to them? In my experience, we typically tell ourselves the symptoms are the things causing us pain, and the way to get out of the pain is to suppress the symptoms. Let's just think about that for a moment. Let's say you ingest a poison—maybe your food contains some bacteria that would be dangerous to your body. The symptoms that result will—most likely—be vomiting and diarrhoea. Most people don't find those symptoms pleasant to experience. If offered a way to suppress them, I suspect most of us would happily take up that offer. However, those symptoms are the mechanisms through which your body deals with a threat. Imagine if your body didn't begin to eradicate the bacteria. What would happen then? The bacteria would take up root, begin using your energy to feed itself, and potentially cause damage to your cells. In the worst case, the results can be fatal. In the best case, your biological eco-system is simply supporting something that doesn't belong and is draining you of energy better spent on supporting your own cells.

This is a part of what is happening with chronic fatigue. Remember, this can be happening on a physiological level—for example, with a chronic Lyme infection—or on an emotional level—a traumatic event which caused a powerful emotion to become stuck. Your body will adapt to these challenges: the fatigue is a symptom of those adaptations. However, if you begin to take a treatment that really addresses the root issue, it is going to end up dislodging whatever has taken up residence in your cells. It will stimulate your immune system to remember those things aren't meant to be there and to take action. So, you may end up experiencing an unpleasant immune response. Again, this can be physiological—e.g., a fever—or emotional—e.g., suddenly experiencing a flood of anger that you had previously suppressed. So, if that happens, what is your natural inclination? To feel like everything is going wrong and try to suppress the symptoms and blame the treatment for "making you worse"? Or to recognise this as a healing event, ride it out, and experience some lasting improvement on the other side?

The truth is, healing is very much a *process*. So, we're talking marathon here, not a sprint. Whilst I cannot tell you exactly how your personal route is going to look, I can give you a few pointers. This may not be what you want to hear, but you will thank me in the end. Imagine if you were really running a marathon, and you announced this to two friends who had previously had this experience. One friend might say something like "Brilliant! I loved it when I did it. It was much easier than I thought. I barely did any training—a couple of sessions at the gym, maybe. But, basically, I just turned up on the starting line and, three hours later, I was crossing the finish and getting my medal."

That might sound like a pretty nice experience that makes you glad you've decided to take on the challenge. Then your second friend comes along and says something like "I'm not going to lie. This was really hard work. I had to spend months training. I started in January, and it was freezing. I was forcing myself to get up before work and run in the dark, freezing cold streets. I kept wondering what I was doing, but I found a way to picture myself crossing the finish line and thinking how great that was going to feel. So, that kept me going. The training really helped, so don't skip that, but you should know it still felt challenging on the day. You know that "wall" everyone talks about? Well, I hit it around mile fourteen, and I really wanted to give up. I'm not sure what kept me going, but somehow I managed to limp across the finish line and the experience of euphoria was like nothing I could have imagined. So, yeah, it was hard, but I'd do it again."

Maybe that doesn't sound so great. Maybe, after that conversation, you are wondering if you might be better off giving up on the whole idea and offering your place to someone else. Yet assuming you do go ahead with the project, which friend's advice will you be more grateful for? Well, as I said, the healing process is a bit like a marathon. Yes, there are great periods where you are making progress and you feel very hopeful and grateful you committed to whatever treatment you've decided to try, but there are also challenging periods where symptoms you thought you had healed will resurface. You begin to wonder if you're stuck and will never make it to the finish. You even begin to question where the finish line is. You may want to stop altogether and just wallow in despair.

The difference between the recovery path and the marathon is you don't have to run all twenty-six miles. You can simply get yourself to a place that feels more comfortable and stop. That may mean resting there forever, or it may be that after a while you feel like you want to experience more, and you try another treatment. The point is, you are the one writing the script here. So, what kind of script do you want to write? Would you like to experience *Nightmare on Elm Street* or *Mary Poppins?* Your choice rests on how you react to your experience. That is an active choice one hundred percent within your control. So, if I could rewind the clock ten or twenty years and give myself some advice about approaching this marathon, I would say this:

"Invest as much time in trying to learn how to accept where you are today, as you invest in looking for, or pressuring yourself to follow, the latest treatment. At the end of the day, nobody can guarantee where you will be tomorrow, but you can choose where you spend today. Ironically, the place

where you spend today is going to impact what happens tomorrow. So, learn to cultivate more acceptance and more compassion, and the entire experience will feel a whole lot better. You aren't going to succeed in accepting or loving yourself every day: all you can do is try your best and try to be at peace with the process."

ENERGY SAVING AID

These are the essential points that are helpful for you to take away from the following section:

- *Finally, it is important to spend a little time contemplating how you will know you have recovered. What exactly will your life look and feel like when you have recovered from CFS? Are those expectations realistic? If you are expecting to never get tired again, never catch another virus, and suddenly be running marathons, that may be unrealistic. You may be chasing a rainbow really about future growth, not just basic recovery.*
- *You also need to recognise the process of moving from "basically recovered" back into "normal life" requires some conscious attention. Even though your cells may now be functioning optimally, long periods of physical debilitation may mean that you need to do some basic body reconditioning. Some people also need to address some PTSD attached to having the illness. You can end up being triggered by perfectly "normal" symptoms, and those triggers causing a psycho-emotional response that appears to manifest a physical relapse. If that is happening, it is important to recognise this is an issue to address through psycho-emotional support.*
- *The final stages of recovery are still a time where you need to*

show yourself a great deal of self-compassion. Even if you do recognise yourself responding with emotions you would rather not face, know that these responses are coming from patterns that have kept you alive in the past. You are not faulty, or shameful, or to blame: the re-appearance of these emotions or patterns is simply their way of asking to be let go because you are moving on to greater things than you could possibly have imagined.

How Will You Recognise You Have Recovered?

Let's just go back to another nuance about the idea of expectations. I also want to remind you to try to remain realistic about what you think life is going to look like after you have recovered. Having experienced huge physical and mental discomfort, it is easy to imagine a "healthy person" would not have those experiences. So, check-in, here. Are you imagining, once recovered from CFS, you will never feel tired, never catch a virus, and never find yourself in a challenging emotional situation? If that is your expectation, then you are going to find yourself chasing the pot of gold at the end of the rainbow. Somehow this is never quite going to materialise. Whilst you are busy chasing it, you are also missing out on life's other adventures. Having experienced the rollercoaster of peeling back the layers of your metaphorical onion, you will reach a point where you have the physical and mental capacity to work, socialise, and follow your favourite hobbies once more, but this point requires another physical and mental adjustment that can feel very confusing.

On the physical side, you will need to do some basic reconditioning. Again, though, think about realistic expectations. If you believe recovery is defined by being able to run a marathon, is that realistic? Are your healthy friends all running marathons? Would you be running a marathon right now if you had not experienced CFS? The answer? Running a marathon requires a level of training and physical fitness that is "above healthy." It would be a new growth step for you to take, not the final stage of recovery. Similarly, in the early days of experiencing recovery or remission, you are going to experience things that may trigger you. We talked about PTSD in chapter thirteen. Well, it is possible to get a form of PTSD from having CFS. Your experience of illness may have felt so traumatic, it leaves scars that need healing. For example, catching a simple cold might trigger your fear this is the first step towards another relapse. Working a longer-than-normal day and experiencing tiredness at the end may trigger a fear you are relapsing. Having also explored the placebo and nocebo effects, it is easy to see these fears can even end up manifesting the very thing you are trying to avoid. So, even if your CFS symptoms are wholly caused by physical issues, the side effect of PTSD-style trauma from experiencing the illness may be another layer you need to address as you reach the final stages of your recovery journey. You can reach a point where your physiology is fully recovered, yet your PTSD response to a situation is causing the physical symptom to manifest. So, in this case, the symptoms have a root cause at the psycho-emotional level and a little extra psycho-emotional healing may be necessary. At the very least, the adjustment process is something of which you need to be aware, and you must allow yourself the time to adjust, with compassion.

So, I hope that has given you something to contemplate. Perhaps you have already spent a while on the recovery path, and maybe some of the things I have shared are resonating with you. You may even be recognising patterns accidentally sabotaged the progress you have been making. If that is the case, this book invites you to recognise an important lesson about acceptance and self-forgiveness. Despite the fact there is a psycho-emotional component, both in the illness and in the recovery process, this is not saying you are to blame. Nobody deliberately sabotages themselves. In fact, the very patterns that may be causing accidental sabotage right now are also the patterns that have guaranteed your survival in earlier parts of your life. So, this is simply an invitation to become aware of them, to accept them, to make peace with them, and to allow yourself to let go of whatever is no longer of service in your current experience.

> *ENERGY SAVING AID*
>
> *Don't skip the following section. This part will help you map your personal recovery path. It's OK if you don't have the energy to answer all the questions in one go—you can journal entries over time. It's also OK to keep your answers short, but please don't miss this opportunity to really get in touch with how you honestly think and feel about your situation.*

Your Invitation to Practice

For this invitation to practice, I would like to invite you to simply complete the following set of questions. You can also journal about this chapter and what you have learned from it if you wish. However, most importantly, let's bring some awareness to any misconceptions you have about what your recovery journey will look and feel like. That will empower you to avoid the common mistakes that keep people stuck in chronic fatigue.

- What do you expect your life to look and feel like when you have recovered? In detail, what job or other activity will you be doing? What will your social life look like? How about your family structure? When you have outlined all of that, do a sanity check. Are all of these things really about recovery, or are you perhaps confusing some with growth steps that you want to go on and take after your recovery has stabilised?

- If you have already been following a recovery path, look back at your experience. Have there been times when you did any of the following?

    - Abandoned one type of treatment and replaced it with another: if so, do you feel that was wise, or had you slipped into the trap of making substitutions when you might have derived greater benefit from layering up new support?

    - Experienced a recurrence of symptoms and interpreted that as a sign that things were going wrong: is this really what was happening, or was your body trying to eradicate something weighing it down it wants to let go?

    - Fallen into patterns of despair or given up hope because you haven't recovered to the degree that you expected in the time you hoped: was this really a sign you can't recover, or were your expectations actually a little unrealistic?

- What wise and compassionate learnings can you take to move forward and support yourself now?

Chapter 16

Overcoming Roadblocks on the Recovery Path

Before I guide you through planning your exit from the CFS maze, I need to warn you about one last pitfall that might catch you unawares. The roadblocks in your maze. Now, at first glance, these may look like dead ends. It may seem as though you have just hit an impassable hedge, and you need to turn back and retrace your steps along the path. Before you fall into despair or about-turn too fast, there's something you need to know about roadblocks. These are, in fact, very sneaky things. Despite their appearance, the blocks we are about to discuss in this chapter are not dead ends. In fact, if you're willing to step a little outside your comfort zone, you can dissolve these roadblocks, possibly faster than you imagine. So, if you succeed in doing that, you will see the hedge in front of you simply disappear, allowing you to continue along your path and potentially travel faster to the exit point. Are you interested in that?

Before I explain the details, let me share another journal entry to set up this discussion. You see, the information about roadblocks may just challenge you a little. You may feel I am layering blame and shame onto you or even asking you to do something totally impractical and ridiculous. I am not doing either of those things. Regarding the blame and shame, I hope you are beginning to practice non-judgement towards yourself. I will also add the reminder that none of this—whatever "this" means to you—is your fault. Regarding the practicalities of the learnings from this chapter: I am sharing the lessons I learned through experience. So, I am only asking you to do things I have already done for myself—which is why I feel I need to remind you that back in 2015 I was not in the headspace to be taking the advice I am sharing in this chapter. You may feel you are closer to the 2015 version of me. Or you may find you are already nodding sagely as you learn about roadblocks. Neither version is better than the other: my example is simply an illustration that growth, change, and recovery are possible for everyone.

ENERGY SAVING AID

The following journal section is here to set the scene and share my personal story. It is not essential for understanding recovery, so you can skip it if you need to conserve your energy.

Journal: November 2015

Well, here I am again: As it happens, about five hours after I finished my last entry and went to bed. Clearly, less than five hours is not enough sleep for anyone, but this is something else that frequently happens to me, and for the past three or four weeks it has been happening pretty much every day. I find myself wide awake, even though I am still tired and haven't managed the recommended eight hours of sleep, but there's not a hope of going back to sleep. So, the only thing is to get up and get on with the day. If necessary, I can take a nap later on. Or maybe it will catch up with me eventually, and I'll have a really early night and sleep through. Or maybe this is all going to end in another "crash." I really have no idea. I just spend my life trying to listen to my body and trying to be more aware of doing what it wants me to do, not what I want it to do—all this in the vain hope it's going to wake up and realise that I'm not the enemy and it should stop punishing me. Or is that the other way round: my body isn't the enemy, and I need to stop punishing it? Here I am back to that divide between body and mind—but that isn't what's in my thoughts today.

Maybe now is a good time to talk about the impact this illness has on friends and family. As with everything else about CFS, the big picture is simple, but the details are complex. I should start by saying I'm lucky: I already had a lot of good people in my life. I've always had a very close, loving, and supportive immediate family, and I have a good supply of friends who have supported me and not judged any of this—to my knowledge! See the paranoia slipping in there?

I have also had some friends who have not been so kind: One in particular springs to mind; someone who knew me all through school, who knew how hard I drive myself, how ambitious I am, and who still felt it necessary to give me the advice that "Maybe it's time to just pull yourself together and start living your life again." Coming from a very intelligent person and a person who I thought knew me well, this made me both angry and sad. Why would this person think I had taken a decision to "stop living"? Why would I, or anyone else, do that? You might be looking in on all of this from the outside and thinking it's not so bad to find yourself being paid to sit at home and watch daytime TV all the time, as I was doing between 2002 and 2007. Well, have you ever tried sitting and watching daytime TV for a week even? Believe me, however good it sounds in theory, you will quickly reach a point where you long to "start living" again, however annoying your job may be or whatever little curved balls life throws your way. What this person misunderstood, and what a lot of people misunderstand, is that this illness—and many, many others like it—doesn't take away your desire to "live"; it takes away all those choices that everyone else takes for granted. You don't choose to take a step out of life and spend a day in front of the TV pretending that life isn't happening to you. You don't choose when you want to go back out and fight again. You don't get to choose if you want to go to work, or if you want to change jobs, or if you want to go and get blind drunk, or just go out for a chat with a friend. All those choices are taken away from you. The question you constantly find yourself asking is, "Can I do this?" or "If I do this, what am I going to be dealing with tomorrow?" I've tried ignoring these questions and just doing what I want anyway: it catches up at some point.

So, I find myself sitting here dealing with issues I frankly don't want to deal with. I don't want to be thinking about why I've now had a sore throat for over a month—again—and what, if anything, I'm going to do about it. I don't want to be wondering how I'm going to work through the feelings of loss that are re-surfacing at the moment. However, if you do choose to believe that the theories behind Mickel Therapy or CBT are correct, and that these are valid treatments for this illness, then in order to treat the sore throat and swollen glands, I do need to be sitting here and thinking about why I'm feeling the loss and frustration. I need to find answers to those questions and—or so the theory goes—the sore throat that is a symptom of something I am suppressing or not dealing with will go away.

That entry is one of many in which I found myself musing over how I "should" be approaching the reality of CFS and the potential reality of recovery. As you see, I had some awareness of the theoretical links between mindset and recovery, simply because other people had pointed this out to me. Yet, facing those suggestions felt incredibly confronting to me. If you are being asked to accept that your mindset can determine your success in recovery, then it's difficult to separate that from the suggestion your mindset somehow got you into this mess in the first place. That suggestion leads to some pretty toxic self-blame. So, I hope that the last section, in which we explored trauma and your nervous system, has set you up with the framework to understand it's not your fault you found yourself in this situation. At the same time, you really do have the capacity to step into your power and support your recovery.

ENERGY SAVING AID

These are the essential points that are helpful for you to take away from the following section:

- *Are you someone who has heard about or explored treatments in the past and decided not to pursue them simply because you feel you can't afford the price?*
- *This can be a legitimate reason. It can also be something masking some deeper issues relating to your beliefs about your own self-worth and beliefs about money.*
- *Money is just energy. That means it is simply a tool to empower us to enjoy things we desire or need. It also means it is in constant flow. Yet, we are often brought up with beliefs about whether it's "good" to spend money on certain things or beliefs that money is scarce and finite. All of those beliefs can be examined, addressed, and potentially overcome—if you desire.*
- *So, ask yourself this: If you come across a treatment or practitioner you believe can help you, would you view that as a "cost" or an "investment" in your future? And if you choose not to take the opportunity to get help, what is the cost of making that choice: How will your life look five or ten years from now? Is that a choice you really wish to make? Spoiler alert! There isn't a "right" or "wrong" answer to those questions.*

Roadblock Number 1 – Your Finances

So, let's start by looking at these roadblocks. They can come up in any order, but I have chosen to look at finances first because it is often the first block that reaches our conscious awareness. Now, before we dive into this, I also need to emphasise that financial roadblocks can be very real. I am not suggesting you bankrupt yourself in your efforts to recover. As with all these roadblocks, the issues around money have the potential to get out of balance in two directions. At one extreme, we have self-deprivation, in which you are deciding to avoid spending money even though you have that money available. At the other extreme we have reckless spending where you simply throw your cash at everyone who offers you a solution, without considering whether or not their offer is really likely to help you. There is a middle path where you will find balance. That path stems from understanding a few basic principles about money, cost, and investment.

Every single one of us grows up with stories about money. These stories originate from social memes, belief systems that our parents give us, and also our own personal experiences. There is a sense in which all of these stories are symptoms of our core beliefs. These, in turn, can be their own trauma patterns. In case you are wondering, yes, I do see trauma in a lot of areas because it is all-pervasive. We are now living in a reality in which trauma has become normalised.[89] So, if you find the word trauma a little triggering, perhaps we could replace it with "being human."

So, let's look at one of the social memes you may have heard. *"Money is the root of all evil."* I believe that originated in the text of the Bible. Interestingly, though, the actual words written in 1 Timothy 6:10 are *"For the love of money is the root of all evil."* We will return to that in a moment. This link between money and evil has also been

---

89 If you are interested in exploring this idea more deeply, I invite you to read Dr. Gabor Mate's book, *The Myth of Normal.*

promoted in popular culture for centuries. To give you just one example, Shakespeare's character, Shylock, in *The Merchant of Venice* is a money-lender and portrayed as the villain of the piece. To be honest, you may feel that view is justified. Have you ever witnessed or read a story about someone who has a huge amount of money in their bank account and also behaves in ways that are "not so nice"? On the other hand, you can probably also find examples of billionaires who use their wealth to set up charities and try to support others. So, that brings us back to that original misquote. The important words often left out of the Biblical quote are *"the love of."* In other words, money itself is neither good nor bad. Our relationship with money, though, is another matter.

In fact, money is simply a form of Energy. Let me give you a couple of definitions of Energy from the dictionary:

- According to the Britannica website, Energy is the ability to do work.
- The Cambridge dictionary defines Energy—relating to the human body—as the power and ability to be physically and mentally active.

So, how does that relate to money? Well, money gives you the ability to do or experience or have things. In and of itself, it is neither good nor evil. The good or evil comes from the actions you choose to pursue with your money. So, in this case, money gives you the ability to pay a practitioner to share their expertise and support your recovery. Probably, you have already realised that. If you have been ill for a while, you may also be looking at your bank account and seeing a smaller figure recorded there than you would like. So, you might not like where you think this is going right now, but hang in there. If you are feeling a little triggered, just pause to take a breath to centre and calm yourself again and notice the trigger: this could be important information for you.

That brings me to the next social meme, *"Money doesn't grow on trees."* How often have you heard that one—or said it yourself? Well, this meme speaks to the idea of scarcity. Many of us have a notion that money is a finite resource. When we spend it, that's it; it's gone. In fact, I have very fond memories of my dad's favourite catchphrase regarding money, *"Spend it if you like, but when it's gone, it's gone."* Interestingly, he was born near the beginning of World War II, and so his formative years had been shaped by financial scarcity. In fact, his parents were almost declared bankrupt at one point, and this had clearly made a huge impression on Dad. Consequently, he was always very careful with money, and some of that rubbed off on me. I will share a little story with you later.

However, if money really is Energy, then let's look at another quality of Energy: It cannot be created or destroyed, simply change form. Is this true of money? Yes. You exchange money for something. It might be a physical item, or it might be an experience—service. So, yes, your money has, like Energy, simply changed form. However, your perception of what this means is going to be tied very closely to your perception of the item or service your money turned into. Did this thing bring you joy? Even more importantly, did it fulfil your expectations? If your thing or experience didn't end up matching up to your expectations, then you may well perceive that you have "lost" something. In a sense, you really have. You exchanged your money for something that turned out to be disappointing, which means you cannot exchange that *same* money for something else unless you are able to return the item and get a refund. In some cases, that refund will not be available. Specifically, in the CFS recovery field, you are not going to find a practitioner who offers you a refund if you don't fully recover. In fact, you—hopefully—won't find a practitioner who is selling you a promise of recovery. So, this is where things get a little complicated. As we explored in the last chapter, what are your expectations of the treatment for which you are paying?

Before we go on to explore expectations and some important ideas about cost and investment, let me mention one more interesting thing about this idea of scarcity. Energy is also about flow. Money is always flowing: It comes in, it goes out—unless you somehow block that flow. How would you do that? The same way you might accidentally block the flow of Energy in your biofield: through your beliefs about what is possible, or about what you deserve. Maybe you look at people who appear to attract wealth or possess a lot of wealth, and you simply view them as "lucky." But what is luck? According to the story of Helen Hadsell,[90] luck is about mindset. Once you clear the blocks that interrupt your flow, then life just flows. Quite literally, we all create our own "luck."

That idea may really challenge—even anger—you. It certainly challenged me, as you may have noticed in my journal entry. Yet, it links into the work of Bruce Lipton and the study of Epigenetics that we explored in earlier chapters. It also links to the Intention studies being carried out by the Institute of Noetic Science—IONS. In particular, their research using Random Number Generators and Intention has shown, on multiple occasions, that a human observer

---

90 Helen Hadsell was born in America in 1924 and died in 2010. She was nicknamed the "Contest Queen" because she entered and won a huge number of contests for prizes ranging from smaller household items through to all-expenses-paid holidays and even a house. In 1971 she published a book sharing her philosophy of "believe you can win, and you will." During the 1960s and 1970s, she studied mind control, becoming involved with Jose Silva and the *Silva Mind Control* approach in 1972. Incidentally, that approach now underpins the *Mind Valley* organisation. In summary, these various approaches are all concerned with the idea of intention. We are all manifesting our reality all the time, so what we intend will come to pass. The reason that feels so difficult to believe largely comes from the fact that so many of our intentions are subconscious, so we aren't aware that we are manifesting from places which may also be self-sabotaging.

intending a particular outcome can increase the statistical probability of that outcome occurring. This, in turn, links into the theories about consciousness—we are creating our reality, not the other way around—and also ties into areas in Quantum Physics around the Double Slit Experiment and the power of the observer—all a surface-skim approach to saying you have far more power than you realise. Your mindset and beliefs may easily be blocking the natural flow of Energy in many forms. If you have heard about a treatment you feel might be beneficial for you, are you going to go for it or will you hold back because of the way in which you perceive your finances?

What types of mindset and beliefs might impact the way you view your financial situation? Let me share a personal story with you. I had the opportunity of working one to one with a coach who had been getting amazing results. This coach was well-qualified, so this didn't seem like someone who was just good at marketing: It looked like the "real deal." I felt this person had something to offer that would help me. So, I signed up for a discovery call with them. I knew exactly what they were charging for their services and, from my perspective at the time, this was a large sum of money. Yet, I still wished to pursue this opportunity. I found myself on the discovery call, explaining my situation. The coach saw straight to the foundation of my problem—in a way that I had struggled to put into words. They offered a simple set of steps we would take together should I choose to work with them. Then they asked me what I wanted to do. I felt confidence in their ability to diagnose my problem and offer a sensible solution. I also liked this person and could see myself being able to work comfortably with them. However, when I was asked if I wanted to go ahead and sign up for the program, my instinctive reaction was to fall back into the pattern of saying, *"Thank you. I don't think I can afford this at the moment."* This person was very gracious and said that was fine, it had been great speaking with me, and if I wanted to think about it, I could get in touch if I changed my mind, but no hard feelings if I didn't. So, our call ended, and I continued on with my day, but all the time with a niggling feeling of doubt. Clearly, I had felt drawn to this person and their approach. Everything in our phone conversation had indicated they really would be able to help me, and I had found them kind and approachable. The price of their services was *significantly* higher than any investment I had ever made in myself before. So, when it came to decision time, I had decided I couldn't justify that expense. It wasn't that I couldn't *afford* it: if I had said yes, I would still have been able to pay my bills, feed myself, and do all the basics, but, obviously, I wouldn't have been able to spend that money on something else. I would have removed that money from my personal savings, and that felt scary.

So, I began exploring this, and I made several interesting discoveries about my belief system. First, I believed I didn't *deserve* to spend that amount of money on myself. Yet, this was a little nonsensical. The help this person was offering me would improve my health and energy and open me up to new opportunities. So, why didn't I *deserve* that? I was spending my time saying I wished to recover, and now I had someone offering to help me, and no reason to suspect they wouldn't be able to—other than the inherent risk that nothing is guaranteed. What was *really* blocking me from taking this opportunity? Then, I noticed I was assuming if I spent that sum of money on this item, the money would be gone, never to return. Was this really true? If I invested that sum and the program increased my energy and improved my health, then it would open up my capacity to return to earning money, so more could potentially flow in and replace what I had spent. Even if it was true this particular sum of money never flowed back to me, what did that mean? Well, now I was getting to some pretty deep survival fears. Guess where they came from? Yes, most likely from Dad's experience, and even that was distorted. His parents hadn't *actually* gone bankrupt. He hadn't found himself destitute or homeless at any point; he simply feared that might happen, and he allowed the fear to determine what he experienced and enjoyed in life. In other words, to keep himself safe, his nervous system had learned that money was finite and had to be carefully guarded in order to survive. That's not a "bad" philosophy at all. It just represents an extreme swing of the pendulum in one direction, which can result in self-deprivation in other areas of life.

So, you're probably wondering how my story ended. I used the tools I had—by this time—learned to help work through trauma and unlock some of those limiting beliefs. I ended up taking the risk and signing up for the program. The funny thing is, the more you choose to invest, the more this supports your intention to really experience growth and change. I also recognised that part of the "success" of the program would depend on my own intentions and my own willingness to spot and work through new blocks as they came up. The ticket price of any item reflects its quality. At the same time, it also reflects the value to you. For most of us, the greater value we place on something, the more of ourselves we invest in nurturing or looking after that thing. In terms of a treatment program, that investment means showing up physically to appointments, and mentally or emotionally as we follow the guidance offered to us. Did I make a "good" decision? I believe I did. Not only did I receive the benefits I desired from the program itself, but this experience also paved the way to clearing more subconscious blocks, and that improved multiple areas of my life. After all, our beliefs around money end up affecting every single area of life. If you are someone like me who feels a little guilty about spending money on yourself, then imagine how lovely it will feel when you are able to buy something you desire and simply enjoy the item without the feeling of guilt.

Before I wrap up this section, I would like to draw your attention to one other subtle nuance. You may or may not have noticed this, but I have been using the terms *cost* and *investment*. They are the same thing.

One term is about loss, and the other is about gain. So, when you are asking, *"What will this treatment cost?"* you are asking from a mindset of loss. You may not have recognised this before. That little word *cost* implies there is going to be some kind of penalty for following this path. In this case, the penalty is specifically twofold:

- First, the number on your bank statement, which represents your wealth, is going to become smaller. So, what does that mean for you?
- Second, whatever number you are being asked to hand over in exchange for this treatment cannot then be spent on anything else. So, what else were you going to purchase with that money?

A large element of your perception about what you can and cannot afford relates to what you value. So, by parting with that sum of money, will you end up being unable to provide for your basic survival needs like food, clothing, and shelter? If not, then what else were you planning to do with the money? Perhaps exchange it for a holiday or use it to fund a hobby that you enjoy? Well, let me ask you this: do you really value those things more highly than you value your health? There isn't a "right" or "wrong" answer to that.

In order to have a fully rounded perspective of the proposal, have you also asked yourself this question about cost? *What does it cost me if I don't undertake this treatment plan?* Maybe that means your condition deteriorates. Or maybe you are going to remain the same. What will your life look like in five or ten years? Will you regret that decision, or is it something you could do later on? These are all things to consider. I'm not saying I have any answers, nor am I advising you which course of action to take. I simply invite you to consider there are two paths opening up. Even if you do nothing, that is still a choice. It is a choice to remain where you are, and maybe a choice to end up somewhere that feels worse. Of course, underpinning it all is the fact any treatment is a risk. This doesn't just apply to CFS or even just to alternative medicine. There is no medical intervention for any illness or condition 100% guaranteed to give you a specific outcome 100% of the time. So, I invite you to consider what it is you are really expecting.

So, let's look at the other word: *investment*. What does that mean? An investment has the energy of growth about it. Yes, you are still exchanging money, but your intention is that the exchange will bring a benefit to you in the future. That benefit may or may not arrive. Simply, the intention behind your exchange is now inviting growth rather than fearing loss or stagnation. So, how do you perceive a treatment? Do you see it as a cost to your bank balance or an investment in your well-being?

ENERGY SAVING AID

These are the essential points that are helpful for you to take away from the following section:

- *This second roadblock can feel triggering because it taps into some of the grossly unfair ideas the general population has come to believe about CFS. The illness is not something created by the person living with it, and it is not a matter of conscious choice to live with—or recover from—CFS.*
- *At the same time, the unconscious mind can inadvertently end up influencing the course of recovery. There may be parts of the unconscious that view some of the practical implications of CFS as being beneficial. For example, if you are someone who prefers to be quiet and unseen, CFS achieves that result beautifully. There is a way to recover and honour the needs of the subconscious mind, which are only ever trying to protect you.*

- *Unconscious blocks can accidentally create nocebo effects, which will mean even beneficial treatments won't work. So, if you are going round in circles, it is worth at least considering whether there are any parts of you that benefit in any way from living with CFS and whether those parts can enjoy the same benefits within a life in which you are free from pain and feel energised.*

Roadblock Number 2: Secondary Gain

Some of the themes we have explored above are going to come up again in this next roadblock. I have to warn you that this one may really trigger you. If it does, that is just interesting information. So, I invite you to simply notice your response, notice whether it is towards yourself or towards me, and try to use your practice of stepping out of judgement as you become aware of whatever is happening inside you.

What is this roadblock? Secondary gain. It is a big topic, and one that can end up accidentally causing a nocebo effect with any treatment or practice you decide to try. So, the sooner you can become aware of this, the sooner you can support yourself by working through it. Secondary gain is basically the idea that your experience is serving you in some way. The reason that idea feels so triggering is because it speaks to all those accusations that have been levelled against those who are living with CFS. Namely, that you are making a choice to live this way, and you could simply make a different choice if you wish.

Now, secondary gain is NOT a conscious choice, which is why most of us are completely unaware of the fact we may be doing this. Also, secondary gain is NOT something that applies specifically to CFS. It can apply anywhere in life. For example, you may declare you desperately wish to give up smoking, or lose weight, or stop being late for work, or stop forgetting to phone your friend Emily—and, yes, one hundred percent of your conscious mind does desire those things. How about your unconscious mind? What does that think? Maybe there is a part of you that resides in your unconscious and just loves the satisfaction you gain from smoking. Maybe there is a part of your unconscious that really hates your job but doesn't feel brave enough to speak up about it. Instead, it keeps making you late in the hope your boss is going to notice and fire you!

If you are thinking this is all rather silly and childish, you might just be right. Remember, the unconscious mind contains the survival patterns we set up in early life and forgot about. So, if your tactic seems more like something a five-year-old would do, then maybe that's because you were five years old when you installed that program. Now, as an adult, you can see there would be a better way of dealing with the issue, but until you acknowledge your five-year-old part and create a sense of safety for it, you are going to struggle to retrain it. No matter how vigilant your conscious mind tries to be, that sneaky but oh-so-clever five-year-old part is going to jump in there somehow and sabotage your adult efforts. Thank goodness it does because, at the age of five, that pattern guaranteed you survived and are sitting here today getting frustrated with yourself. So, that's the slightly bad news. Now for some good news. You can integrate your five-year-old part and help it grow into alignment with your current conscious self. If you are really willing to do this, the process can be very quick and simple, as I discovered. That is precisely what Neuro-Linguistic Programming is designed to achieve,[91] and it does. I have watched people change

---

91 I have to acknowledge that NLP has gained "bad press" in some circles because of its ability to control the mind. Now, if I asked you whether mind control is a good thing, you might say "no." If mind control means other people controlling your mind, then I agree with you. Yet have you considered that is already how you are living? You are already running subconscious programs other people installed without your conscious agreement. So, wouldn't it be nice to examine all your programming and consciously decide which you wish to keep and which you prefer to let go? Well, when used with integrity, that is precisely what NLP offers. Sadly, as with many other tools, it can also be used without integrity as a way to try to control

in minutes as I work through an NLP practice with them. I have experienced the changes for myself as other people have guided me through NLP practices, or I have worked my way through them on my own. These changes can truly feel miraculous.[92]

I began inviting you to explore secondary gains in your journaling practice at the end of chapter seven. I just didn't give it that label. So, you may already have recognised there are aspects of your CFS experience that give you things you might desire. There is no shame in that. After all, as we have explored, if this illness is about making sensible adaptations, then it is natural some of your experience will reflect hidden desires. So, here we have another choice point. Right now, your choice may be unconscious. It is still a choice, though. I am now inviting you to bring it into awareness and make it conscious. Examine those things that are benefits and ask yourself two questions:

1. Is this still something I wish to experience? Your answer may be "yes" or "no." There is nothing wrong either way, as we will explore in a moment.

2. If the answer is "yes," then ask yourself whether it is essential to have CFS in order to retain this benefit or could you get the same benefit via a different route? What might that route look like? If the answer is "no," then which practice is going to help you make the necessary changes to create a different experience?

---

or influence. For example, an advertising campaign is likely to be using NLP-type practices to influence your subconscious mind to prompt your conscious mind to behave in a certain way. So, again, wouldn't it be lovely to understand how that happens and take back your power to make conscious choices?

92 I have created a membership on https://findmyenergy.co.uk where you can learn more about NLP tools to help you integrate parts of yourself that may be accidentally blocking your recovery. Depending on your budget and desires, you can work through some blocks on your own, or you may choose to engage with my one-to-one coaching services to support yourself in this area.

So, let's spend a little time unpacking those ideas.

First, here is a radical idea for you. What is "wrong" with living with CFS? For me, it was about being in physical pain and also feeling mental frustration at not being able to follow the same lifestyle as the world around me. Well, the not desiring physical pain is pretty reasonable, right? Yet, actually, even that can have a secondary gain if it means you are given sympathy and looked after. In some cases, there are people who enjoy that. I don't say you are one of them. I wasn't, so that aspect of the illness didn't offer me any secondary gain.

What about the aspect of not being able to follow the same lifestyle as society suggested I should? Well, there, things become a little less crystallised. Let's say you, like me, are an introvert. A lot of our current society is set up to cater for extroverts. Desiring to spend time alone or being happy sitting in a quiet corner of an office without being disturbed may not be part of your company's culture. So, being signed off work legitimately may present a benefit. Could this be a secondary gain? If so, is there another way to achieve the same benefit? Yes: Find a different job. Interestingly, I had that opportunity in 2012. Through mutual agreement, I left my career in Strategy Consultancy. This opened the path for me to set up my own business in the craft industry. I loved this. Funnily enough, there was a short time during which my symptoms improved dramatically. So, did the process of changing to a lifestyle that suited my personality better act like a form of treatment for the illness? Yes—and no. In 2016, I crashed for the second time. I was still loving life, and I still crashed anyway. Also, in 2002, I wasn't aware of *hating* my job. Far from it: I relished the intellectual challenges and the salary if I'm honest. Many aspects of the lifestyle that came with it—lack of sleep, most notably—were not enjoyable, nor were they conducive to good health for anyone. So, perhaps there was no secondary gain for me in that area either. Not everyone has secondary gain. Even if you do have some element, this secondary gain is unlikely to be the *entire* cause of your illness. If only it were that simple!

The significance of exploring secondary gain is to give you the power to remove some roadblocks. For example, maybe you are currently using a treatment that is really helping you, and you start to plateau. Yes, as we discussed in earlier chapters, it could be that this treatment is only a part of your story, and the plateau is now telling you to add another layer. On the other hand, that plateau can also come from you reaching your edge of safety. Maybe there is a subconscious part of you getting some secondary gain from your remaining ill. So, even if you try to layer up multiple different treatments, your roadblock will remain in place until you address the part that experiences a gain from CFS. This can be the point at which you feel as if you are going round in circles.

I mentioned that secondary gains can cause a nocebo effect. Well, this occurs when you are out of alignment. As we explored in the last chapter, if there is a part of you that does not agree with your movement towards recovery, that part is going to put up resistance and blocks. What does resistance do? It slows the flow of Energy. So, this is the nocebo effect at work. You are legitimately working with the best available treatment. It is doing everything it is supposed to be doing. Yet you aren't recovering because of this block that you haven't addressed. Although I have been focusing on the psycho-emotional secondary gains, it is also possible to have a secondary gain that is physiological. In effect, this is where the nutritional protocols I used were coming into play. Until my body had sufficient supplies of critical vitamins and minerals, it was not safe for me to be living at "normal speed." So, rather than seeing a secondary gain as something shameful or "bad," let's look at what it really is: another clever protection mechanism to keep you safe.

ENERGY SAVING AID

These are the essential points that are helpful for you to take away from the following section:

- *I wish to end by reminding you that everything is a choice, whether you make that choice consciously or unconsciously. I know you are making the perfect choice for you.*
- *Living with CFS doesn't have to be "bad." We do not have to pathologize the illness. If you can find a level of acceptance in which your experience allows you to enjoy life as much as you desire, that is wonderful.*
- *So, this book is not about forcing anyone to follow any particular path. It is here to open your eyes to different ideas and allow you to continue making your choices, trusting they are right for you and making them from a more conscious perspective.*

Do You Have to Recover?

Leading on from the question of secondary gains is another very interesting question. What if you are actually happy living in the maze? OK, so if you have already reached that conclusion, you probably aren't reading this book. Most likely, you're happily enjoying life within your personal capacity. That is also great. I did not write this book with the intention of telling anyone that it's "bad" to have CFS. I wrote this book for those who, like me, desire a different experience.

So, in this final section, I invite you to consider another perspective. Who told you that you need to live your life a certain way? Whose life are you actually trying to live? Maybe the key to unlocking your discomfort is Radical Acceptance. CFS is an illness all about feeling a lack of energy. This may manifest a host of other symptoms. What if you were to develop the acceptance of your body being how it is? Accept that you need to eat a certain diet. That you need to follow a particular pattern of rest and activity. Accept everything you personally need to live in a way that feels comfortable to you. Can you even live with pain from a place of accepting and observing it rather than resisting it? What would happen if you tried that? Radical Acceptance is not about paying lip service to the limitations or giving up on yourself. It is about wholeheartedly accepting who you are. In other words, if you are still aware of a little voice—maybe it belongs to you or maybe it has the personality of someone you know—questioning why you feel and behave as you do, then you have not reached Radical Acceptance. The level of acceptance I am talking about requires you to be able to simply observe everything that you think, feel, or experience and just accept it. No judging it. No telling stories about why it has to be this way—or why it shouldn't be this way. Just complete peace with what is. If you can attain that state, you are removing resistance. Maybe that is the answer to re-opening your flow. Just maybe your experience will change without you "efforting" to make things happen. After all, we are human beings, not human doings![93]

So, you can think of these roadblocks as choice points. Every time you meet a block, you choose how you respond to it. You get to make that choice anew every day. If you choose to keep searching, then I invite you to complete the final practice here and then move on to the conclusion of our tour of the CFS maze and start plotting your escape route. You may discover that the first path out of your personal maze requires you to examine and address your beliefs around money in order to pave the way for feeling at ease paying for treatments. On the other hand, you may now be wondering if there are any secondary gains standing in your way and creating nocebo effects. Until you explore

---

93 Interestingly, Dr. David R. Hawkins, M.D., PhD, used a similar idea to recover from multiple complex conditions. He details his experience and learnings in the book *Healing and Recovery*.

and address those areas, even the best treatments are unlikely to help you find complete recovery. There is nothing wrong with choosing to stay in the maze. If you choose the path of Radical Acceptance, then that is also awesome. In fact, practicing Radical Acceptance alongside your other paths can ease your journey considerably. I know with one hundred percent certainty that whichever path you take is perfect for you, and you have the power and potential to experience whatever you desire.

ENERGY SAVING AID

Don't skip the following section. This part is going to help you map your personal recovery path. It's OK if you don't have the energy to answer all the questions in one go—you can journal entries over time. It's also OK to keep your answers short, but please don't miss this opportunity to really get in touch with how you honestly think and feel about your situation.

Your Invitation to Practice

For the final time, I invite you to grab your journal and answer the following questions:

What are your beliefs around finances? Write down some memes that come to mind for you. Write down the values around spending and saving that your parents taught you. Add in any other beliefs you have gained through your adult life, and make a note of how and why you came to believe these things.

How do you feel about spending money on yourself? Write down where these beliefs came from—your own experience or things that other people have told you or shown you.

How do you see money? In particular, think about your views on scarcity and flow.

How do you look at the price of a treatment: as a cost or as an investment?

What would you need to know or understand in order to be willing to pay for a treatment? As you consider this, do you feel your expectation is realistic?

Do you believe that your mindset can control how you feel physically, and why do you believe this? Your belief could come from your personal experience or from things other people have told you.

Revisit the notes you made in the practice at the end of Chapter 7 and see if you can identify any secondary gains. How do these benefits serve you? Is there another way in which you could attain the same benefit? You can let your imagination fly there—anything can be possible.

How do you think and feel about the information in this chapter? What learnings can you take forward and apply to your own circumstances?

Conclusion
Drawing your Roadmap

Conclusion

Exiting Your Maze

Journal: January 2024

I am now past twelve months without any kind of relapse of my CFS symptoms. That feels like something to celebrate. As I reflect on this, I cannot help noticing it is difficult to declare myself "recovered" when we still lack a diagnostic test for this illness. Some might argue that I never really had anything wrong with me. I somehow decided to create my symptoms—maybe even imagine them—and then decided I had had enough and simply decided to stop experiencing symptoms. Not everyone will be of this opinion. I can point you towards a plethora of diagnostic tests looking at my digestive system, my mitochondrial function, and the levels of vitamins and minerals in my body. Repeat tests show improvement in those areas. I can also point you to improvements in my NES health scans, monitoring what is happening in my biofield. Yet, critically, none of this is about diagnostic tests or "proof" of illness or recovery. All of this is about how I feel.

I no longer experience a sore throat. My lymph glands, which were swollen for twenty years, have now returned to normal. I am enjoying life without fatigue. January is the annual Yoga with Adriene thirty-day journey, and I am enjoying that fully, without feeling any post-exertional malaise or delayed fatigue. I am working full-time hours, albeit still for myself. I can plan a social life without worrying about resting before and after my chosen activity. It had become a "tradition" for me to collapse between Christmas and the New Year. In fact, I remember Christmases when I found myself needing to spend part of the day in bed in order to survive. That is all a dim and distant memory. The restrictive diets designed to bring my microbiome and nutrients back into balance are all a thing of the past now. Once again, I can take for granted the small pleasures like chatting to a friend on the phone, following a normal daily routine, and going for a walk. I am able to do a ballet class—although I do not have the level of fitness I did in my early twenties! I could keep on listing the many small and large things that have changed for me.

In short, I am now looking at a vista of potentials. Did my life return to its pre-illness place? No. I recognise that flogging my body and depriving it of sleep or nutrition is not serving me. The insecurities that drove me to feel I needed to prove myself through achievement or pleasing others are healed. That doesn't mean I no longer achieve or no longer think of others: I pursue those aims from a place of greater self-love. The more self-love I find, the more energy comes with it. So, this feels rather like the closing of one chapter and the opening of another. It's not the end of the road; it's the beginning of a new adventure.

It seems only fitting to bring this book to a close with another journal entry. If nothing else, those of you who have been noting the dates on my journal entries may have noted the change in me. Recovering from something as massive as CFS only happens through deep, deep change. I can honestly look back upon this experience and see it as an incredible gift. It brought me the opportunity to know myself, an experience I doubt I would have gained from pursuing my career through Strategy Consultancy and wherever else life took me—or would I? In truth, I will never know the answer to that.

So, where does this leave you? Well, if you have been following the practices at the end of each chapter, you are currently in possession of your roadmap and ready to begin your journey in earnest. You see, whatever information you may have gathered from these pages, it will only create change when you begin acting upon it. Until then, you are still standing in the centre of your maze, just holding a map. I invite you to now begin stepping forth.

The Five Steps to Recovery

So, here's the part you've been waiting for: the steps you need to take on your recovery path. You have been using your journal to gather the data that you can use to support these steps. So, let's look at them.

STEP 1: Setting your intention. You did this in the introduction, and your journal entries should have been helping you to refine this. The thing about intentions, though, is they need to be positive. Unity Consciousness is all about creating. It will create wherever you place your focus. If you place your focus on the things you don't want, you end up creating them. If someone tells you not to think about elephants, say, what is the first thing that pops into your head? An elephant! In order to not think about it, you need to know what you're not thinking about. So, if your intention for recovery is based upon things like "not feeling tired" or "not being in pain," change the focus. What do you desire instead? Start imagining and feeling gratitude for that experience. Place your focus squarely on the life you are going to create. With that focus set, keep showing up and moving forward, one day at a time.

STEP 2: Awareness. This is what you have been cultivating throughout all the practices: self-awareness. Again, how can you solve a problem you don't understand? So, by this time, you should have a clear picture of how you feel, what you think, your preferences, your beliefs, the people and things that support you, and the people and things that do not. If you feel like you don't have that clarity, then just continue to return to the journaling practices and ask yourself more questions.

STEP 3: Safety. This is key to supporting your nervous system. Remember, the nervous system is the master controller. If it detects danger in its internal or external environment, it is going to remain on alert. In that state, it will be lacking the energy to maintain itself or iron out any glitches in the system. It will also lack the incentive to create positive change. If it believes it is walking into a dangerous environment, then it will avoid that at all costs and choose to remain wherever it is right now. That place may not feel comfortable, but it may be relatively safer. So, what needs to change in order for your intended new life to be safer than your existing life?

STEP 4: Support and acceptance. This is the means through which you maintain safety. As my NARM therapist[94] kept reminding me, *"Get comfortable with being uncomfortable."* In other words, when you are feeling discomfort—physical or emotional—instead of trying to distract from it or avoid it, get curious about it. What is the pain or emotion trying to communicate to you and how can you follow that instinct to support yourself? I have been encouraging you to let go of judgement and replace it with discernment. This is the path for creating support. It validates your experience; it acts with love and compassion; it guides you with wisdom and integrity. Acceptance allows you to move forward with minimal resistance. Know that whatever you are experiencing is OK, and it is temporary. Tomorrow will bring in a new experience. Accept whatever is coming up: the good, the bad, and the ugly. Create as much safety and support as you can throughout the process.

STEP 5: Change. Being willing and open to change is key. Using your awareness to see where you need to change and how, you can work with symptoms, behaviours, and habits, using appropriate tools or treatments to let them go or transform them into supportive patterns. Change is an ever-evolving process—a spiral in which you are constantly cycling through greater awareness, bringing in safety and support. Change can also be bumpy and uncertain. Know that it's OK to go off track from time to time. Holding onto your firm intention will bring you back onto the path you seek. Recovery is not

---

94 NARM—NeuroAffective Relational Model. This is the trauma treatment program I used to work through my own developmental trauma, in conjunction with the encoded meditations that sped up the process hugely.

About the Author

Katie Dean is a writer, award-winning artist and energy coach who specialises in supporting people to reconnect to their true self and empowering them to live with self-love, peace and joy. She holds a Bachelor's, Master's, and PhD in history, all from Cambridge University.

Katie worked as a Business Strategy Consultant in London before becoming ill and being diagnosed with Chronic Fatigue Syndrome in 2003. Her illness ended that career, and opened the door to starting her own business as a beadwork artist, designer, and tutor. Her beading designs reached the finals and won numerous international competitions. She has published more than thirty beading books.

In 2022, during the final stages of her recovery from illness, Katie pivoted her career once more, training as a Bioenergetic Health Coach and a Colour Therapist whilst studying NLP, life-coaching, and trauma therapy. She combined all of these skills to create the Kolorlan System, a Blueprint for Wholeness and Metamorphosis.

Katie lives just outside of London, in the UK, and enjoys walking in nature, watching the Royal Ballet Company, spending time with her family, and indulging in just about anything creative.

Acknowledgements

I have been truly blessed to have met with and been supported by so many different people throughout my life. All of you, whether you know it or not, have contributed to my eventual recovery, helped me to write this book, and continue to contribute as the next chapter of my life unfolds. It doesn't feel possible to name each of you: it would be a long list, and I would feel terrible if I left anyone off. So, I'm going to mention a few, and to the rest, you know who you are: I love you and am deeply grateful to have met you. Thank you.

I literally would not be here without my family and closest friends. My mum and brother are a constant source of love and support and have pulled me through the bad times and celebrated the good times with me. Thank you, and I love you forever! My dad probably wouldn't have told me to my face (that wasn't his style!), but he would have been very proud to have held a copy of this book in his hands. I'm sad he isn't here to do this in reality, and I also know his soul is celebrating right now and has always supported me in the best way he knew how.

To my closest friends, Chloe, Melissa, Serena and Rachel, thank you! You've supported me and been there for me in so many ways: Never questioned my illness, my need for rest, my desire for companionship, listened to me and shared with me. I am truly blessed to have met you and grown up with you. And to Vivienne, originally my beading book editor, who then became a wonderful friend and encouraged me as I was starting to write this book – thank you for all the chats, wisdom and support.

I also wish to thank the work colleagues and mentors who believed in me and supported me through the earliest years of my illness, especially David, who I came to think of as a friend as well as mentor.

And this story could have taken a very different shape without the generous help and support of many different doctors, practitioners and healers along the way. Every single one of you has provided me with a piece of this jigsaw: some large, some small. Even the moments of frustration and misunderstanding gave me nuggets of wisdom that made my journey possible. I cannot mention everyone, but I do wish to mention Dr Bajwa, Dr Sharma, Tammy, Julia, Maya, Doris, Niki, Christine and Jeff. Thank you!

Then, there are the practitioners and healers who never came into direct contact with me, but who, by generously sharing their knowledge through books, interviews, podcasts, and conferences, allowed me to come to the understanding of CFS that supported my recovery, boosting the help I was receiving from practitioners in person. Thank you for the time you all spend researching, seeking to understand, and thank you for championing the cause of everyone with CFS who cannot always voice their needs.

I am also deeply grateful to the friends I have made, and friendships that have deepened because of a common problem: chronic fatigue syndrome. So, David, Heather, Cheryl, Lesley, Siobhan, Alex, thank you for sharing your journeys, your discoveries, and continuing to have the courage to seek energy and live your life to your fullest.

Finally, these pages would not be in print without the skill and support of the amazing team behind this book. Thank you to Dr Karen Kan who (among other things) introduced me to Keith and Maura, and to Maggie who has been such an incredibly supportive and kind editor, Autumn and the team who have brought the text to life with such love and kindness. To each of you, it has been a privilege and a blessing, to have received your support, wisdom and practical help in manifesting my dream of sharing my story in this book. Thank you.

Printed in Great Britain
by Amazon

62875376R00238